CONTAINING MISSILE PROLIFERATION

Containing Missile Proliferation

Strategic Technology, Security Regimes,
and International Cooperation
in Arms Control

DINSHAW MISTRY

UNIVERSITY OF WASHINGTON PRESS

Seattle and London

Library of Congress Cataloging-in-Publication Data

   Mistry, Dinshaw.
     Containing missile proliferation : strategic technology, security
  regimes, and international cooperation in arms control / Dinshaw Mistry.
     p. cm.
   Includes index.
   ISBN 0-295-98294-2 (alk. paper)
    1. Arms control.   2. Ballistic missiles.   I. Title.
JZ5665 .M57   2003
327.1'743—dc21

                               2002035697

CONTENTS

TABLES

PREFACE

This is a study of international efforts to contain the proliferation of a particularly deadly military technology—long-range ballistic missiles. Ballistic missiles enable states to rapidly deliver weapons of mass destruction over vast distances. Missile proliferation is therefore among the foremost concerns on the international security agenda. When faced with mutual challenges and concerns, states often coordinate their national policy responses through multilateral regimes. International regimes deal with a wide spectrum of issues ranging from interstate trade and commerce to environmental management to the control of armaments. Drawing upon well-established frameworks of international cooperation and regimes, this study examines multilateral responses to the challenge of missile proliferation. The study critically examines how well key technology suppliers such as Western states, Russia, and China have complied with the Missile Technology Control Regime (MTCR); it explores the missile programs of major regional powers—Argentina, Brazil, South Africa, South Korea, Taiwan, Egypt, Syria, Iraq, Israel, India, Pakistan, North Korea, and Iran; and it outlines five practical ways to strengthen the MTCR and better contain missile proliferation.

Such a study adds to cooperation theory by highlighting how cooperative regimes can be attained on particularly tough military security issues. It also provides a valuable policy blueprint on how regimes may tackle the missile threat and offer crucial safety nets if missile defense falls short.

This book had its origins in my 1999 doctoral thesis, sections of which appeared in *Contemporary Security Policy* and *Security Studies,* and in conference papers presented to policy-makers developing the MTCR's Code of Conduct and other missile nonproliferation initiatives. This study was supported by fellowships from the Belfer Center for Science and International Affairs (BCSIA) at Harvard University; the Center for International Security and Cooperation (CISAC) at Stanford University; and the Program in Arms Control, Disarmament, and International Security (ACDIS) and Department of Political Science at the University of Illinois. I am particularly grateful for their support, and also thank Stephen Cohen, Paul Diehl, Edward Kolodziej, Scott Sagan, Lynn Eden, Richard Speier, Aaron Karp, Evan Medeiros, Steven Miller, John Garofano, Sean Lynn Jones, John Reppert, Michael Barletta, and many friends and colleagues at BCSIA, CISAC, ACDIS, Cincinnati, and Brookings for insightful comments and assistance that greatly enhanced this study. This book also owes intellectual debts to a select group of missile experts whose writings on missile proliferation made my own research much easier and are extensively cited in the following pages. Finally, I thank Michael Duckworth, Marilyn Trueblood, Leila Charbonneau, and the University of Washington Press for their assistance with the publication of this study.

ABBREVIATIONS

ABM: antiballistic missile, Anti-Ballistic Missile Treaty

ACDA: Arms Control and Disarmament Agency

ADD: Agency for Defense Development

BWC: Biological Weapons Convention

CAT: Conventional Arms Transfer

CBMS: Confidence-building measures

COSTIND: Commission on Science, Technology and Industry for National Defense

CWC: Chemical Weapons Convention

DPRK: Democratic People's Republic of Korea (North Korea)

DRDO: Defense Research and Development Organization

ESA: European Space Agency

FMCT: Fissile Material Cutoff Treaty

GCS: Global Control System

IAEA: International Atomic Energy Agency

INF: Intermediate Nuclear Force Treaty

ICBM: intercontinental ballistic missile

IRBM: intermediate-range ballistic missile

MIRV: multiple independently targetable reentry vehicle

MTCR: Missile Technology Control Regime

NBC: nuclear, biological, and chemical weapons

NMD: national missile defense

NPT: Nuclear Nonproliferation Treaty

NSG: Nuclear Suppliers Group

ROK: Republic of Korea (South Korea)

SAM: surface-to-air missile

SLBM: submarine-launched ballistic missile

SLV: satellite launch vehicle

SRBM: short-range ballistic missile

START: Strategic Arms Reduction Treaty

TMD: theater missile defense

UNSCOM: United Nations Special Commission on Iraq

WMD: weapons of mass destruction

ZBM: zero ballistic missile

CONTAINING MISSILE PROLIFERATION

1

Introduction

In a February 2001 report to Congress, the Bush administration called attention to a looming missile threat. It noted that "in a world where more than a dozen nations possess ballistic missile technology, and a number of nations are racing to acquire weapons of mass destruction, America's most pressing national security challenge is to reduce our current vulnerability . . . against missile attack."[1] The previous year, President Clinton had also stated that a missile threat to America was "real and growing."[2] Fears about the spread of ballistic missiles had greatly increased since August 1998, when North Korea stunned the world by launching a three-stage rocket over Japan and into the Pacific. Many Japanese were shocked to the point of terror; headlines in Europe ominously declared, "Europe Comes into Range";[3] and the U.S. media warned of a "serious" future missile threat from North Korea and Iran.[4]

Ballistic missiles enable states to rapidly deliver nuclear, chemical, and biological weapons over vast distances. Missile proliferation is therefore among the foremost international security concerns. When faced with mutual challenges and concerns, states often coordinate their national policy responses through multilateral regimes. In 1987, the Missile Technology Control Regime (MTCR) was initiated to contain the missile threat. During the MTCR's first decade, several regional powers such as Argentina, Brazil, Egypt, South Africa, South Korea, Taiwan, Iraq, Syria, and Libya were thwarted from advancing their missile ambitions. In light of these positive developments, MTCR members expressed satisfaction with the regime at its tenth anniversary. Yet in subsequent years, other states such as North Korea, Iran, Pakistan, India, and Israel tested medium-range missiles, and several additional states retained missile arsenals and missile ambitions. These developments demonstrated the MTCR's weaknesses and raised critical questions about its ability to halt further proliferation.

What accounts for the MTCR's successes and limitations? How well can it continue to curb missile proliferation? What measures may enhance its effectiveness? More fundamentally, how well can multilateral regimes manage security affairs? Can regimes such as MTCR contain deadly technological advances that undermine international security? Are technology control regimes only useful for ten years and not much longer? These questions are examined in this book, which explains the operation and effectiveness of the MTCR through the framework of international regimes.

THE ARGUMENT

The MTCR is a multilateral agreement of over thirty states to restrict their transfer of missiles and related technologies. The MTCR's basic premise is that denying foreign technology and expertise to regional powers can curb their missile programs. A typical missile program requires expertise in chemicals (for rocket propellants), metals and materials (for airframes and re-entry vehicle heat shields), and electronics (for guidance systems), and an engineering capability to design and integrate various missile components.

The first chapters of this book examine how well and why major suppliers such as Western countries, Russia, and China complied with the MTCR's policies against missile exports. The Western states, which were not selling complete missiles but were important technology suppliers, largely curbed their technology transfers. Russia and China halted sales of complete missiles and adopted stronger export controls but their firms still transferred some technology to regional powers. The political dynamics of the MTCR are also worth noting. While cooperation is essential for building regimes, conflicting interests, power politics, and the use of sanctions and incentives are behind the bargaining processes that lead to cooperation. These factors influenced the primary suppliers to rein in their missile technology transfers.

This book then examines the MTCR's impact on target missile programs. Nine regional powers—Argentina, Brazil, South Africa, South Korea, Taiwan, Egypt, Iraq, Syria, and Libya—restrained their missile efforts in the 1990s. They either ceased missile activity or limited their missile projects to cruise missiles, artillery rockets, and 100–300 km range ballistic missiles. Yet five other states—Iran, Pakistan, North Korea, India, and Israel—built and tested 1,000–2,000 km range ballistic missiles.

Moreover, and somewhat paradoxically, although the technologically stronger target states would be more likely to overcome the MTCR's embargo and advance their missile activity, this outcome has not materialized. Instead, many technologically strong states (for example, Argentina, South Africa, Taiwan, and South Korea) *curbed* their missile programs, while some technologically weaker states (Iran, Pakistan, and North Korea) *advanced* their missile activity. This suggests that technology embargoes alone do not explain missile outcomes. Technological obstacles are sufficient to halt missile programs in technologically very weak states (such as Libya and, for about a decade, Syria). But for other states, such barriers mainly hinder, delay, and raise the costs of missile programs, and during these delays, political pressures critically influence national missile decisions.

Two political factors—security pressures from their regional system and political-economic pressures from the global system—affect national missile decisions. In cases where regional security improves (thus reducing the security-related demand for missiles), and states are susceptible to international leverage (because of their strong ties with external powers, or due to economic liberalization which requires foreign aid and investment), missile proliferation has been curbed. In other cases, missile proliferation continues. Thus, Argentina, Brazil, South Africa, South Korea, Taiwan, and Egypt constrained their missile programs. For the first three states, the regional security environment improved, while for the latter three, the United States offered an external security assurance. In addition, these states had strong economic or security ties with the United States and were consequently susceptible to U.S. pressure (and U.S. influence was more pronounced because, in a unipolar system, the U.S. was the major source of foreign aid, trade, and investment). Israel, India, Pakistan, Iran, and North Korea continued missile activity because they faced security threats and were less vulnerable or more resistant to external political-economic pressure. Moreover, the latter three states collaboratively advanced their missile programs (North Korea's Nodong missile formed the basis for Iran's and Pakistan's missiles), which were also assisted by foreign technology transfers.

This analysis suggests that one policy approach to restraining proliferation would be through a stricter technology embargo, combined with international engagement strategies to influence missile proliferators. Such engagement that increases political-economic ties with and results in leverage on regional powers, and also positively influences their security perceptions, could restrain their missile activity. This approach would work if the number of proliferators remains small and if they are susceptible to U.S. influence. However, under changing political conditions where regional powers perceive new security threats, or changing economic conditions such as a growing demand for space rockets, regional powers may revive their rocket ambitions. In addition, under a different international system—such as a multipolar system where regional powers have stronger ties with other major powers and consequently weaker ties with Washington—or if the United States disengages from regional theaters, U.S. influence on regional powers could decrease. Under changing political and systemic conditions, engagement strategies may be unable to contain renewed missile programs, and would have to be complemented with more robust non-proliferation institutions.

What types of arrangements can strengthen the missile nonproliferation regime? This question is dealt with by critically examining the missile nonproliferation regime's institutional design. The exclusive technology-focused scope of the MTCR has limitations compared with other arms control regimes. The nuclear, chemical, and biological nonproliferation regimes have technological, political, and legal components. They function through global treaties that ban entire categories of weapons; they address national security concerns; and they offer political and economic incentives for compliance with the regime. In contrast, the MTCR has only a technological component. It lacks legal components (there is no global treaty banning missiles) and has few political and security components, which could serve as incentives for states to restrain their missile aspirations. Such a regime does not address key issues like the elimination of missile forces, the halting of continuing missile programs, and the diffusion of space-related technology. It also cannot adapt to political changes and technological advances. In the long term, therefore, additional policy approaches may be necessary to contain missile proliferation. The five most feasible policy options to enlarge the missile nonproliferation regime are agreements on global intermediate-range missile bans, regional missile-free zones, flight test bans, verification mechanisms, and space service incentives for countries to restrict missile activity. These explanations and policy prescriptions borrow from and add to three areas of scholarship. They provide new insights for the study of proliferation; they add to debates on the ability of regimes to manage security affairs; and they stress a critical line of analysis for public policy studies—a line that goes beyond the pros and cons of, and explores supplementary approaches to and safety nets for, policies such as missile defense.

THE STUDY OF PROLIFERATION

Scholarship on nuclear and missile proliferation has mainly sought to explain *national proliferation decisions* and the *causes of proliferation,* or the question of why states seek nuclear weapons and ballistic missiles. This book examines the largely unexplored issue of *international responses to proliferation* and the *effectiveness of nonproliferation regimes* in containing proliferation.

Theories about proliferation argue that states pursue nuclear and missile programs for five reasons—because of technology-pull (the availability of a given technology), bureaucratic political pressures, prestige considerations, security threats, or economic motivations (to develop a nuclear infrastructure for nuclear energy, and to build rockets for launching satellites or to gain revenue from missile exports).[5] Each of these theories provides important insights on particular cases of proliferation, but no single theory explains every case. Instead, more than one cause is often prominent in the same state, and the factors that lead to proliferation in any given state may be absent in other states. For example, North Korea's missile program has been driven by both export and security considerations; prestige and security reasons to match North Korea influenced South Korea's missile ambitions; Brazil's space program was guided by a strategic quest for technological autonomy; and domestic political pressures, security concerns, and prestige motivations all influenced India's nuclear and missile projects.

Finding that there are multiple causes of proliferation provides no firm policy prescription as to which cause to address when tackling proliferation. Therefore, it is important to study proliferation from another angle, by examining the actual impact of arms control regimes on proliferation; this examination may then be linked with the causes of proliferation to provide a more complete explanation for proliferation outcomes. Such an analysis is undertaken in this book to assess how well a regime—but one built primarily around technology barriers—may curb proliferation.

INSTITUTIONS AND INTERNATIONAL SECURITY

The issue of whether institutions and regimes can solve security problems remains highly contested. Cooperation is generally difficult in the zero-sum environment of security issues. Yet, as discussed in the next chapter, security and arms control treaties certainly exist and have been effective. Therefore, scholars note that "institutions sometimes matter, and that it is a worthy task of social science to discover how, and under what conditions, this is the case."[6] This book draws upon these themes by specifying the political, technological, institutional, and structural conditions that influence nonproliferation and security regimes.

The two main arguments of this study are that, first, institutional design has a significant impact on international cooperation and regime effectiveness. Regimes that are exclusively technology-focused and lack more robust political-legal foundations may be temporarily successful, but are eventually undermined by technological advances, commercial and economic pressures, and political change. Second, two political influences affect the operation of regimes and may compensate for their institutional deficiencies. In the first instance, regional security considerations affect state participation in global security regimes. In areas of regional tension, an external security guarantee or improvements in regional security increase the effectiveness of nonproliferation and security regimes. The second political influence is that structural and domestic political-economic factors affect national decisions to comply with regimes. Increased interdependence in a globalized system makes regional powers vulnerable to external pressure to join regimes, especially when they pursue economic reforms that require integration with global markets. These arguments provide crucial insights into the MTCR's operation.

THE MISSILE THREAT AND MISSILE DEFENSE

Which countries have missiles that can threaten the United States and its European and Asian allies? Why are missiles a deadly and threatening military technology? What options do missile defenses provide against the threat?

National Missile Arsenals

Several countries have short-range ballistic missiles (SRBMs), a handful have intermediate-range ballistic missiles (IRBMs), and very few have long-range intercontinental ballistic missiles (ICBMs) that can reach the United States, but the ICBM threat could grow in time.

Over twenty-five countries in the Middle East, South Asia, Northeast Asia, and Eastern Europe have SRBMs such as Scud missiles that weigh 5 to 10 tons and have a 300 to 600 km range (see Table 1.1, pages 10–11). Some of these countries have a few tens, others have a few hundreds, of such missiles. Most of these missiles were bought from foreign suppliers, though many states are building their own SRBMs.

Five regional powers—Israel, India, North Korea, Iran, and Pakistan—have built and tested IRBMs that typically weigh 10 to 25 tons and have ranges of 1,000 to 2,000 km.[7] These states typically have ten to fifty, but in a decade could build (and possibly export to other states) hundreds, of such IRBMs. In addition, Saudi Arabia bought IRBMs from China, and China builds its own IRBMs. The United States and Russia scrapped their IRBMs under the INF treaty.

Five countries, the five NPT-defined nuclear states, have 5,000 to 10,000 km range ICBMs and submarine-launched ballistic missiles (SLBMs)—the United States (550 ICBMs and 430 SLBMs), Russia (750 ICBMs and 300 SLBMs), France (48 SLBMs), Britain (48 SLBMs), and China (20 ICBMs, plus about 100 IRBMs, 12 SLBMs, and several hundred SRBMs). Thus the United States faces missile threats from these states, but U.S. territory is beyond the range of regional power missiles. Major U.S. cities such as New York are 7,500 km from Libya and 9,500 km from Iraq and Iran, while North Korea is 8,000 km from Seattle and 6,000 km from Alaska. However, future missile threats loom over the horizon. North Korea's 4,000 to 6,000 km range Taepodong-2, whose range could be extended with a third stage or a lighter payload, was near a prototype test in 1999. North Korea can initially build about two such missiles each year. These could be exported to other states such as Iran and Iraq, who, later this decade, may develop similar long-range missiles. Regional powers could also acquire

Russian or Chinese ICBMs, or, technical obstacles notwithstanding, fire SRBMs and IRBMs from ships near a target coast. Moreover, the heavy capability (5,000 to 10,000 km range) space launchers of Japan and India and medium capability (3,000 to 5,000 km range) space launchers of Israel and Brazil could be upgraded into ICBMs.

Thus the missile threat is real (hundreds of short- and medium-range missiles can strike states in Europe and Asia), but its most dangerous aspect (the proliferation of ICBMs) is still limited. The threat could either expand or remain limited in the coming years: it would increase significantly if regional powers obtain foreign technical assistance to build greater quantities of more powerful missiles; it could be limited if foreign technical assistance remains embargoed and political initiatives and institutional barriers restrain target missile programs.

The Strategic Consequences of Missile Proliferation

Ballistic missiles are particularly deadly nuclear delivery systems and terror weapons because they cover distances of hundreds to thousands of kilometers in a matter of minutes, and are hard to defend against. Missile attacks and deployments therefore have serious strategic, political, and military consequences.

On *strategic* grounds, missile proliferation undermines the nuclear, biological, and chemical nonproliferation regimes. Ballistic missiles enable states (and nonstate actors and terrorist groups) to quickly deliver weapons of mass destruction (WMDs) to distant regions, thereby exacerbating the WMD threat and weakening the nonproliferation regime. Conversely, halting missile proliferation mitigates the WMD threat, strengthens the nonproliferation regime, and enhances international security.

Missile attacks are a significant *military* threat to armed forces, international peacekeeping forces, and civilian populations. Missiles have been used in several international and civil conflicts: Germany fired thousands of missiles against London and Antwerp in World War II; Iraq launched hundreds of missiles against Iran and several dozen at Israel and Saudi Arabia; Afghan groups fired hundreds of missiles in their civil war; and missiles were used on a smaller scale in other conflicts. The military impact of missiles in these conflicts should not be exaggerated, because missiles are not very accurate, most missiles did not hit any significant targets, and they did not result in mass fatalities. Yet the occasional missile caused dozens, even hundreds, of casualties. In the Gulf War, a Scud strike on an American military barracks caused 28 fatalities, which was the largest number of allied fatalities in a single engagement. Another Scud landed some 300 meters from cargo and oil facilities and would have caused high casualties if it had hit these targets. Missiles can be even more deadly against civilian populations; in World War II, a V-2 strike on Antwerp's Rex cinema caused

Table 1.1. The Global Inventory of Ballistic Missiles, 2001

Country	Short Range		Intermediate Range			Long Range or SLVs
	(100–250 km)	(300–700 km)	(1,000–1,500 km)	(1,800–2,200 km)	(>2,500 km)	(>5,000 km)
Afghanistan		Scud-B				
Argentina	*Alcaran*					
Armenia		Scud-B				
Azerbaijan		Scud-B				
Bahrain	ATACM					
Belarus	ss-21	Scud-B				
Bulgaria		Scud-B				
Egypt		Scud-B, *Scud-T*				
Georgia		Scud-B				
Greece	ATACM					
Iraq	*Al Samoud*					
Kazakhstan	ss-21	Scud-B				
Libya		Scud-B				
Romania		Scud-B?				
Slovakia	ss-21	Scud				
South Korea	*NHK*, ATACM					
Syria	ss-21	*Scud-B*, Scud-C				

Taiwan	*Green-Bee*					
Turkey	ATACM					
UAE		Scud-B				
Vietnam		Scud-B				
Yemen	ss-21	Scud-B				
Saudi Arabia					DF-3	
Pakistan	*Hatf-1, -2*	M-11, *Shaheen-1*	*Ghauri*	*Shaheen-2**		
Iran	M-7	Scud-B, -C	*Shehab-3*	*Shehab-4**		
North Korea		*Scud-B, -C*	*Nodong*	*Taepodong-1*	*Taepodong-2**	
Israel	Lance	*Jericho-1*	*Jericho-2*		*Shavit* (SLV)	
Brazil					*VLS* (SLV)	
India	*Prithvi*			*Agni-2*	*Agni-3**	*PSLV* (SLV)
Ukraine	ss-21	Scud-B				*SLVs*
France						*SLBM, Ariane*
China	*M-11, M-9*			*DF-21*	*DF-3A, DF-4*	*DF-5, SLVs*
Japan						*H-2* (SLV)
U.K.						*SLBM*
U.S.	*ATACM*					*ICBM, SLBM, SLVs*
Russia	*ss-21*	*Scud-B*				*ICBM, SLBM, SLVS*

Italicized text indicates indigenously built missiles; other missiles were purchased from foreign suppliers.
*System under development but not tested by 2001.
SLV: Satellite launch vehicle

270 fatalities. Moreover, the above examples involved missiles with conventional warheads. A WMD missile attack would be far more catastrophic.

Missile activity has destabilizing *political* consequences in both wartime and peacetime. Missile strikes that terrorize a target population and increase pressures on political leaders to retaliate can considerably escalate conflicts. In the Gulf War, Iraq's missile strikes against Israel could have had a very serious political impact. The Coalition might have fractured as Arab states left it if Israel had retaliated against Iraq. Further, ballistic missiles escalated tensions in the prewar phase (because of Iraq's declared policy of threatening Israel), widened the war's parameters once the fighting began, and diverted significant air power and special force resources away from other military tasks.

Even when they are not used in wars, missile deployments and tests exacerbate interstate tensions. Three examples illustrate this point. First, Soviet missile deployments in Cuba provoked the 1962 missile crisis that brought the two superpowers to the brink of a nuclear exchange. Second, Chinese missile tests off Taiwan in 1995 and 1996 led to a tense standoff between the United States and China, and two U.S. naval battle groups were sent to the Taiwan Strait. Third, North Korea's August 1998 rocket test over Japan terrorized Japan's population. Tokyo demanded an apology and explanation from Pyongyang and suspended its economic aid. North Korea responded harshly, declaring "Japan's behavior is ridiculous," adding, "We warn Japan to . . . act with discretion and renounce its anachronistic hostile policy."[8]

Missile proliferation can also increase the likelihood of interstate conflict in the long term. International conflict studies suggest that neighboring states are more likely to fight wars with each other, and that proximity correlates positively with conflict.[9] Ballistic missiles can quickly strike distant states and thereby bring distant states "closer" to each other, which (especially if deterrence stability cannot be attained) could increase interstate tensions and the likelihood of regional conflict. Moreover, missile deployments can be provocative in a region where nuclear weapons are vulnerable to a preemptive strike. Missiles then undermine the stability of deterrence.

Missile proliferation is therefore a particularly serious security challenge. Further, there is a new urgency to tackle the missile threat because it is directly linked with the controversial missile defense issue.

Missile Defense

In its first year in office, the Bush administration pulled out of the antiballistic missile agreement (ABM Treaty) to pursue an ambitious national missile defense (NMD) initiative.[10] This book does not explore the pros and cons of missile defense or of other options such as deterrence and counterproliferation against the missile threat.[11] It mainly notes that a policy of excessive, indeed exclusive, reliance on NMD leaves few backup options if NMD falls short. Shortcomings are a concern because missile defenses have had many technological, economic, and political problems.

Missile defense technology is not yet proven (missile defense tests have had a mixed record) and is expensive (costing a few billion dollars annually).[12] Some of the technology may eventually work, but missile defenses can still have negative political-strategic consequences. If NMD expands unchecked over the long term, this may strategically pressure Beijing, and in the middle term Moscow, to maintain large offensive forces and reject deeper arms control accords. Moscow may hesitate to reduce its nuclear force much below levels of 2,000 strategic warheads. Beijing may build up a few hundred multiple warhead ICBMs (compared with its 20 single warhead liquid-fuel ICBMs that would be replaced by 50 to 100 solid-fuel ICBMs and SLBMs under a modest modernization program) and reject any fissile material treaty (a treaty that would halt its production of nuclear weapons material). India, and consequently Pakistan, may then respond with their own expanded nuclearization. Noting these potential negative consequences, the Senate Foreign Relations Committee chairman argued, "The cost of unilaterally walking away from the ABM treaty and forging ahead with missile defenses includes . . . the likelihood that we will unleash a new arms race that will create a nuclearized Asia."[13] Washington's NATO allies and the broader international community similarly cautioned about such developments.

Even the less controversial theater missile defense (TMD) systems that counter IRBMs and SRBMs have had problems. Giving defensive interceptors to states can actually increase missile proliferation by causing neighboring states to seek additional offensive missiles. Moreover, TMD has complicated regional security, especially in Asia. Beijing viewed U.S.-Japanese security and TMD cooperation as "an attempt to encircle Asia." It warned of "grave consequences" if a U.S.-supplied missile defense system were to cover China and it began deploying missiles in the Nanjing Military Region opposite Taiwan, illustrating the sensitivity and potential explosiveness of missile defense issues.[14]

Arms control regimes that contain the missile threat can crucially supplement and provide safety nets for missile defense. If the missile threat is contained, NMD deployments could be safely limited to preserve strategic stability; TMD deployments can also be regulated to maintain regional stability.

ORGANIZATION

This book is organized into nine chapters. Chapter 2 explores issues of theory and method, and analyzes how international regimes, technology embargoes, and political pressures influence proliferation. Chapter 3 surveys the establishment of the missile nonproliferation regime. It notes major trends in this area such as the shift from ad hoc U.S. missile control policies from the 1950s to the 1970s, to multilateral approaches and the MTCR's formation in the 1980s, and the regime's expansion to cover Russia and (informally) China in the 1990s.

Chapters 4 through 7 review the missile nonproliferation regime's effect on target states. Chapters 4 and 5 examine states that constrained their missile programs—Argentina, Brazil, South Africa, South Korea, Taiwan, Egypt, Iraq, Syria, and Libya. Chapters 6 and 7 examine states that advanced their missile programs—Israel, India, Pakistan, North Korea, and Iran. Chapter 8 analyzes whether the sources of cooperation in the MTCR can consolidate and perpetuate the regime. It notes the MTCR's institutional limitations and examines policy options to strengthen the regime. Chapter 9 summarizes the main lessons of this book for the study of proliferation and our understanding of security regimes and international cooperation.

2

Regimes, Technology, Politics, and Proliferation: The Theoretical Foundations of the MTCR

International efforts to contain missile proliferation originated in the Missile Technology Control Regime (MTCR). The first section of this chapter defines the important concept of regimes and clarifies issues concerning their institutional design and operating components. Because the MTCR's initial scope was restricted to technology barriers, the second section assesses scholarship on technology and its control. Technology barriers delay rather than halt missile programs, increase their costs, and cause a target state's missile decision to shift from technical to political considerations. The third section of this chapter examines how political factors such as security considerations and political-economic pressures influence national defense policies and missile decisions. The fourth section discusses how missile proliferation is linked with the proliferation of weapons of mass destruction.

INTERNATIONAL REGIMES

The MTCR as an International Regime

Regimes are defined as "sets of implicit or explicit principles, norms, rules and decision-making procedures around which actor expectations converge in a given issue-area."[1] Each of these terms may be clarified through the example of the missile nonproliferation regime.

Principles are theoretical statements about how the world works and include beliefs of fact and causation. The principles behind the missile nonproliferation regime are that the proliferation of ballistic missiles is detrimental to international security; conversely, international security is enhanced by curbing missile proliferation.[2] *Norms* specify general standards of behavior for participants in the regime and are defined in terms of rights and obligations. The norms of the missile regime, or obligations undertaken by MTCR members, are that missile proliferation should be halted: missile sales and related technology transfers should be curbed. The *rules* of a regime are specific prescriptions for action. The rules for the missile nonproliferation regime, specifying the particular technologies that should not be exported, are indicated in the MTCR guidelines and technology annex. *Decision-making procedures* are practices for making and implementing collective choice. Such procedures are not always centered around an autonomous international organization or treaty.[3] They may also be informal, as in the MTCR, where decision making primarily involves intergovernmental consultation at annual MTCR meetings. The decisions taken during MTCR meetings are then implemented by the national legislation of member states. For comparison, regimes concerning security, economic, and environmental issues are illustrated in Table 2.1.

Two additional points should be noted. First, the relation between a regime's rules and principles is crucial. The rules of a regime can be changed without

Table 2.1. Security, Economic, and Environmental Regimes

Broad Issue Area:	*Security*	*Economics*	*Environment*
SPECIFIC ISSUE:	MISSILE PROLIFERATION	WORLD TRADE	GREENHOUSE GASES
Principles (Beliefs of fact and causation)	Missile proliferation diminishes international security	Trade barriers hinder global economic advancement	Greenhouse gas emissions cause global warming and degrade the environment
Norms (Standards of behavior for regime participants)	Halt missile proliferation	Eliminate trade barriers	Restrict greenhouse gas emissions
Rules (Specific actions to attain regime norms)	Deny missile-related technology to states	Reduce trade barriers in all economic sectors as specified by WTO	National quotas: Reduce greenhouse gas emissions to 5% below 1990 levels by 2012
Decision-making Procedures	Loosely institutionalized in the MTCR	Strongly institutionalized in WTO	Evolving under Kyoto framework

altering its principles and norms. Changes in the rules (changes *within* the regime) do not jeopardize the regime. However, challenges to the principles and norms can result in a change *of* regimes, and may lead to the disappearance of a regime and the rise of a new one. Thus the missile regime may be undermined if its norms to *curb* technology exports are challenged by other norms on the economic and trade agenda, such as norms to *promote and expand* technology exports for economic and trade reasons. Second, a more critical examination of the MTCR's norms and rules (to halt missile proliferation by halting technology *exports*) reveals that they are different from the Nuclear Nonproliferation Treaty's norms and rules, which are to prevent proliferation by banning not just the *export* but also the *possession and development* of nuclear weapons. This issue is better understood by examining the regime's scope and domain.

Institutional Design, Scope, and Domain: Comparing the MTCR, NPT, and CWC

A regime's scope is defined as the issues addressed by the regime. In general, three issues are relevant to missile proliferation: supply-side issues of restricting missile sales and technology transfer; the development of missiles in target states; and legal bans on missiles and steps toward missile elimination. The missile regime mainly addresses the first two issues through a multilateral supplier cartel, the MTCR, and also seeks transparency through a Code of Conduct.

The nuclear and chemical nonproliferation regimes, while containing a technology control cartel (the Nuclear Suppliers Group and the Australia Group, respectively), operate largely through international treaties such as the Nuclear Nonproliferation Treaty (NPT) and the Chemical Weapons Convention (CWC) (see Table 2.2). The NPT and CWC ban the possession and development of nuclear and chemical weapons. The CWC goes even further, calling for the destruction of existing weapons stockpiles within ten years. Moreover, the NPT and CWC have verification mechanisms such as inspection provisions and safeguards to detect violations. These safeguards may be imperfect, and can be more easily circumvented in the chemical and biological areas;[4] in November 2001, Washington charged Iraq, Iran, North Korea, Libya, and Syria with developing biological weapons. Safeguards are tighter in the nuclear area, though even nuclear safeguards were violated by Saddam Hussein's government, but they have since been strengthened.

The NPT regime also deals with (or at least attempts to address) security concerns in two ways. First, the NPT contains a contract between the nuclear and nonnuclear states. Under this contract, nuclear states agree to eventual nuclear elimination. Further, outside the NPT, nuclear states have given political (but not legal) assurances to not threaten nuclear use against nonnuclear states that are not allied with a nuclear power (but with some exceptions, such as concern-

Table 2.2. The Missile, Nuclear, Chemical, and Biological Nonproliferation Regimes

Institutions	Missile	Nuclear	Chemical	Biological
Supplier cartel restricting technology transfer	MTCR	NSG	AG	AG
International treaty banning system	–	NPT	CWC	BWC
Verification agency	–	IAEA	OPCW	–
Other measures banning or limiting system	-INF and START for U.S., Russia -UNSCOM for Iraq -Missile restrictions for new MTCR members -Transparency measures of MTCR Code of Conduct	-Regional NWFZS -CTBT -FMCT -Security assurance		

AG: Australia Group
CTBT: Comprehensive Test Ban Treaty
FMCT: Fissile Material Cutoff Treaty
IAEA: International Atomic Energy Agency
INF: Intermediate Nuclear Force Treaty
NSG: Nuclear Suppliers Group
NWFZ: Nuclear Weapon Free Zone
OPCW: Organization for the Prohibition of Chemical Weapons
START: Strategic Arms Reduction Treaty

ing WMD use by a regional power). Second, collective action principles such as the logic of reciprocal restraint operating among the nonnuclear states address security concerns about each other. Under this logic of collective action, states legally refrain from acquiring WMDs with some confidence that their neighbors will reciprocate. For any pair of states A and B, state A refrains from acquiring WMDs, and neighboring state B reciprocates, because if B did not reciprocate, this would cause A to reconsider its earlier non-WMD decision, a step that could escalate into an undesired arms race between A and B.[5] This dynamic of reciprocal and multilateral restraint from WMDs, backed by verification of compliance, is intended to enhance the security of all parties and thereby persuade states to renounce WMD programs. A third security mechanism, outside the NPT, stems from major external powers (principally the United States, and previously also the former Soviet Union) who have military alliances with or provide security assurances to other states, thereby dissuading them from pursuing independent nuclear programs.

Finally, treaties and regimes are not perfect. Commentators note that "the anthrax attacks against Americans show that a treaty is not the be-all and end-all to stopping the spread of biological weapons or preventing and dealing with germ attacks."[6] States of concern that do not join regimes, or states that join but then violate regimes, or nonstate actors (rebel groups and terrorist groups) who acquire WMDs, can be real and serious security threats. Such cases must be addressed through means outside treaty regimes (such as the UNSCOM system for Iraq), but the regime provides the international mandate to bring such states in line with the regime's norms.

A regime's domain, similar to the breadth of an international organization, is the number of members it has. The NPT and CWC seek universal membership. The MTCR has a more restricted domain of thirty-three members and a few more adherents. Although the MTCR does not desire universal membership, it nevertheless seeks universal compliance with its norms against missile technology exports. At the MTCR's formation in 1987, its members noted that they "would welcome the adherence of all states to these [MTCR] guidelines in the interest of international peace and security."[7]

Three points on the completeness of regimes follow from this discussion. First, the missile nonproliferation regime was somewhat incomplete in its first decade: it contained a supplier cartel (the MTCR) but not legal bans on missiles or a verification agency. Second, and following from the first point, the MTCR is one component of a missile nonproliferation regime whose other components (legal bans and verification mechanisms) had not been created. Since these other components did not exist, the MTCR was essentially the entire missile nonproliferation regime for this period, and therefore the terms "MTCR" and "missile nonproliferation regime" are used interchangeably. If and when the other components are created, these terms should be more carefully distinguished.

Third, the above definition of the MTCR as a regime would then be modified to note that although the MTCR fits the definition of a regime, it is actually a subregime, or one component of a regime. The norms and rules of this subregime are to halt missile proliferation by undertaking to *not export* missile technology. The norms and rules of any more complete regime would be to halt missile proliferation by undertaking to *not possess* missiles—just as the norms of the complete nuclear nonproliferation regime are to *not possess* and *take steps toward the eventual elimination of* nuclear weapons.

Institutional Design and Regime Size

A regime's optimal domain and scope, and the paths to regime formation, warrant further analysis.[8] A successful regime must include those states whose exclusion jeopardizes the regime. Yet the MTCR left out important missile suppliers like Russia and China when it was formed in 1987. Why was this strategy pursued, and what are its drawbacks?

Cooperation among states is essential for regimes, and limiting the number of participants increases the likelihood of cooperation. As Mancur Olson notes, unless the number of players in a group is small or unless there is coercion or some other special incentive, rational self-interests alone will not compel group members to act to achieve their common interests.[9] Elaborating on this theme, Downs, Rocke, and Barsoom argue that, all other factors being equal, large multilateral arrangements that start out with a small number of participants will achieve considerably greater depth in cooperation than those that start out with a large number of participants.[10]

However, the benefits of small groups do not apply to all situations. For example, Duncan Snidal argues that a larger membership enhances the stability of regimes.[11] Miles Kahler notes that institutional devices such as voting rules, representation, delegation, and horizontal minilateralism provide avenues for multilateral collaboration with large numbers.[12] Eventually, as observed by Kenneth Oye, reducing the number of players has both positive and negative effects.[13] Player-limiting strategies may diminish the gains from cooperation while they increase the likelihood and robustness of cooperation. Further, player-limiting strategies may impose substantial costs on third parties, by excluding them from a public good or targeting or sanctioning them. These costs may motivate third parties to undermine the area of cooperation or may be an impetus for the third party to enter into and enlarge the zone of cooperation.

Finally, although a formal treaty or organization can institutionalize cooperation, treaties are not always the optimal means to create regimes. On this issue, James Caporaso notes that multilateral activity without an organization to facilitate and enforce agreements may raise the problems of distrust, defection, and reneging.[14] Yet negotiations on a formal institution may be lengthy and detrimental when states seek rapid consensus on an issue. The MTCR is not a treaty. In terms of its degree of legalization measured on a scale of 1 (hard law) to 8 (nonlegalized arrangement), the MTCR ranks at level 7; it has a low level of legal obligation and no delegation to third parties for enforcement, but has higher levels of precision.[15]

Regime Operation: Power, Interests, and Knowledge

Regimes are sustained by strong normative foundations, but regime politics also involve interaction between three basic causal variables—state power, national interests, and knowledge on an issue.[16] State power can secure cooperation in regimes and also influence the distribution of benefits from cooperation. The realist "hegemonic stability theory" notes that a dominant power (the hegemon) supplies the leadership and resources to build regimes.[17] Hegemony does not exclusively imply coercion but also incorporates leadership, which uses entrepreneurial, managerial, and organizational skills in pursuit of specific objectives.[18] Neoliberal theories emphasize that rational interests prompt states to participate in regimes. Cognitive or knowledge-based theories focus on the origins of and the norms and information that shape national interests, thus partly complementing neoliberal theories.

Beyond the basic causal variables, strategic interaction and issue-linkage are prominent in regimes.[19] Thus, even if states agree on an issue, they bargain further to maximize their interests by linking issues.[20] The linkage of sanctions and incentives to a supplier state's compliance with the regime has been a key feature in the MTCR.

The issue of regime continuation warrants further examination. Although regimes may be created by a dominant power, they do not necessarily disintegrate upon the decline of this dominant power.[21] Several functional, interest-based factors perpetuate regimes. First, regimes persist because they provide functional benefits such as supplying information and reducing transaction costs. Second, states comply with regimes because of the costs of noncompliance; these include the social costs of a damaged reputation, and political and economic costs arising from the fear of retaliation and the effects of precedents.[22] Third, regimes are more easily maintained than created as states learn more about their utility over time.[23]

States also comply with regimes independently of cost-benefit calculations. The force of inertia and the absence of an alternative maintain a system. In the absence of new ideas, existing practices may simply continue.[24] Also, patterns of institutionalized cooperation keep regimes functioning. With repeated interactions, regularized behavior patterns develop, and these acquire a normative aura and constrain state behavior. These factors have sustained the MTCR.

Security Regimes

The MTCR is an example of a security regime, representing cooperation among states on the security issue of missile proliferation. In general, several types of security regimes exist, including informal alliances (ententes, nonaggression pacts, consultation pacts), formal alliances,[25] collective security mechanisms, cooperative security structures, regional security regimes, and strategic arms control. Such institutions can promote cooperation in several ways. They internationalize a set of norms and define a range of permissible behavior, and by doing so alter a state's expectations about how other states will behave in the future and how their own actions will influence the behavior of other states. This institutional dynamic persuades states to reject power-maximizing policies and accept outcomes (such as limits on missiles and nuclear weapons) that may weaken their relative power positions (in this case by limiting their strategic weapons).

Yet scholars of international relations have expressed skepticism about the concept and utility of security regimes. They argue that regimes may be easier to attain in economic and environmental situations, but are harder to attain in the zero-sum conditions typical in international security, where states seek to maximize the difference between their utilities and those of other states.[26] Further, the perilous consequences to a state's vital national interests and national survival arising from swift and decisive defection by another hinder security cooperation. The immediate and potential grave losses to a player who attempts to cooperate without reciprocation, and the risks associated with inadequate monitoring of the decisions and actions of others, are key differences between cooperation in the security and economic areas.[27] Scholars are also skeptical of the persistence of alliances and other security complexes, arguing that they break down and are replaced with balancing and multipolarity if external threats decrease.[28]

Realists make three further points on the nonproliferation regime. First, cooperation over trade-related aspects of proliferation such as export controls and technology transfer is different from cooperation over a military national security issue. Second, realist factors such as power and national interests, rather than nonrealist factors such information, values, and norms, perpetuate the nonproliferation regime.[29] Third, great powers or hegemonic states play a vital role in security regimes. These three themes are all manifest in the MTCR. But this study also highlights how knowledge and information crucially complement state power and national interests in the MTCR's operation.

Different strategic structures also influence prospects for regime building. Cooperation is easier when states are playing a coordination game such as allying against a common threat or choosing common technical standards.[30] However, cooperation is harder in prisoners-dilemma type situations typical of international security issues. The formation of the MTCR resembles a coordination game, which made cooperation on the issue easier. But how was the zone of cooperation widened and why was it not deepened? These questions are explored in this study, which analyzes how the lack of depth and legal foundations in the MTCR affects its ability to tackle missile proliferation.

TECHNOLOGY AND ITS CONTROL

The Study of Technology Export Controls

The MTCR aims to curb proliferation by denying missile-relevant technology to target states. It is essentially a trade ban seeking to impair the military capability of a target state. Other types of military impairment bans include the denial of economic goods that may strengthen an opponent's military machine, and arms embargoes that deny military equipment to adversaries or states engaged in wars (see Table 2.3). Scholars of international security and political economy clarify certain aspects concerning the scope, controversies, and effectiveness of trade and technology embargoes.

In scope, economic embargoes range from broad ranging sanctions aimed at the entire target economy to narrow sanctions directed at a specific sector.[31] Broad and comprehensive trade embargoes are supported by the mercantilist school, which emphasizes that military power is based on economic power, and therefore favors a complete trade embargo on a target state because even the smallest amount of trade will boost its economy and release resources for military use. Narrower and refined forms of economic warfare only control the supply of key items such as raw materials or components used for arms manufacture. Trade embargoes on critical bottleneck commodities, or items for which demand is highly inelastic and the cost of domestic production is prohibitive in the short run, are particularly effective. Other embargoes restrict the transfer of design and manufacturing know-how and technology rather than finished products. This was suggested in the 1976 Bucy Report, which also recommended curbing active technology transfer (occurring through turnkey projects, licensed production, and training) because it enabled a recipient to utilize the transferred technology more effectively.

Under contemporary technology embargoes, three types of goods are restricted—dual-use industrial technology, conventional arms or munitions, and nuclear and WMD materials. These restrictions are incorporated in U.S. legislation and the export control policies of other states. They were also part of the Cold War export control regime Cocom, under which Western states denied technology to the former Eastern bloc. A strategic technology embargo like Cocom, withholding only items that directly contribute to a target's military capacity, minimizes interference with overall trade.

Technology control regimes are controversial because of the tensions between security reasons to maintain technology embargoes on the one hand, and the economic spinoffs of technology and commercial and trade pressures for tech-

Table 2.3. Military Impairment Export Controls

Types	Examples of Items Banned	Policy/Regime
ECONOMIC EMBARGO: Bans a broad range of items including dual-use economic infrastructure and technology	Oil and gas pipeline and drilling equipment to former Soviet Union	Cocom
ARMS EMBARGO: Bans a broad category of weapons	Tanks, aircraft, small arms, to specific regions of conflict, at times of conflict	UN embargo on South Africa, Iraq, Serbia
ARMS CONTROL EMBARGO: Bans a few specific military systems	Ballistic missiles to all states at all times	MTCR
TECHNOLOGY CONTROL REGIME: Bans dual-use industrial items	Rocket engines, rocket fuels Machine-tools, hi-tech electronics Precursor chemicals Nuclear technology	MTCR Cocom / Wassenaar Australia Group Nuclear Suppliers Group

nology exports on the other. In general, technological advances are ubiquitous in world affairs and have both economic and military spinoffs.[32] The use of technology in mass destruction weapons drives efforts to control its transfer. Yet WMD-related technologies also have widespread civilian applications. Nuclear power is a source of energy; chemical and biological agents are used in the industrial, pharmaceutical, and agricultural sectors; and rockets are used to launch communications satellites and remote sensing satellites. Rocket technologies such as chemicals (for rocket propulsion), electronics (for rocket guidance), metals (for airframes and heat shielding), and machine tools (for building missiles) also have several nonmilitary industrial applications.

Moreover, commercial pressures to export technology for profit, and international free trade norms to remove barriers on trade, both conflict with arms control measures to restrict technology transfer. Export controls are challenged by economic lobbies seeking increased trade balances, and by groups losing revenues (estimated by some studies to be several billion dollars annually) from such embargoes. These tensions were prominently manifest when the U.S. firm Loral provided technical assistance to Chinese rocket launching firms. Such assistance generated profits for U.S. firms but enabled China to improve the accuracy of its ballistic missiles.

Summarizing export control dilemmas, a UN report notes, "it is difficult to reduce transfers for security reasons, and at the same time, to open markets for economic reasons," and yet a balance must be struck "to accommodate economic and scientific development for the beneficiaries [of technology] with the preservation of security imperatives for everyone."[33] The MTCR seeks to impair only missile production (and not all military-related production) in target states. It thus controls only missile-relevant technology and has therefore been less controversial than broader national export controls and Cocom.

The effectiveness of economic sanctions has been computed to be (at best) roughly 20 to 30 percent.[34] However, few studies compute specific success scores for technology embargoes. Instead, social science research on export controls has mainly analyzed their theoretical and political aspects. One line of research explores why supplier states join export control regimes. Bertsch, Cupitt, and Elliott-Gower note that geopolitical, economic, societal, governmental, international institutional, and technological factors determine export control policy. Cupitt, Grillot, and Murayama provide a membership-fee explanation for why states adopt nonproliferation export controls.[35]

A second line of arguments explores the outcome of export controls. For example, some studies assert that "there are no technical barriers to nuclear proliferation, only hurdles of greater or lesser size which can be leaped over at greater or lesser cost and . . . time scales."[36] Others assert that technology embargoes are actually counterproductive because they cause the target state to acquire its own technology and thereby become invulnerable to further embargoes. Reflecting this argument, Radio South Africa noted that the international arms embargo against South Africa "has achieved the opposite of what it was intended to achieve. In the last two decades the country [of South Africa] has built up the tenth largest arms industry in the world and this achievement was the direct response of the misguided attempt to isolate South Africa."[37] Since these assertions have not been tested over a large sample of cases, this study empirically tests the above propositions.

Measuring National Technological Capacity for Missile Production

Technology embargoes are expected to be most effective against technologically weak states, and least effective against technologically strong ones. These differences in the expected impact of the MTCR are incorporated in the following propositions:

Proposition T1: *Technologically strong states overcome the MTCR's embargoes and advance their missile programs.*

Proposition T2: *Technologically weak states are thwarted by the MTCR's embargoes and halt their missile programs.*

Proposition T3: *For states that continue their missile activity after the MTCR's advent, the technologically stronger states develop more powerful missiles, while the technologically weaker states develop less powerful missiles.*

Three sets of data can be used to measure a state's technological strengths and capability for missile production—its economic and industrial base, its prior arms production record, and its expertise in critical technologies.

First, macroeconomic indicators and data on the key industries required for missile development—chemicals, iron and steel and metals, electronics, and skilled manpower—are shown in Table 2.4. These figures are highly correlated.

Second, data on arms production and national defense industries usefully supplement macroeconomic indicators. This is because although states with a high GDP generally build more sophisticated weapons, some states such as Israel have a small economy but still have a large defense industry.[38] Studies of arms industries and aircraft production have ranked Brazil, India, Israel, and South Africa as high-level producers; South Korea, Argentina, and Taiwan as midlevel producers; Egypt, North Korea, and Pakistan at mid to low levels; and other states at low levels.[39]

Third, a state's prowess in critical technologies can significantly boost its missile program. Data on these technologies are found in the Military Critical Technologies List of fifteen items: materials, industrial production, electronics, computers, telecommunications, navigation-guidance-vehicle controls, sensors and electronic combat systems, marine systems, propulsion-vehicular systems, laser-optic-power systems, direct and kinetic energy systems, survivability-hardening systems, and nuclear-related technology.[40] The top five regional powers in these categories (indicated on a 0–1 scale) were Israel (0.456), India (0.303), South Korea (0.232), Brazil (0.182), and South Africa (0.126).[41]

National ranks across economic-industrial, arms production, and technological indicators are moderately correlated; Table 2.5 combines these three sets of indicators into an aggregate level of national technological capability. Relative to other regional powers, Brazil, India, Israel, and South Korea are technologically

Table 2.4. National Economic and Industrial Data

UNIT	GDP ($ BIL.) 1990	GDP 2000	Industrial Share of GDP (%)	Industry Size ($ BIL.) 1990	Industry Size 2000	Chemicals (%) 1990/97	Electrical (%) 1990/97	Metals (%) 1990/97	Steel (MIL. TONS) 1998	Economic-Industrial Relative Size
Brazil	648	836	23	149	192	13.9	13.5	11.0	25	High
S. Korea	340	616	30	102	185	10.7	22.1	15.1	40	High
India	280	486	17	48	83	10.5	7.1	4.4	24	High
Taiwan	253	472	25	63	118	12.5	20.5	11.9	17	High
Argentina	188	294	27	51	79	3.2	2.6	6.7	4	High
S. Africa	133	157	22	29	35				7	Mid
Israel	66	112	22	15	25				0.2	Mid
Iran	60	89	13	8	12		0.8	1.8	5	Low
Egypt	54	82	22	12	18				3	Low
Pakistan	47	70	16	8	11	1.5	1			Low
N. Korea	19	13	25	5	3				8	Low / Very Low
Libya	34	37	5	2	2				1	Very Low
Iraq	15	24	10	2	2				0.3	Very Low
Syria	10	18	3	1	1					Very Low
	(a)		(b)	(a x b)						

SOURCE: GDP data in 1996 dollars is from Economist Intelligence Unit, Country Reports. Percentage indicators for industrial chemicals, electrical machinery, and metal products (metals) reflect each state's share of developing country production for the industry; data are average of 1990 and 1997. United Nations Industrial Development Organization, International Yearbook of Industrial Statistics (Vienna: UNIDO, 1995 and 2000). Steel data is from New Steel, March 1999; figure for Libya is from Illustrated Book of World Rankings (New York: M.E. Sharpe, 1997); figures for Israel, North Korea, and Iraq are from Industry Commodity Statistics Yearbook 1997 (New York: United Nations, 1999).

Table 2.5. National Technological Capability for Missile Manufacture (Relative Levels)

	GDP & Industry	Arms Production Record	Technology	Aggregate Capability
Brazil	High	High	High	High
India	High	High	High	High
S. Korea	High	Mid	High	High
Israel	Mid	High	High	High
S. Africa	Mid	High	Mid	Mid
Argentina	High	Mid	Mid	Mid
Taiwan	High	Mid	Mid	Mid
Iran	Low	Low	Low	Low
Egypt	Low	Mid/Low	Low	Low
N. Korea	Low	Mid/Low	Low	Low
Pakistan	Low	Mid/Low	Low	Low
Iraq	Very Low	Low	Low	Very Low
Syria	Very Low	Low	Low	Very Low
Libya	Very Low	Low	Low	Very Low

highly capable states, while Argentina, Taiwan, and South Africa have midlevel capacities for missile manufacture. North Korea, Pakistan, Egypt, and Iran have technologically lower capabilities, while Iraq, Syria, and Libya have technologically very low capabilities. It should be clarified that, while they differ significantly from each other in relative levels, almost all the regional powers in this study have at least some basic industry and technically trained manpower. For example, North Korea has a substantial steel industry, Egypt has the major military industry in the Arab world, and Iran has skilled science and technology manpower and publishes many technical journals.

POLITICAL INFLUENCES ON PROLIFERATION

During the space (or window of opportunity) generated by technology embargoes, target states encounter domestic and external pressures on their missile decisions. What are the sources of these pressures?

In general, any regime operates within a broader system that shapes not only the nature of the regime but also the behavior of states toward the regime. The MTCR operates in the post–Cold War international system characterized by unipolarity, globalization, increasing interdependence between states (especially between regional powers and the remaining superpower), democratization, and economic liberalization. These factors generate external and internal political-economic pressures on regional powers. In addition, regional powers encounter another set of pressures—security threats—from their regional system. Thus both political-economic pressures in the globalized world system and security pressures from their regional system influence national missile decisions.

External Factors: Security Considerations

Proposition S1: *States facing low security threats curb their missile programs.*
Proposition S2: *States facing high security threats retain missile programs.*

Realist theorists and policy makers argue that proliferation is the result of perceived or actual military security threats to a state. In an anarchic international system, military capability (including missile and nuclear weapons capability) is the only assured form of survival. This reasoning suggests that states seek nuclear and missile capability when they face military threats from regional or distant states. Conversely, they may abstain from proliferation if threats diminish, or if threats can be countered by alliances and a related security guarantee from a major power. In a forty-country study, Stephen Meyer noted that alliance commitments with a nuclear superpower were important in dissuading proliferation.[42]

Two clarifications on security threats and proliferation should be noted. First, proliferation may be the *cause* as well as the *consequence* of security threats. A state's acquisition of nuclear and missile capability can increase the security concerns of neighboring states and lead them to respond with similar capabilities, providing the original state with an important security reason to refrain from proliferation. Second, the questions of whether a nuclear and missile deterrent actually enhances a state's security, and whether deterrence averts interstate conflict or is even stable, remain contested. Debates on deterrence stability are beyond the scope this study.

Four criteria can be used to measure the presence and intensity of security threats. First, a state is determined to face security threats if it has fought a recent war or has a serious and militarized territorial or political dispute with an adversary, and faces an offensive military threat from the adversary. Second, the threat is more acute if the adversary has a WMD program (indicated if it has not signed international WMD-control arrangements, or has attempted to break out of such arrangements). Third, the threat is also substantial if an adversary has overwhelming conventional military and economic superiority. Fourth, if a state faces international political and economic isolation, or loses (or perceives itself to be losing) a major ally, its insecurity increases. Conversely, when adversarial states resolve territorial or political disputes or renounce WMD programs, then the security threats they face from each other are reduced. Overall, this four-criteria assessment of security threats provides a more appropriate measurement than, and can be cross-checked against, international relations data on militarized inter-state disputes and the correlates of war.

In the 1990s, military threats to national security were low for Argentina, Brazil, and South Africa; security threats were at low to mid levels for Libya and Egypt; they were mid to high for Iran, Iraq, Syria, and India; and they were high for North Korea, Pakistan, Israel, South Korea, and Taiwan.

While security motivations are important in missile acquisition, security threats do not fully explain the timing of many national nuclear and missile decisions. When threats recede, some states still maintain nuclear and missile programs. Therefore, a comprehensive explanation for proliferation must include other political and economic factors.

External Factors:
Political-Economic Influences, Interdependence, International Leverage

Missile programs raise global proliferation concerns, and therefore states pursuing missile activity encounter international opposition to halt these programs. External powers may offer incentives to regional powers, or exert political and economic pressure on regional powers, or pursue both strategies, to curb their missile programs. The following discussion analyzes how such strategies allow for leverage on target states. It explores how leverage is induced by structural factors such as interdependence and by psychological factors such as the national will to withstand external pressure. It then elaborates upon how interdependence is measured, and examines the conditions influencing the degree of interdependence between states. It also explores the effects of security interdependence.

In general, interdependence between states allows them to influence each other. Scholars analyzing the links between power and economic interdependence note that "the influence which country A acquires in country B by foreign trade depends in the first place upon the total gain which B derives from that trade; the total gain from trade for any country is nothing but another expression for the total impoverishment which would be inflicted upon it by a stoppage of trade."[43] Elaborating upon this theme, Keohane and Nye note that states that are interdependent are *sensitive* and *vulnerable* to each other's economic actions.[44] Thus, if a regional power's economy is substantially dependent upon trade with and aid from external powers, as well as sensitive (to short-term shocks) and vulnerable (to long-term embargoes, because of the unavailability of alternative trade or aid partners), it would be more susceptible to external pressure.[45]

Four qualifications to the principle of interdependence and leverage should be noted. First, noneconomic factors also influence relations between states and the preferences of target states. If a weaker state values its security and sovereignty more than the stronger nation is bent on dominating it, then the weaker state will more intensely resist external political-economic pressures and would bear economic losses for security gains. This discussion ties in with the national will to resist external pressure and the psychological components of power and bargaining. States facing security threats would not only give higher priority to security-relevant missile programs, but may also have a stronger national will to resist external pressure (though national will can be induced independently of security concerns; it can be the result of other cultural, political, or historical factors). Second, domestic politics influence interstate bargaining. Domestic lobbies in a stronger state that derive economic gains from or have political-cultural ties with a target state can prevent the stronger state from fully exerting pressure on the target state.[46] Third, a weaker state may have reverse leverage on the stronger. The weaker state's geopolitical importance to the stronger, and the stronger state's reliance on strategic commodities from the weaker, can restrain the stronger from pressuring the weaker. Finally, issues such as coercive diplomacy and the links between foreign aid and leverage are also relevant to interstate bargaining.

The extent to which a regional power was susceptible to external pressure in the 1980s and 1990s can, in most cases, be determined from its ties with one principal external power—the United States. At that time, the United States was the primary external power exerting diplomatic and economic pressure on regional powers. Other major powers (Russia, China, Japan, and West European states) also have economic or security ties with some of the regional powers in this study or offer large aid packages to them. These major powers have sometimes engaged or sanctioned regional powers for nonproliferation reasons,[47] but this engagement has not been as intense as that pursued by the United States. Economic dependence between regional powers and the United States (measured as the sum of regional power exports to and imports and aid from the U.S., as a percentage of GNP), for the 1980s and 1990s, is as follows: Taiwan (20%, 19%); South Korea (12%, 12%); Israel (14%, 15%); Egypt (11%, 10%); South Africa (3%, 3.5%); Brazil (2%, 2.4%); Argentina (1%, 2%); India (1.3%, 2.1%); Pakistan (4.7%, 3.8%). These figures were below 1 percent for Iran, North Korea, Libya, Syria, and Iraq in the 1990s. A regional power's other foreign economic ties include aid from international organizations and foreign investment, which account for up to 3 percent of their GNP.[48]

Thus, South Korea, Taiwan, Egypt, and Israel have a high degree of interdependence with the United States; Argentina, Brazil, India, and Pakistan have middle levels of interdependence; and North Korea, Iran, Iraq, Libya, and Syria have very low degrees of interdependence with the United States. Further, trade with target states is a negligible component of U.S. national trade; it is barely

3 to 5 percent for large trading partners such as South Korea and Taiwan, 1.5 percent for Brazil, and under 1 percent for other states. This asymmetry allows for substantially greater U.S. leverage on regional powers. In addition, the regional powers in this study had little reverse leverage on the United States because the United States is not highly dependent on strategic commodity imports from these states.[49]

Three factors affect the magnitude of interdependence between states—the conscious engagement strategies of an external power, the globalization of the world economy, and the economic liberalization policies of a regional power. Interdependence may be consciously created through a foreign policy of engagement that promotes economic and strategic ties to gain leverage on a trading partner. Interdependence also arises from increased trade which either naturally accompanies the globalization of the world economy or is the result of a regional power's conscious economic liberalization policy. On this issue, Robert Gilpin notes that the economic benefits of participating in the marketplace are too great for most states to resist becoming entangled in trade relationships, even at the price of their sovereignty.[50] The failure of the Soviet model left regional powers with little alternative than to adapt to the market- and trade-based economic model in the 1990s. The success of market reforms has been tied to trade, aid, and credit from the West. This enables these external powers to gain leverage on regional powers. The structurally unipolar international system further increased a regional power's dependence on the dominant power—the United States—because alternative economic options (that may have been available from other major powers in a bipolar or multipolar system) were not viable.

Beyond economic interdependence, a regional power's security ties with an external power also affect its missile decision. Security ties with a major power can alleviate the security concerns of a regional power (and thus reduce its security need for a missile program). They also make the regional power further susceptible to major power leverage. Three indicators determine the strength of security ties between a regional power and the United States—a defense or security pact, a U.S. military presence in the state, and U.S. military sales.[51] Based on these indicators, four regional powers have high levels of security interdependence with the United States: South Korea, Taiwan, Israel, and Egypt.

Security interdependence is considerably asymmetric for Taiwan and South Korea, because they rely heavily on the United States for their national security while Washington does not strongly depend on these states for its own geostrategic interests. In contrast, Israel and Egypt have some reverse leverage on Washington because they are vital for U.S. strategic objectives. They are major U.S. allies in the geostrategically important Middle East, and a strong Israel lobby in the United States also gives Israel additional leverage.

One further means to leverage is through positive incentives. Irrespective of the level of interdependence, meaningful security and economic incentives (including the incentive to lift sanctions) can influence the defense policies and missile decisions of regional powers.

Another measure of a state's capability and willingness for missile programs comes from its defense budgets. Military expenditures in 1990 and 2000 in billion dollars were as follows: Brazil (5.8, 10.1); South Korea (7.8, 10.0); India (7.5, 12.3); Taiwan (8.0, 7.2); Argentina (3.9, 4.5); South Africa (3.6, 2.1); Israel (7.6, 8.9); Iran (3.8, 7.1); Egypt (2.5, 2.5); Pakistan (3.1, 3.1); North Korea (2.1, 1.3).[52]

Table 2.6 summarizes overall economic and security ties between regional powers and the United States, and the factors influencing national missile decisions.

In addition to international factors, domestic political and economic considerations also influence (either singularly or by interacting with external factors) nonproliferation outcomes. Democratization and economic liberalization are prominent contemporary domestic political-economic developments; further, both have coincided with and reinforced each other.[53]

Domestic Economic Factors: Liberalization and Reforms

Economic liberalization makes regional powers more interdependent with external powers and therefore susceptible to external pressure on their missile programs. Moreover, as Etel Solingen argues, domestic coalitions pursuing economic reforms are more likely to embrace regional and international nuclear regimes than their inward-looking nationalist and radical-confessional counterparts.[54] This is because a state's decision to remain outside the nonproliferation regime involves costs such as the denial of access to foreign technology, markets, capital, and investments. As a result, domestic coalitions emerge that favor or reject tradeoffs and linkages. Groups that might otherwise pay little attention to the country's nuclear posture become more attentive to the international bargain involved. They are thus willing to renounce nuclear options in exchange for foreign technical and financial assistance.

South Korea and Taiwan have liberalized their economies since the 1960s; Argentina, Brazil, South Africa, India, Pakistan, and Israel pursued varying degrees of economic liberalization in the 1990s; Egypt and Iran pursued limited economic liberalization. Regional power economic-freedom scores for 1995 and 1999, on a scale of 1–5 (with 1 representing most free and 5 representing least free), were as follows: Taiwan (1.95, 1.95); South Korea (2.15, 2.4); Argentina (2.85, 2.5); South Africa (3.0, 2.9); Israel (3.1, 2.8); Brazil (3.3, 3.25); Pakistan (3.15, 3.35); Egypt (3.5, 3.35); India (3.7, 3.7); Syria (4.2, 4.4); Iran (4.7, 4.7); Iraq (4.9, 4.9); Libya (4.9, 4.7); North Korea (5.0, 5.0).[55]

Table 2.6. Factors Influencing National Missile Outcomes

State	(+) Capability Technical[a]	Financial[b]	(+) Security Threat[e]	(−) U.S. Influence Economic[c]	Security[d]	Other	Indigenous Missile Program
South Korea	High	High	High	High	High		SRBM
Taiwan	Mid	High	High	High	High		CM, SRBM
Argentina	Mid	Mid	Low	Mid	Low		
Brazil	High	High	Low	Mid	Low		AR, SLV
South Africa	Mid	Low	Low	Mid	Low		
Egypt	Low	Low	Low/Mid	High	High		SRBM
Iraq	Very Low	Low	Mid/High	Low	Low		SRBM
Syria	Very Low	Low	Mid/High	Low	Low		SRBM
Libya	Very Low	Low	Low/Mid	Low	Low		
Israel	High	High	High	High	High	U.S. compromise	IRBM
India	High	High	Mid/High	Mid	Low		IRBM
Pakistan	Low	Low	High	Mid	Low		IRBM
North Korea	Low	Low	High	Low	Low	Talks with U.S.	IRBM
Iran	Low	Mid	Mid/High	Low	Low		IRBM

+/: Factor Increases (+) or Decreases (-) likelihood of missile program.

a   Technical capabilities are determined from a state's economic size, industry (size and presence of key industries such as metals, chemicals, electronics), technology base, and conventional arms production.

b   Financial capabilities are calculated from average annual military expenditure, and their relative levels are ranked as low (below $3 billion), midlevel ($3 billion to $7 billion) or high (over $7 billion).

c   U.S. economic ties are calculated from the sum of trade with and aid from the United States, as a percentage of a state's GNP. States for which this figure is over 10 percent have relatively high ties with (and are thus highly dependent on) the United States; those where this figure is 2–10 percent are moderately dependent; and states where it is below 1 percent have a low degree of dependence.

d   U.S. security ties (and the resulting U.S. influence on a state's security) are calculated from U.S. arms sales to, a U.S. troop presence in, and U.S. military or security treaties with, the respective state.

e   Security threats are measured from four criteria—threats are higher if a state has fought a recent war or has an acute interstate dispute with an adversary, if the adversary has a WMD program, if the adversary has overwhelming economic and conventional military superiority, and if a state faces international political and economic isolation and loses (or perceives losing) an ally.

Relative levels: Low, Mid, High

CM: cruise missile; AR: artillery rocket; SRBM: short-range ballistic missile; IRBM: intermediate-range ballistic missile; SLV: Satellite launch vehicle

Domestic Political Factors:
Bureaucratic Politics, Civil-Military Relations, Democratization

Two aspects of domestic politics—bureaucratic politics and regime type—can influence national proliferation decisions. First, bureaucratic politics, or rivalry among domestic actors and bureaucracies having different policy preferences, affects missile outcomes. Proliferation is more likely when particular groups (such as scientific elites, the defense-industrial complex, the military, or specific political parties) committed to a WMD program prevail over other groups. Second, the type of regime—democratic or nondemocratic—can influence proliferation. On theoretical grounds, the democratization of both states of a dyad would favor nonproliferation, while democratization by itself would have a mixed impact on proliferation.

At the dyadic level, the democratic peace hypothesis (which has its critics) notes that democratic states do not fight each other. It argues that democratic dyads are peaceful due to the presence of democratic norms and a democratic political culture, and structural and institutional constraints on democratic governments.[56] Based on this logic, democratization in both states of a dyad favors nonproliferation. This is because democratic states may perceive fewer security threats from their democratic neighbors (for both institutional and political culture reasons), which in turn would reduce their security requirement for missile programs.

The effects of democratization at the monadic or national government level are mixed. Democracies are as likely as nondemocracies to fight wars (though not with other democracies), and when they face or perceive acute security threats, democracies may well acquire nuclear and missile programs. Indeed, nuclear and missile programs in three of the five NPT nuclear states and in India and Israel were initiated and sustained by democratic governments. Yet two other effects—one positive and one negative—of democracy on proliferation are worth noting.

On the positive side, democratic institutions provide checks and balances on government policies. An accountable democratic government must pay greater heed to social and economic issues (especially when pursuing economic reforms that require domestic and international support), and may therefore have less enthusiasm for military projects such as missile programs. Civil-military relations are also relevant to this analysis: if civilians exert strong control over the military (as is generally the case in consolidated democracies), then they would be more capable of resisting military pressure for nuclear and missile programs. Further, as noted in a six-country study by Mitchell Reiss, internal considerations such as antinuclear public opinion in democracies play some role in preventing proliferation.[57] Conversely, military or authoritarian governments may be more inclined to advance defense and missile programs at the expense of social development. It should be clarified, however, that even in democracies, political elites allocate budgetary resources to defense industries to cater to domestic lobbies, while authoritarian governments themselves cannot totally ignore domestic audience costs and economic constraints.

On the other hand, the democratic process and political culture can make reversing proliferation harder. A country's leaders must be sensitive to public opinion and nationalism in democracies, which makes it difficult for them to back down on a security issue such as a missile project. George Perkovich has noted that democracy makes reversing proliferation harder in the case of India's nuclear program because public opinion does not allow Indian policy makers to compromise on nuclear issues.[58] Further, leaders may deliberately support prestige projects such as missile programs to generate domestic support and boost approval ratings.[59] Indeed, civilian control of a nuclear program demonstrates that civilians are as capable as the military in providing for national security. Therefore, civilian leaders may benefit from (and actively seek) a nuclear program to bolster their position versus the national armed forces. An illustrative example is in Pakistan.[60]

Argentina, Brazil, South Korea, Taiwan, South Africa, Israel, India, and Pakistan were democratic during the 1990s; Iran and Egypt undertook political liberalization but remained nondemocratic; North Korea, Syria, Iraq, and Libya were nondemocratic. These classifications largely agree with the quantitative democracy scores of Polity III and Freedom House data.[61] In terms of democratic dyads, only the Argentina-Brazil and India-Pakistan dyads (but not the India-China dyad) were democratic in the 1990s; the other dyads in this study were not democratic.

MISSILE PROLIFERATION AND WMD PROLIFERATION

Missile proliferation is partly linked with and partly distinct from the broader proliferation of weapons of mass destruction. Since states acquire missiles to deliver WMDs, this logic suggests that states with WMD ambitions would seek missiles and states renouncing such programs would curb their missile aspirations. A strong correlation between WMD proliferation and missile proliferation supports this reasoning. For example, Argentina and South Africa renounced their nuclear programs and also dropped their missile programs, while India, Pakistan, and Israel retained their nuclear options and built medium-range missiles. This further suggests that states retaining missile programs—North Korea and Iran with medium-range missiles, South Korea and Egypt with short-range missiles, or even other states having satellite launch programs—may have not entirely given up their WMD options despite signing nonproliferation agreements. They may instead be preparing for, or hedging against, a breakout from WMD controls. And states armed with missiles may be in a better security position during any breakdown of WMD control regimes (as discussed below). Of the states in this study, Taiwan, Egypt, Iraq, Syria, Libya, and North Korea had not signed the CWC as of 2001; India, Israel, and Pakistan had not signed the NPT; all the regional powers in this study except Israel had signed the BWC.

Despite the strong correlation, there are also several differences between missile proliferation and WMD proliferation. First, the MTCR's technology blockade slows target missile programs but does not affect target WMD programs. Second, a state's WMD programs and missile programs may be pursued by different national bureaucracies. For example, Argentina's air force operated the Condor rocket project but its navy was more linked with the national nuclear program. Thus, even if a government can persuade its nuclear weapons complex to curb its activities, the government may not ask or influence its missile organization to halt this activity—especially when rocket programs have no connection with WMD programs. This leads to a third point: rocket programs are not always intended for strategic use and WMD delivery. Missiles have other *military* applications that are noncatastrophic. Tactical conventionally armed missiles have been acquired to undertake deep strike missions that cannot be performed by a national air force (though most ballistic missiles are not accurate and not optimal for such missions). Rocket programs also have *civilian* uses as space launchers. Fourth, the timing of advances or restraints in national missile programs differs from that in national WMD programs. For example, South Africa signed the NPT in 1991, but continued its rocket program and only agreed to abandon it in 1993–94. These areas of difference between missile proliferation and WMD proliferation suggest that it is important to study missile outcomes independently from WMD outcomes.

On policy grounds, since ballistic missile strikes are not catastrophic if they are not armed with WMDs, the question can be raised as to whether a missile control regime is less relevant if a strong WMD control regime already exists. A missile control regime still has advantages in strengthening the WMD control regime and mitigating the negative effects of any WMD breakout. First, missile control regimes are less prone to be violated (and thereby possibly break down) than chemical and biological control regimes. This is because missile bans, though harder to verify than nuclear bans, are easier to verify than chemical and biological bans. Second, any breakdown in the chemical, biological, and nuclear control regimes would be less destabilizing if a functional missile control regime is already in place, because states without missiles would not strongly threaten distant states with WMDs. Conversely, in the absence of a missile control regime, states breaking out of a WMD control regime could immediately threaten distant states, thereby gravely exacerbating international tensions. Third, the very existence of several missile-armed states (under no missile control regime) can accelerate the breakdown of a WMD control regime. States may more quickly abandon WMD control regimes at the first signals of their breakdown if they face acute threats from an adversary who can use missiles to deliver WMDs on the state. A state's main security option may then be swift missile and WMD rearmament to build a deterrent against such an adversary. Conversely, if a WMD breakout by a few defectors is not very threatening (which would be the case when the states breaking out do not have long-range delivery forces), then states would be willing to give at least some time to bringing defectors back into a WMD control regime. For these reasons, the establishment of a strong missile control regime would strengthen the WMD nonproliferation regime and mitigate the effects of any breakdown of the nuclear, chemical, and biological nonproliferation regimes.

METHOD AND CASES

In the 1980s and 1990s, fourteen regional powers were attempting to build ballistic missiles—Argentina, Brazil, South Korea, Taiwan, South Africa, Egypt, Iraq, Syria, Libya, Israel, India, Pakistan, Iran, and North Korea. These missile programs were most likely to be affected by the MTCR and are therefore examined in some detail in this book. Other regional powers that bought missiles from foreign suppliers but were not building their own missiles were not the MTCR's direct targets. Similarly, the missiles of the five NPT nuclear states and space rockets in the United States, Russia, the European Space Agency, China, Japan, and Ukraine are not controlled by the MTCR. The above systems are therefore excluded from detailed study, but they are considered when exploring future policy options for the missile regime.

This comparative study of fourteen cases is not the only way to examine the MTCR's impact on missile proliferation, but it may be the most appropriate. Alternative research designs such as single case or "small-n" studies, that examine only one or a few national missile programs in some detail, would provide valuable information about the specific technological obstacles and political pressures behind a nonproliferation outcome. Yet a single case does not allow for comparing positive and negative outcomes.[62] Small-n studies may have variations in outcomes, but still do not facilitate broader generalizations, because certain conditions may be unique to a state or region and cannot be generalized to other regions.[63] The cases in this book vary widely in their technological and political parameters, and this study's conclusions can therefore be more widely generalized.

Finally, a methodological limitation in this study should be noted. Obtaining accurate missile data is difficult because such information is among a country's most closely guarded secrets. Therefore, figures in this book on the number and types of missiles in a country and their payload and range may not be completely accurate. Yet this book's sources represent the most authoritative research on missile proliferation. These include think tank databases and reports; government documents such as several National Intelligence Estimates and Commission Reports (like the July 1998 Rumsfeld Commission Report); and major analytical studies of missile proliferation by Shuey (1990), Carus (1990), Nolan (1991), Stanford (1991), Brauch et al. (1992), Navias (1993), Potter and Jencks (1994), Speier (1995), Hayes (1996), Karp (1996), and others. Moreover, limitations in technical information do not affect this study's wider arguments about how multilateral cooperation and international regimes can contain missile proliferation and manage global security affairs.

3

Building a Supply-Side Regime: Western Countries, Russia, and China

In February 2001, Secretary of Defense Donald Rumsfeld launched a dramatic broadside against Moscow, charging that "Russia is an active proliferator. . . . They are selling and assisting countries like Iran and North Korea and India and other countries with these [missile-related] technologies which are threatening . . . the United States and Western Europe and countries in the Middle East."[1] That same month, Washington's Central Intelligence Agency reported that "the Chinese have continued to take a very narrow interpretation of their bilateral non-proliferation commitments with the United States. . . . Chinese missile-related technical assistance to Pakistan continued to be substantial."[2] It added that "entities in Western countries in 2000 were not as important as sources for WMD-related goods and materials as in past years."[3]

These statements provided Washington's assessment of how well the main missile technology suppliers—Western states, Russia, and China—complied with the Missile Technology Control Regime (MTCR). The MTCR was announced in 1987. In prior years, no formal regime controlled missile proliferation. From the 1950s to the 1970s, the only major curbs on missile exports were through ad hoc U.S. restrictions on space technology transfers and conventional arms sales. In the 1980s, multilateral negotiations to halt missile proliferation led to the creation of the MTCR by the G-7 states. In the 1990s, MTCR members sought to bring other key suppliers such as Russia and China into the regime. Several rounds of diplomacy and the use of sanctions and incentives were involved in this process of building a supply-side regime to contain missile proliferation.

MISSILE TECHNOLOGY PROLIFERATION AND THE ESTABLISHMENT OF THE MTCR

Space Technology and Ballistic Missile Transfers

In the first decades of the nuclear and missile age, interstate nuclear and missile transfers were not strongly and formally curbed by a global regime. Although national governments did not generally share sensitive nuclear technology with other states, this approach was somewhat relaxed under programs such as the Eisenhower administration's "Atoms for Peace" initiative (1954) and the International Geophysical Year (1958). States were then given access to nuclear technology (mainly civilian technology under safeguards) and rocket technology (relevant to small rockets but not powerful missiles); this served as an incentive for them to refrain from the military use of this technology, and to forestall their indigenous development of nuclear programs. Technology transfers also attracted states into the Western and Eastern camps during the Cold War.

Beginning in 1959, the United States, the Soviet Union, and West European states signed technology-sharing memorandums of understanding (MOUs) with a dozen countries in Latin America and Asia, including Argentina, Brazil, India, South Korea, Mexico, Pakistan, and Taiwan.[4] Through these MOUs, they transferred technical data on sounding rockets and on space launch vehicles (the equivalent of short-range and intermediate-range missiles, respectively), and hardware such as satellite tracking stations, launch facilities, and suborbital sounding rockets, to regional powers. The technology in these transfers was generally not directly convertible to ballistic missiles, but was relevant to rocket design, rocket components, and rocket infrastructure.

Both superpowers also considered missiles to be tactical weapons, and exported *short-range* systems to their allies. From the 1960s, the United States selectively transferred short-range Honest John and Lance missiles to its allies, as part of a foreign policy of containment that aimed to strengthen West European defenses and to limit Soviet influence in developing countries. Washington thereby supplied 37 km range Honest John artillery rockets to its West European allies (Belgium, Denmark, France, West Germany, the Netherlands, and the U.K.), and to South Korea, Taiwan, Greece, and Turkey in the period 1959–61. It sent the 130 km range Lance missiles to the U.K., West Germany, and Italy in the 1960s and 1970s. It supplied twelve Lance launchers and over one hundred missiles to Israel in 1976, and also placed these missiles (under U.S. control) in South Korea. In addition, U.S. intermediate-range Pershing-1 missiles were based in West Germany in the 1970s, and were replaced by 108 of the 1,800 km range Pershing-2 missiles in the 1980s (both these systems were under U.S. control). Washington further supplied over one hundred Polaris SLBMs to Britain beginning in 1965, and these were replaced with Trident SLBMs; this was the only U.S. transfer of long-range missiles. Washington initially opposed but from 1972 supplied some missile design, guidance, and spin stabilizing assistance and technology to France. Finally, it transferred space launcher rockets to Japan. At the time, no major U.S. policy clarified restrictions on missile transfers. The only guidelines on this issue were outlined in

National Security Action Memorandum (NSAM) 294 of April 20, 1964, which covered strategic missile transfers and applied to U.S. missiles in NATO states. This document did not deal with tactical missile exports.

In subsequent years, missile technology exports were indirectly curbed in three ways—under space policies, via conventional arms control initiatives (which were concerned with regional security), and through a general technology denial approach—but were not specifically part of the nuclear nonproliferation agenda until the late 1970s.

Space Technology Restrictions

Beginning in the early 1970s, U.S. space technology transfer policy became restrictive for both commercial and national security reasons. Congress denounced the Nixon administration's decision to sell Delta space rocket licenses to Japan, calling it a sacrifice of U.S. technology.[5] The ensuing debate led to a revised export control policy—National Security Decision Memorandum (NSDM) 187 of August 30, 1972, titled "International Space Cooperation: Technology and Launch Assistance." This policy clarified, and to some extent reduced, U.S. cooperation with foreign rocket programs. It defined U.S. space policy concerning rockets, satellites, and participation in international space ventures. By restricting rocket technology transfer even to allies, NSDM 187 protected U.S. commercial interests in space launch services and shielded the space shuttle project. NSDM 187 reflected then-existing U.S. munitions export policy (the policy that applied not to space technology but to conventional weapons). If client states requested U.S. technology, then the transfer of hardware rather than the related production technology (which would enable client states to indigenously build hardware) was appropriate. By curbing technology transfer, NSDM 187 indirectly contributed to missile nonproliferation.

During the late Ford administration and the Carter administration, the Arms Control and Disarmament Agency (ACDA) reviewed and suggested two new U.S. space policy proposals.[6] One option would provide rocket technology to states that restricted their rocket activities to peaceful uses (this led to the 1980 U.S.-Japan space cooperation treaty, and to U.S. space talks with Brazil and India). A second option was to form a multilateral cartel curbing technology transfers. This was further pursued after India's successful rocket launch in 1980. Developments in the conventional arms and technology transfer fields reinforced this move toward restricting rocket technology transfers.

Conventional Arms Control and Regional Security Considerations

The conventional arms control framework partly covered missiles at various times in the 1960s and 1970s. During the Kennedy and Johnson administrations, sections of the U.S. bureaucracy were concerned about the impact of missile pro-liferation on regional security, especially in Egypt and Israel. In a 1963 visit to Egypt, President Kennedy's coordinator for disarmament activities, John McCloy, sought restraints on Cairo's missile activities. In May 1964 the U.S. embassy in Cairo was instructed to inform President Nasser of an arms rivalry with Israel. In late 1964, the Johnson administration sought Cairo's participa-tion in an initiative to limit Egypt's and Israel's missile activities.

From the mid-1970s, Washington was increasingly concerned about the impact of arms transfers on regional conflicts, especially because such conflicts could escalate and drag in the superpowers. For example, although Secretary of State Henry Kissinger favored supplying Pershing-1 missiles to Israel (to bring it aboard a Middle East peace settlement), the Defense Department raised objections. Washington therefore denied Israeli requests for the medium-range Pershing-1 and instead supplied it the short-range Lance in 1976. Thereafter, Washington considered restraining its conventional arms exports to build international sup-port for a global conventional arms control initiative. An American proposal to the Conference on Disarmament on July 29, 1976, noted that the United States had restrained its missile and aircraft transfers. Washington called on other sup-pliers to observe similar restraints and also urged recipients "to forgo acquisition of destabilizing systems not yet introduced into the area, particularly surface-to-surface missile systems having a long range beyond any defensive need."[7]

The Carter administration's emphasis on restraining both nuclear prolifera-tion and conventional arms transfers—through the 1977–78 Conventional Arms Transfer (CAT) talks—resulted in ballistic missiles being placed more promi-nently on the arms control agenda. Within the U.S. bureaucracy's intra-agency discussions on CAT, some groups noted that armed systems "that accorded a country a clear advantage in a preemptive strike, such as long-range surface-to-surface missiles, could be discussed as candidates for comprehensive restraint."[8] By 1978, ACDA was emphasizing the need to curb missile prolifer-ation not only for reasons of regional security, but also because of the implica-tions of missile proliferation for nuclear proliferation. It was concerned that missile production "could be particularly destabilizing if carried out by coun-tries assessed capable of producing nuclear weapons. Thus the availability and spread of technology potentially useful for ballistic missiles, space launch vehi-cles, cruise missiles, and remotely piloted vehicles could cause serious prob-lems for regional stability in the coming decade."[9]

Policy Shifts from Technology Transfer to Technology Denial

In the mid-1970s, the U.S. bureaucracy intensely debated various approaches to conventional and nuclear arms control, and the technology *transfer* policies of previous years gave way to technology *control* approaches. In the area of conventional arms control, sections of the U.S. bureaucracy preferred supplier restraints to any broader treaty. In a 1978 congressional briefing, the director of the State Department's Bureau of Political-Military Affairs noted that "formal agreements probably are not the most effective approach to this complicated arms control problem. Other more realistic possibilities include the development of harmonized national guidelines for transfer restraint, such as the London nuclear export guidelines."[10]

Another group in the U.S. bureaucracy held the opposite view, arguing that "an ongoing supply of technology, and U.S. involvement, could inhibit a recipient country's drive to militarize its space launch program. Arrangements to supply technology for military missile programs would be more selective, require more caution, and be limited to Third World allies. In principle, U.S. supply and involvement could keep military programs from being perceived as nuclear-related."[11] Thus, active supply rather than denial (which could lead to indigenous manufacture or to supply by other states, both of which would reduce U.S. influence on a target program) would ensure U.S. leverage on the end use of a technology.

The above debates on technology denial versus technology sharing approaches to conventional arms control were also prevalent in nuclear nonproliferation policy. In the mid-1970s, technology denial was not perceived as being the most appropriate way to halt proliferation, because Washington recognized that countries with a modest technological capability could still develop a nuclear program. However, under the Carter administration, U.S. technology exports became more restrictive, and the Nuclear Nonproliferation Act of 1978 authorized technology transfer only to states accepting comprehensive safeguards.

U.S. Missile Nonproliferation Policies Preceding the MTCR

The emphasis on technology denial made its way into U.S. missile nonproliferation policy during the Carter and Reagan administrations. Initially, as discussed above, missile nonproliferation was to be pursued through the conventional arms framework, but the CAT talks collapsed in December 1978. However, missile proliferation remained a prominent issue among the U.S. bureaucracy, especially because of four missile developments between 1978 and 1981: South Korea's 1978 missile test; Iraq's 1979 bid to purchase rocket stages from Italy; India's satellite launch vehicle flight tests in 1979 and 1980; and a German firm's (unsuccessful) March 1980 rocket launch in Libya. The Reagan administration then approached missile proliferation through two policies on space and missile technology transfer—NSDD 50, which was less restrictive, and NSDD 70, which was more restrictive.[12]

National Security Decision Directive (NSDD) 50 of August 6, 1982, was titled "Space Assistance and Cooperation Policy." NSDD 50 replaced NSDM 187, and its foreign policy objectives included promoting multilateral cooperation with other nations that would be "similar to on-going U.S. cooperation with the European Space Agency," in order "to demonstrate that the U.S. is a reliable partner in international ventures."[13] It allowed U.S. technical assistance for foreign satellite launch vehicles, but with "adequate assurances to control replication and retransfer and ensure peaceful use" (these restrictions were tighter than those of NSDM 187). It also sought to ensure that U.S. space exports would not contribute to the "development of any foreign weapon delivery system."[14]

NSDD 70 (November 30, 1982), titled "Nuclear Capable Missile Technology Transfer Policy," was an update of NSAM 294. It emphasized technology denial more strongly than NSDD 50, and it more explicitly placed missile proliferation within the nuclear nonproliferation regime. Its aims were to prohibit missile-relevant technology exports, exempt on a case-by-case basis certain U.S. friends and allies, and seek cooperation with supplier nations in export limitations.

Thus NSDD 50 and NSDD 70 both placed technology controls and missile proliferation under the broader nuclear nonproliferation regime, representing a shift from the prior focus of restricting missile exports primarily for regional security considerations. The Reagan administration also held the view that export controls were a national security tool, and not just a diplomatic or industrial issue, through which to halt the security threat of proliferation; the MTCR's export controls reflected these views, and its structure borrowed from the model of the Nuclear Suppliers Group (NSG) and Cocom.

Multilateral Approaches and the MTCR's Formation

In the 1980s, Washington engaged in multilateral discussions on missile proliferation with the G-7. Washington's bureaucracy explored missile controls in talks with the U.K. in May 1982, and with West Germany, Italy, and France in June 1982; the talks subsequently included Canada and Japan at a June 1983 meeting among all G-7 members in Washington. In conjunction with these meetings, by the spring of 1983 the State Department had drafted a set of rules titled "Missile Technology Control," which outlined national policy and multilateral coordination guidelines on the subject. By early June 1983, the Defense Department had drafted a document on the technical parameters of missiles to be controlled—missiles with a range greater than 300 km when carrying a 500 kg payload, and having a 10 km circular error probable.[15] This 1983 document also contained a "short list of denials," which included items (complete missile systems and complete subsystems) whose export would be prohibited. The document was approved by other agencies in the U.S. bureaucracy.

At their June 1983 meeting, G-7 officials outlined two categories of items that would be controlled. The first was a small group that would not normally be exported; it was based on the Defense Department's "short list" noted above, and eventually became category I of the MTCR. The second category was a long alert list of items (missile components and related technology) that would be subject to control and monitoring, but could be exported depending on the end user.

At a second missile nonproliferation meeting in Rome on December 1–2, 1983, the G-7 reached a broad agreement on the category I short list, but some states sought to exempt satellite launch vehicles (SLVs). There was also disagreement over procedure and rules. States were reluctant to create Cocom-like rules, where they would have to notify and consult each other prior to exports, because they feared commercial losses. Prompt notification was especially problematic because it alerted potential competitors, although bulk notifications on a monthly or annual basis were more acceptable.

No multilateral missile meetings took place in 1984. At this time, the U.S. bureaucracy also disagreed internally on whether the MTCR should ban SLV exports. The State Department sought flexibility on this issue, both to facilitate cooperation among the G-7 on the broader missile regime, and not to hurt U.S. relations with states such as Brazil and India that had SLV interests. On the other hand, the Defense Department desired a strict policy banning SLV exports. In March 1985, the G-7 agreed to informally implement the MTCR despite not reaching consensus on its final rules.

At a December 1985 London meeting, the issue of banning SLV transfers remained unresolved, but G-7 negotiators reached consensus on most other issues. By the spring of 1986, the G-7 states agreed on the definitions of category II items whose export would be controlled. Martin Navias notes that the regime's formal announcement was still delayed because France sought concessions from the United States and Britain that they would not sign the Treaty of Raratonga.[16] In February 1987, the last state holding out finally agreed to the regime, and on April 16, 1987, the MTCR was publicly announced.

Even after reaching agreement, the G-7 states differed over the mode of the MTCR's announcement. The U.S. bureaucracy desired a high-level public announcement, while the other G-7 states preferred low-key statements for fear of jeopardizing their relations with the international community. The MTCR's technology embargoes could curb scientific and commercial ventures between states and thereby hurt diplomatic ties between the G-7 and their trading partners. European states were also reluctant to enthusiastically embrace the export control philosophy, because they had strong export ministries and vigorous trade ideologies and were less willing to sacrifice even small export markets.

Eventually, most G-7 states made only low-key announcements, while in

Washington the White House press secretary, and not President Reagan, made the MTCR announcement. This one-page statement began by noting that "the President is pleased to announce a new policy to limit the proliferation of missiles capable of delivering nuclear weapons."[17] It ended with the line, "The United States, and its partners in this important initiative, would welcome the adherence of all states to these guidelines in the interest of international peace and security." By targeting nuclear delivery systems (i.e., ballistic missiles), the MTCR was intended to complement and strengthen the nuclear nonproliferation regime.

At the time of its formation, the MTCR's scope and domain were deliberately kept limited. The regime was concerned only with establishing guidelines among the G-7 for restricting missile technology exports. These guidelines were relatively simple, defining two categories of items whose transfer would be restricted. The MTCR mandated a strong presumption of denial for the export of category I items that included complete rocket systems and complete subsystems such as engines. But it had more flexibility for category II items such as chemical propellants and electronics (which were already on existing control lists); they were subject to a case-by-case review and could be exported if deemed appropriate.

The MTCR's initial narrow scope, low degree of formalization, and consciously gradualist approach stemmed from prior experience with failed conventional arms talks. The CAT negotiations generated much enthusiasm for a comprehensive regime before the implementing infrastructure was in place. Over time, dispiritedness over the regime's complexities caused the issue to be abandoned.[18] Recognizing the drawbacks of a comprehensive approach, the MTCR's scope and domain were limited; yet the regime was also recognized as inadequate in several areas.[19] It would be ineffective for states such as India and Israel that had an independent technological capability to construct rockets, and it did not offer incentives for countries seeking to buy or build missiles to abandon those activities. It also did not seek the elimination of existing missile forces.

EXPANDING THE MTCR

When the MTCR was established in 1987, it was an incomplete regime. Many missile technology suppliers remained outside the regime, and Russia, China, and North Korea were still exporting missiles. Four events in the late 1980s further heightened concerns about missile proliferation, and spurred efforts to expand the MTCR. These events were Iran's and Iraq's 1987–88 missile attacks against each other's cities; the March 1988 discovery of China's CSS-2 missile sale to Saudi Arabia; increasing knowledge about the Argentina-Egypt-Iraq Condor missile project; and India's 1989 Agni missile test.

At their December 1989 London meeting, MTCR members sought to expand the regime's membership. The impetus for expansion arose because several years after the MTCR's establishment, its limitations were more prominent than its achievements. Outlining these in March 1990, Rear Admiral Thomas Brooks, head of U.S. naval intelligence, stated that "the MTCR and other efforts had been largely ineffective and are likely to remain so."[20] Brooks noted that the regime required only pledges of compliance but no firm commitments from its members; the Soviet Union and China had not joined the regime; and a substantial pool of Western or Western-trained scientists, engineers, and technicians had been successfully tapped by states willing to pay for these human resources. Former ACDA Assistant Director Kathleen Bailey enumerated further weaknesses of the MTCR. Bailey noted that indigenous missile programs like those of India and Israel could proceed irrespective of the MTCR; export controls could be circumvented; the MTCR addressed only nuclear delivery systems; and the MTCR allowed space technology transfer.[21]

In light of these concerns, the MTCR was expanded with the goals of tightening the supply embargo and enlarging the regime's domain by bringing all relevant suppliers into the regime. On the first issue, as a result of strong congressional interest in missile proliferation, the United States incorporated the MTCR into its domestic legislation. It did so under the Missile Technology Control Act (MTCA), which was Section 17 of the National Defense Authorization Act for Fiscal Year 1991, and was signed by President Bush on November 5, 1990.

The MTCA legislation added new items (those in the MTCR Annex) to two earlier acts of export control legislation, the Export Administration Act (EAA) of 1979 and the Arms Export Control Act (AECA). It also specified sanctions for MTCR violators (these were adopted by Congress despite the Bush administration's concerns on the issue). Under the EAA, for the transfer of category II items (missile components), a violator would be denied "for a period of 2 years, licenses for the transfer . . . of missile equipment or technology . . . controlled under this Act." For the transfer of category I items (complete subsystems or complete missiles), sanctions were stricter: the violator would be denied "for a period of not less than 2 years, all licenses for . . . items the export of which is controlled under this Act." This meant that not just *missile-related* technology, but *all items and technology* covered by U.S. export control laws (the EAA and the AECA munitions list), would be denied to a violator. In addition, for both category I and II transfers, the violator was prohibited from importing items into the United States for two years. This law was used to sanction several foreign entities (discussed later in this chapter).

In the following years, Congress passed further sanctions legislation. For example, a February 2000 bill required the president to inform Congress semiannually of entities that transfer items or information that could help Iran's missile, nuclear, chemical, biological, or advanced conventional weapons programs. The president could then either impose sanctions or inform Congress why he did not. The bill would also withhold subsidies to Russia for the International Space Station unless Moscow demonstrated a sustained commitment to nonproliferation.

The second method of strengthening the MTCR was by bringing major missile suppliers such as Russia, China, and West European states into the regime.

RUSSIA

Moscow's missile exports and export controls can be analyzed in three parts. First, Moscow exported short-range ballistic missiles to clients in the Middle East and Eastern Europe from the 1960s to the 1980s. Second, after negotiations with Washington from 1987 onward, Moscow formally joined the MTCR in 1995. Third, although Russia halted exports of complete ballistic missiles by the early 1990s, Russian firms still transferred some missile-relevant technology to Iran and other states during the middle and late 1990s.

Soviet Ballistic Missile Exports

Moscow exported Frog series artillery rockets, the 300 km range Scud-B, and the 120 km range SS-21 to over a dozen clients such as Algeria, Egypt, Kuwait, Iraq, Libya, North Korea, North Yemen, South Yemen, and Syria. These exports were often part of larger conventional arms packages that included aircraft, tanks, and surface-to-air missiles (SAMs), and missiles were considered to be a conventional system.[22] Overall, Moscow exported some three thousand Scud-Bs, including hundreds to its Warsaw Pact allies, approximately eight hundred to Iraq, several hundred to other Middle Eastern clients, and over a thousand to Afghanistan between 1988 and 1991. Beyond its Scud sales, Moscow supplied about seventy 500 km range SS-23s to three Warsaw Pact allies: twenty-four missiles and four launchers to East Germany, eight systems to Bulgaria, and several to Czechoslovakia. Moscow did not export longer range missiles. It denied the 900 km range SS-12 to Iraq in 1985 and also denied the SS-22 and SS-23 to Syria in 1987 and 1989. Much earlier, Moscow had assisted China's rocket programs in the period 1955–60.[23]

Early Missile Talks, 1987–90

Washington informed Moscow about the MTCR when the regime was publicly announced in April 1987; after three years of talks, Moscow agreed to abide with the regime. Initially, the G-7 could not formally invite Moscow into the MTCR because intelligence sharing with Moscow was not politically feasible.

But at the May–June 1988 Moscow summit, Washington and Moscow agreed to hold talks on missile nonproliferation issues, which took place on September 27, 1988, in Washington. The talks were essentially exploratory, but in a memorandum and in later discussions, Moscow raised a number of issues that differed from the MTCR's requirements (Washington therefore rejected the memorandum in December 1988). Moscow sought to control a larger category of missiles and wanted the MTCR to cover 150 km range / 200 kg payload systems (these were typical parameters for artillery rockets). It supported a global ban on missiles with ranges under 5,500 km (this built upon the INF treaty parameters), and sought limitations on aircraft transfers. It favored a World Space Organization (a proposal earlier made in 1986) that would allow the sharing of SLV technologies. Moscow viewed the MTCR as similar to Cocom and criticized it for negatively influencing international technology sharing. Moreover, Moscow wanted the MTCR to include regional missile manufacturers such as Israel and China. It also sought restraints on Western missile defense.

Despite Moscow's initial reluctance to join the MTCR, U.S.-Russian missile nonproliferation talks continued through the late 1980s; they were pushed ahead by the State Department's concerns over Russia's prior record of exporting missiles. Missile issues were raised at the 1989 Wyoming summit, the May 1989 Baker-Scheverdnadze meetings, and the December 1989 Malta summit. By 1990, Moscow became more supportive of the MTCR for several reasons.

Pressure from the United States was influencing Russian decision making. Washington linked the strengthening of U.S.-Soviet economic relations to Moscow's compliance with U.S. nonproliferation objectives, and Secretary of State James Baker explicitly made this linkage in 1989. Russian policy makers were also concerned about the detrimental diplomatic consequences of the use of Soviet missiles. In particular, Iraq's firing of Soviet-supplied Scuds on Iranian cities complicated Moscow's relations with Tehran. Further, Soviet territory was falling within range of Middle Eastern ballistic missiles. Thus, following Israel's May 1987 Jericho-2 test, Radio Moscow noted that the missile could strike Soviet Caspian Sea oil fields and Black Sea naval bases. It warned that further Jericho development might cause Israel "to encounter consequences that it could not possibly handle."[24] Moscow was also concerned about American sales of nuclear capable aircraft to Israel and Pakistan. And in 1989, it expressed concern about both the Jericho-2 and Saudi Arabia's CSS-2s that could also strike Soviet territory. In addition, under a "new thinking"in foreign policy guided by President Gorbachev and Foreign Minister Scheverdnadze, Moscow sought to be a cooperative actor in world politics. This new thinking emphasized flexibility and compromise, and mutual security and interdependence.

Moscow then moved toward the MTCR in two ways. First, it formally agreed with the MTCR in two statements in February and June 1990. In a joint statement following a Baker-Scheverdnadze February 1990 meeting, both sides agreed to adhere to the MTCR's bans against exporting 300 km range 500 kg payload missiles. However, Moscow sought to continue its Scud sales to Afghanistan. After the May–June 1990 Washington summit, the two states again declared that they supported the MTCR's objectives and were taking measures to restrict missile proliferation. Second, after its Scud transfers to Afghanistan ended in 1990–91, Russia halted exports of complete ballistic missiles. (The only known subsequent exception was the transfer of eight Scud launchers and twenty-four to thirty-two Scud-B missiles to Armenia, beginning in late 1992; these transfers were made without the formal permission of the Russian government, and the missiles were previously based on Armenian territory.) Thus, Moscow broadly agreed to MTCR principles by 1990, but these 1990 statements were mainly a nonbinding understanding about its intentions and did not contain formal commitments or specific guidelines for technology transfers. Several controversies then delayed Moscow's MTCR membership for five more years.

Bringing Moscow into the MTCR, 1990–95

The most significant controversy over Moscow's adherence with the MTCR involved a space deal between the Glavkosmos space agency and the Indian Space Research Organization (ISRO). After unsuccessfully raising the issue since late 1990, Washington sanctioned ISRO and Glavkosmos in May 1992.[25] After further negotiations, Moscow and Washington reached a compromise on July 16, 1993, and confirmed it in September 1993. Glavkosmos was permitted to deliver complete cryogenic engines but not the production technology to ISRO. As a result, U.S. sanctions against additional Russian firms were avoided and transactions that could have been blocked by sanctions went ahead. U.S.-Russian accords on July 16 and September 3 allowed Russia to launch eight U.S. commercial satellites (through which it gained several hundred million dollars), permitted joint missions between the U.S. space shuttle and Russia's Mir space station, and allowed Russian participation in the international space station project (which was worth a few hundred million dollars).

Even after the cryogenic rocket sale controversy was resolved (but remained an irritant, as Glavkosmos may still have transferred some technology to ISRO), discord over a dozen suspected technology transfers (discussed below) delayed Moscow's entry into the MTCR. Moscow applied for MTCR membership at the regime's October 1994 Stockholm plenary. The Clinton administration formally supported Moscow's MTCR entry at the June 1995 Gore-Chernomyrdin meetings. It did so after Moscow admitted to missile-related transactions, particularly to Brazil's space program, and pledged to halt such transactions (which allowed Washington to waive sanctions). Russia became an MTCR member on August 8, 1995, and attended the regime's Bonn plenary in October 1995.

Russian Export Control Legislation and Missile Technology Transfers

In the years leading up to and following its entry into the MTCR, Moscow established a tighter export control system. An April 11, 1992, Russian presidential decree itemized five categories (later expanded to six) of goods for control, covering nuclear, chemical, biological, dual-use industrial, advanced conventional, and missile items. Moscow issued a revised MTCR-compliant control list on January 11, 1993. After Moscow's July 1993 understanding with Washington, the list was modified closer to MTCR standards by presidential decree 744 (November 19, 1993) and presidential directive 193 (April 25, 1995). These modifications were necessary for Russia's entry into the MTCR.

Moscow's 1995 Law on State Regulation of Foreign Economic Activity, a 1995 Law on Nuclear Energy, a 1999 Law on Export Controls, and several government resolutions formed the basis for a stronger Russian export control system in the late 1990s.[26] The Export Control Department of Russia's Ministry of Economic Development and Trade grants export licenses for WMD-related technologies. These licenses are reviewed by the atomic energy ministry, the defense ministry, and the Russian Space Agency.

Despite stronger Russian export controls in the 1990s, several Russian technology transfers were reported in the press. Alexander Pikayev notes that some of these may have been minor violations, some charges have been rejected by Moscow, and some reports may have been pressure tactics.[27] He adds three further points. First, the reported transfers may refer to preliminary negotiations before concluding a contract (the signing of contracts cannot be blocked under Russian regulations, which can only block the implementation of contracts). Second, they may involve permissible technology transfers. Third, the issue of whether the training of foreign personnel by Russian educational institutes is a violation of the MTCR remains disputed. The MTCR specifically bans the transfer of missile-relevant technical assistance (training, instruction, consulting) and technical data (blueprints and instruction manuals), but explicitly does not cover technology "in the public domain" and "basic scientific research."[28]

Washington counted a dozen Russian missile technology transactions until 1995; these and transfers in 1996–97 (after Moscow joined the MTCR) include the supply of sensors and engines to China (1991 and 1995–96); the airlifting of seven Scud launcher chassis from North Korea to Syria by Russian transport aircraft in August 1993; a shipwheel-tracking radar sale to India (in a February

1994 meeting, Moscow clarified that the radar could not provide measurements of velocity and position in real time); transfers of nose cone design and manufacturing equipment to Brazil; suspected transfers of missile parts and expertise to Syria and fuel to Libya via Ukraine; the transfer of gyroscopes to Iraq by the Research and Experimental Institute of Chemical Machine Building in Sergiyev Posad, which were interdicted by Jordan in November 1995; and assistance to Iran involving wind tunnels (used for testing nose cones) and the design of guidance and propulsion systems in 1996–97.[29]

Moscow further tightened missile export controls from mid-1997. During 1997 and 1998, U.S. and Russian officials held consultations, and Washington provided Moscow with a list of specific violations. On January 22, 1998, after further U.S. pressure to curb sales to Iran, the Yeltsin administration issued a "catch-all" resolution. This required Russian exporters to be particularly alert about any contracts with foreign WMD-suspected parties—meaning Iran and Iraq. In April 1998, a stainless steel consignment still crossed the Russian border but was intercepted in Azerbaijan on its way to Tehran. In the spring of 1998, after Congress passed the Iran nonproliferation act that could have sanctioned Russian firms (the act was vetoed by President Clinton), Moscow again tightened controls.

In May 1998, a Russian Federal Security Service statement denied allegations of Moscow's noncompliance with the MTCR. It noted that as far back as November 1992, Moscow had prevented scientists from going to North Korea, and added several positive developments in 1997–98. These included banning transactions with Iran's Sanam industries, which had ordered missile engine parts under the pretense of gas-pumping equipment from Trud Scientific and Production; detecting an Iranian embassy official who sought missile engine blueprints; and halting work on missile-relevant materials at a Moscow educational institute. On July 15, 1998, President Yeltsin ordered an investigation of nine Russian firms, though these did not include previously suspected exporters Trud, TsAGI, and Rosvooruzheniye; by early 2001, some twenty firms had been investigated by the Federal Security Service. Two companies and one research institution were warned about further dealings with Iran, one company was administratively sanctioned, and another two remained under investigation.[30]

In January 1999, Washington sanctioned three additional Russian firms for transfers to Iran.[31] In April 2000, the Clinton administration lifted sanctions on the Inor Scientific-Production Center and the Polyus Institute.[32] In June 2000, press reports noted that Russian and Uzbek firms sold aluminum alloy, laser gyroscopes, and connectors and relays to a North Korean firm, and that Scud-related gyroscopes were supplied to the Changgwang Sinyong company in Kazakhstan and resold to Yemen.[33]

Assessing Russia's MTCR Policy

In the late 1990s, despite Moscow's strengthened export control legislation, its firms still supplied technology, primarily to Iran. Fred Wehling aggregates such Russian missile assistance to Iran into three forms: transfer of materials and components, transfer of manufacturing and testing equipment, and training and know-how.[34] Moscow's willingness and ability to curb these exports remain uncertain, and would be influenced by three issues—domestic acceptance of the regime that includes ideological perceptions of the regime and bureaucratic factors; economic considerations; and strategic interests.

In terms of domestic and ideological acceptance, the MTCR did not have substantial support within Russia in the mid-1990s; at the 1997 Carnegie conference, analysts made three points on this issue.[35] First, the MTCR had not been submitted to parliament; many Duma members were critical of the regime; and the MTCR lacked a public basis of acceptance. Second, from the Russian perspective, deterrence rather than the MTCR or arms control was considered a more immediately effective approach to the missile threat; many states surrounding Russia had missiles, and therefore proliferation had already occurred. Third, the circumstances under which the MTCR emerged in the 1980s, and the fact that Moscow was left out of the initial negotiations, made it appear as an instrument of the Cold War. Thus, for Moscow to view the MTCR positively, it must be implemented in an environment of partnership. Otherwise, it could be set aside.

By the late 1990s, Moscow overcame some of its initial ideological reservations about the MTCR, and also strengthened its export controls institutionally. Further, both the government bureaucracy and private firms became more aware of export controls (and 33 workshops had sensitized some 550 Russian enterprises to technical export control issues). Yet, as a Center for International Trade and Security report notes, several bureaucratic obstacles hindered the strict implementation of export controls.[36] First, frequent changes in licensing procedures confuse exporters, regulations are difficult to interpret, and firms cannot easily determine whether an item is controlled. Second, lobbying and corruption undermine the system. Third, military-technical cooperation with former Soviet states is exempt from licensing, and these states can become middlemen for Russian technology exports. Fourth, government agencies are hesitant to sanction entities that they oversee because this raises the problem of self-indictment; sanctions on other countries have also been rare, and have only been imposed publicly on Iran's Sanam industries. Fifth, and partly related to ideological factors and the ideology of particular bureaucracies, Russian policy makers generally reject the practice of blacklisting states, but must closely scrutinize exports to states appearing on U.S. blacklists. Thus Russian control agencies scrutinize exports to Iran, but Russian officials also encourage trade with Iran. This sends mixed messages to firms.

Economic motives also influence Russia's adherence with the MTCR. In general, given Russia's economic decline and the removal of state subsidies in the 1990s, its firms increasingly relied on exports for their survival. At the macroeconomic level, there is only a rough positive correlation between economic decline and technology exports. Russia's economic growth rates were negative from 1990 to 1998 (except for 1997) and positive from 1999 to 2001; Moscow hesitated to halt the cryogenic rocket deal with India at a time of economic distress in the early 1990s, but has taken stronger steps to curb technology exports since the mid-1990s. However, Russian technology exports to Iran continued in the late 1990s when its economic growth rates were higher.

Microeconomic and political explanations then account for these exports. For example, Pikayev mentions one reason for Russian technology transfers in the late 1990s. He notes that "the United States is not offering adequately attractive incentives to compensate the losses Russian industry would suffer as a result of decreased cooperation with Iran."[37] He adds, "Many enterprises in the missile/aerospace sector have reaped no benefit from U.S./Russian cooperation, and have had to contract with Third World countries in order to survive. Sanctions, imposed by the United States on a few Russian enterprises in 1998 and 1999, have fomented the trend of establishing an 'archipelago' of Russian missile enterprises and universities oriented exclusively toward non-Western markets."

Moreover, economics are tied to sovereignty considerations. Thus, when the Yeltsin government suspended the cryogenic engine contract in July 1993, Russian parliamentary speaker Khasbulatov reflected both economic and sovereignty concerns by calling the developments a "national disgrace."[38] Editorials in the Russian press pointed out flaws in the MTCR, arguing that "proliferation control . . . becomes a kind of tool to maintain the competitiveness of [Western and U.S.] domestic high technology companies and to limit infiltration of Russian firms into capacious arms and space markets," and that even though "the U.S. will partially compensate Russia for corresponding losses . . . the damage to Russian-Indian relations and the commercial reputation of Russian firms has already been done."[39]

On international political and strategic grounds, Moscow has mixed reasons for complying with the MTCR. On the one hand, since missile proliferation provides the impetus for expanded U.S. national missile defense (NMD) programs that undermine Moscow's deterrent, Moscow would be interested in curbing proliferation and limiting its technology exports. On the other hand, Moscow may reject the MTCR if relations with the West deteriorate. Thus analysts argued that, faced with potentially threatening NATO expansion or an expanded NMD, conservative Russian lobbies may seek closer ties with China, India, Iraq, and Iran to offset U.S. power in the international system.[40] In that case, arms exports (including missile technology exports) to these countries would be deemed essential, not only for Russian industry, but also for Russian strategic interests. Under those circumstances, it would be easier for Moscow to drop out of the MTCR.

To summarize, Moscow's future compliance with the MTCR will hinge on prevailing economic and political conditions. In 2002, Russia's economy was growing, and political differences with the United States were being cooperatively resolved. Moscow had adopted a conciliatory stance on Washington's ABM treaty withdrawal and NMD plans. Moscow's signing of a strategic arms reduction treaty and an accord with NATO signaled closer ties with the United States and the West. These conditions enhance prospects for Moscow's maintenance of strict export controls. In contrast, economic growth had slowed and relations with the United States were mixed for another major missile supplier, China.

CHINA

China has not formally joined the MTCR, but it halted sales of complete missiles, and made missile nonproliferation pledges in 1992, 1994, 1998, and 2000. Yet Chinese firms still exported missile components and production equipment (that in many cases were dual-use technologies) and antiship cruise missiles. Beijing did not officially join the MTCR because of ideological differences with the regime, bureaucratic obstacles, economic motives, and its desire for strategic concessions from Washington.

Beijing had undertaken three missile transfers in the late 1980s and early 1990s. It exported about thirty 2,500 km range CSS-2s (that it was retiring) to Saudi Arabia in 1987–88 for $2–3 billion; it supplied over one hundred 150 km range M-7s (derived from SA-2s) to Iran since 1989; and it transferred thirty-four 300 km range M-11s to Pakistan in 1991–92. China's policy makers considered missiles to be a conventional weapon, and observed that missiles were widely used in the Iran-Iraq war. Domestic lobbies such as the Ministry of Foreign Affairs (that sought to establish ties with Saudi Arabia, which then had diplomatic relations with Taiwan), the People's Liberation Army (PLA), through its marketing firm Poly Technologies, and defense industries under the Commission on Science, Technology, and Industry for National Defense (COSTIND), furthered these missile transactions. Beijing may also have been considering M-9 exports to Libya and Syria; influenced by U.S. diplomacy, it stopped these exports.

U.S.-China Missile Talks, 1987–94

The Reagan, Bush, and early Clinton administrations held a series of missile talks with Beijing between 1987 and 1994. During this period, Beijing halted its exports of complete ballistic missiles, and gradually shifted its stand from opposing the MTCR to making an adherence commitment in 1994.

Washington raised missile nonproliferation issues with Beijing after Iran fired Chinese-supplied Silkworms on U.S.-flagged Kuwaiti tankers in 1987, and when Washington learned of China's CSS-2 sale to Saudi Arabia in March 1988. It discussed Chinese missile transfers during visits to Beijing by Secretary of State George Shultz in July 1988, and by Secretary of Defense Frank Carlucci in September 1988, but Beijing would not agree to direct missile talks. Following the June 1989 Tiananmen Square incident, Washington suspended all government exchanges with China and imposed financial sanctions. Beijing may then have resumed discussions to sell M-9s to Syria; news reports noted that Libya would finance a May 1989 $170 million Syria-China deal (dating to before the Tiananmen Square incident) for 140 M-9s, of which eighty missiles would go to Syria and the rest to Libya.[41] This issue was raised in a December 1989 visit to Beijing by National Security Adviser Brent Scowcroft and Deputy Secretary of State Lawrence Eagleburger, after which Beijing froze or canceled the missile deal. In subsequent weeks, Washington extended financial loans to China and permitted three U.S. communication satellites to be launched on Chinese rockets. Yet U.S.–China missile controversies persisted. From 1991 to 1994, Washington and Beijing clashed over Beijing's M-11 missile sales to Pakistan.

Beijing declared that the M-11 had a 290 km range and fell below the MTCR's prohibitions. It initially transferred a single training missile and launcher to Pakistan and therefore incurred U.S. sanctions in June 1991.[42] In November 1991, following negotiations between Secretary of State James Baker and Foreign Minister Qian Qichen, Beijing agreed to abide by MTCR guidelines. On February 1, 1992, Qian provided a written adherence commitment (although this document has not yet been publicly disclosed), and Washington lifted its sanctions on March 23. Canceling missile agreements with Islamabad and Damascus caused controversy within China because of the political costs (hurting foreign relations with allies and clients) and economic costs; Chinese moderates expected Washington to stabilize cooperation when they annulled these agreements.[43]

Beijing therefore reacted harshly to the Bush administration's September 2, 1992, announcement of F-16 sales to Taiwan. It declared a nuclear cooperation deal with Iran on September 8 and raised issues at the P-5 Middle East arms transfer talks. It also resumed M-11 supplies to Pakistan, and these missiles were reportedly unloaded at Karachi in November 1992.[44] Beijing may have further transferred missile components and manufacturing equipment to Pakistan and Syria.[45] As a result, after examining the issue for several months, the Clinton administration imposed sanctions on Chinese and Pakistani entities on August 24, 1993.

Beijing became more willing to comply with the MTCR after a year of additional negotiations. On October 4, 1994, Beijing agreed to observe MTCR guidelines, and Washington waived sanctions on November 1. However, Beijing's October 1994 commitment was to the MTCR guidelines and parameters of 1987. It pledged not to export missiles "featuring the primary parameters of the MTCR— that is, *inherently capable* of reaching a range of at least 300 km with a payload of at least 500 kg." This agreement did not commit Beijing to the MTCR revisions of 1993 which covered all WMD-relevant missiles and closed the range/ payload loopholes.

The above discussion highlights some key reasons Beijing initially opposed and subsequently acknowledged missile export restraints.[46] In the mid-1980s, Beijing did not know about the MTCR; after that it stayed out of the regime for four economic and ideological reasons. First, on economic grounds, Beijing had reduced state subsidies to its defense sector, which was then required to be more autonomous financially. In this context, the aerospace ministry's First Academy developed M-series missiles (the M-7, M-9, and M-11) specifically for export. An M-9 (the export version of the DF-15) was displayed at the First Asian Defense Exhibition in Beijing in November 1986, two months before the missile's design work was completed, and Beijing was considering transactions with Iran, Syria, and Pakistan. Second, on political-ideological grounds, Beijing sought to maintain sovereignty over its arms trade and noted that it was not any less responsible than the West in military sales. For example, Beijing had denied Libyan requests for both the CSS-2 and M-9 missiles. Third, Beijing expressed annoyance at being asked to conform to rules (such as the MTCR guidelines) when it had not been included in the negotiations that created these regulations. Fourth, Beijing questioned the rationale behind restricting ballistic missile exports when sales of military aircraft—which were also nuclear delivery systems—were not restricted. Implicit in this last criticism was a reference to U.S. aircraft sales to Taiwan. On this issue, in the 1991–92 P-5 Middle East arms control talks, Beijing objected to ballistic missiles being included under the weapons of mass destruction category unless advanced aircraft were also included. Beijing's November 1995 defense white paper also did not mention missile controls or the MTCR, although China's participation in the IAEA, NPT, CWC, and BWC was discussed.[47]

Beijing became more accepting of the MTCR in the early 1990s for certain economic, political, and ideological reasons. On economic grounds, U.S. sanctions increased the costs of noncompliance with the MTCR. Washington's 1991 and 1993 sanctions prohibited the sale of high-speed computers, missile technologies, and satellite components, and banned U.S. participation in Chinese satellite launches. On the other hand, U.S. space launch incentives (worth several hundred million dollars) compensated Beijing for the revenue it lost by halting missile exports, and the growth of its economy since the late 1980s made China somewhat less reliant on arms exports.

On political grounds, other countries such as Russia, Japan, and Israel pressed China to comply with the missile nonproliferation regime. For example, in his May 1989 visit to Beijing, Mikhail Gorbachev raised concerns over possible M-series missile sales to Libya and Syria. In a May 1993 trip to Beijing, Israel's Foreign Minister Shimon Peres was reportedly assured that China would not sell missiles to Iran and Syria.

On ideological-political grounds, Beijing's willingness to restrict missile exports was part of its broader policy of increasingly accepting the global nonproliferation regime (reflecting this policy, Beijing joined the NPT in 1992).[48] The post-Mao leadership sought to ensure that China's voice would be heard in the world community, and also realized that arms control was going forward with or without Chinese participation. Further, one of China's historical complaints about arms control was that the rules were made by the great powers and then imposed on other states. Therefore, Beijing was deliberately becoming involved in the nonproliferation regime to reverse the previous pattern.

China and the Missile Regime, 1994–2002

After its 1994 missile nonproliferation statement, three developments that moved China closer toward, but then seemed to indicate its backing away from, strong missile transfer restraints are worth noting. First, Beijing adopted formal export control restraints. Second, despite these controls, Chinese firms still exported some industrial missile-related technology. Third, the Clinton administration continued to press Beijing to join the MTCR. Beijing made a missile nonproliferation statement in 1998, froze the nonproliferation dialogue in 1999, but again gave a missile nonproliferation commitment in 2000.

Beijing strengthened and institutionalized its export control mechanism in the middle and late 1990s by passing major laws and decrees on the issue (though most were related to nuclear and chemical exports, and not specifically to missiles). A May 1994 Foreign Trade Law required Chinese firms to have export licenses for goods controlled by international treaties. Beijing issued further chemical and nuclear export control regulations from 1995 to 1998, and adopted control lists similar to those of the NSG and CWC.[49] It still had no formal control lists for advanced conventional weapons or missile-related goods (such as those used by the Wassenar Group and the MTCR), though its November 2000 missile statement indicated that it would soon draft a missile-related list. Beijing also designated key organizations to oversee its export regulations. Its October 1997 Regulations on Export Control of Military Items required firms to obtain licenses from the State Administrative Committee on Military Products Trade (SACMPT), which functioned as an interagency group between the Ministry of Foreign Affairs, COSTIND, and PLA agencies. SACMPT was abolished in mid-1998, and its functions were taken over by groups within COSTIND, the PLA, and the Ministry of Foreign Affairs.[50] Arms control issues were also placed on firmer institutional foundations within various government and defense agencies. For example, in April 1997, a new Department of Arms Control and Disarmament was established within the Ministry of Foreign Affairs to provide expertise on the subject.

As a result of institutionally strengthening its export controls, China's transfers of missile components and technologies were probably more closely scrutinized, but still not completely halted, in the late 1990s. U.S. government and press reports noted that Chinese firms supplied some technology and assistance to Pakistan, Iran, Syria, Libya, and North Korea. Beijing was reported to have assisted Pakistan with production equipment or know-how for a missile plant at Fatehjung outside Rawalpindi, whose construction was believed to have begun in 1995 and was nearly complete by 1998.[51] Beijing also reportedly assisted with a second missile plant; provided steel, guidance systems, and technical aid; and helped Pakistan's Shaheen-II project, in 1999–2000.[52] Chinese firms reportedly supplied Iran with guidance systems and computerized machine tools (1994–95); telemetry equipment used for flight tests (involving the Great Wall Industry, 1997 and 1998);[53] steel and telemetry equipment (1999); and chemicals and metals (involving the Chinese defense industry firm NORINCO, 1999–2000).[54] The *Washington Times* noted that the China Precision Machinery Import-Export Company assisted Libya's Al-Fatah missile program from March 1999, that it supplied wind tunnels to Libya, and that Chinese technicians were linked to the Al-Fatah program from at least June 1998.[55] Chinese firms also reportedly supplied steel, accelerometers, gyroscopes, and grinding machinery to North Korea and helped its satellite program in 1999–2000. The CIA's 2001 report to Congress noted that in the previous year, Beijing's missile-related assistance to Islamabad was continuing (as discussed above), and that Chinese firms helped North Korea with raw materials procurement.

In addition to its missile-component transfers, Beijing exported naval patrol boats with 120 km range C-802 (resembling the Harpoon) antiship cruise missiles to Iran, which Iran tested in January 1996. These cruise missiles fell below the MTCR's range limits, but still threatened the U.S. navy and shipping in the Gulf.

After Iran's C-802 test, Washington further pressed Beijing on its missile exports. (In May 1995, responding to Washington's decision to allow Taiwan's President Lee Tenghui to visit the United States, Beijing had called off missile talks, and the 1995–96 Taiwan Strait crisis also strained Sino-U.S. ties.) In 1997–98, Beijing worked more closely with the United States. For example, Beijing agreed in a September 1997 meeting between Secretary of State Madeleine Albright and Foreign Minister Qian Qichen to halt c-801 and c-802 sales to Iran. At the October 1997 summit between Presidents Bill Clinton and Jiang Zemin, and during Secretary of Defense William Cohen's January 1998 visit to China, Beijing made additional commitments not to sell antiship missiles to Iran or begin new nuclear transactions with that country.

In March 1998, the Clinton administration was considering an offer to "expand commercial and scientific space cooperation" with Beijing if it joined the MTCR and curbed its missile transactions.[56] During a June 1998 presidential summit (soon after India's and Pakistan's May 1998 nuclear tests), Beijing pledged in a joint statement not to export technologies that would help Pakistan develop nuclear-capable missiles. U.S.–China nonproliferation talks broke off in May 1999 (when NATO bombs fell on the Chinese embassy in Belgrade) and resumed in July 2000. In November 2000, following intense U.S. diplomacy, Beijing issued another strong missile nonproliferation statement. It declared that "China has no intention to assist, in any way, any country in the development of ballistic missiles that can be used to deliver nuclear weapons"; and it pledged to reinforce its export controls and to publish a control list of missile-related items.[57] Washington then agreed to resume processing applications for U.S. companies to launch satellites on Chinese rockets. It subsequently began processing, but did not formally approve, such licenses because of Beijing's continued transfers. U.S. intelligence detected twelve ship and truck transfers of missile components by Chinese firms—such as the China National Machinery and Equipment Import and Export Corporation (CMEC)—to Pakistan in the first half of 2001; Secretary of State Colin Powell raised the issue in Beijing in July 2001.[58] U.S. sanctions were imposed in September 2001 on the China Metallurgical Equipment Corporation and Pakistan's National Defense Complex. China published a list of missile-related items subject to export controls in August 2002.

Assessing China's MTCR Position

By the late 1990s, Beijing had observed some of the MTCR's rules (especially against complete missile exports), but had not officially joined the regime, and had not fully halted missile component transfers by Chinese firms. Three sets of ideological-procedural-bureaucratic, economic, and strategic-political reasons explain Beijing's varying stance on these issues.

First, several ideological, bureaucratic, and procedural factors influenced Chinese missile export policy. Beijing's initial ideological opposition to export controls was discussed in the previous section of this chapter: Beijing had objected to the MTCR because it had not been included in the regime's negotiations; because the regime was perceived as inequitable (Beijing criticized Washington and Moscow for continuing their advanced aircraft transfers while requiring Beijing to curb its missile transfers); and because the regime used sanctions. Vice Foreign Minister Liu Huaqiu called Washington's 1993 sanctions a "naked hegemonic act [that] has brutally violated the basic norms governing international relations."[59] Some of Beijing's ideological reservations overlapped with bureaucratic politics. Some bureaucratic groups sought to maintain China's historical ideological opposition to any export controls (which were perceived to have a negative effect on international technology sharing); partly reflecting this theme, Beijing had not joined other export control regimes like the Nuclear Suppliers Group or the Australia Group, although it pledged in 1997 and 1998 to adopt some of their guidelines.

Moreover, although many bureaucratic groups in the 1990s increasingly accepted the nonproliferation norm (for reasons discussed previously), they applied it more strongly to nuclear and chemical issues than to missiles, which Beijing had long considered to be conventional arms rather than a WMD issue, and which also had many dual-use aspects. In addition, on procedural and bureaucratic grounds, some of Beijing's missile-related exports may have been unintentional violations of the MTCR. Ambiguity in the MTCR's technical parameters (especially concerning dual-use technology) or their unawareness of these parameters caused Chinese firms (and the bureaucratic agencies overseeing the exports of these firms) to not be clear about whether their technology sales were barred by the MTCR. This issue applied to at least some firms and for some time, though analysts note that by the late 1990s, because of the persistent U.S. dialogue that sensitized Beijing to the seriousness of missile proliferation, and because Beijing itself had more strongly institutionalized its export control framework, this justification for technology exports was less valid.[60] Finally, different bureaucratic groups have different interests. Beijing's foreign ministry favors greater involvement in multilateral agreements and would generally support stricter export controls; yet the defense industry favors greater trade and looser controls, especially on dual-use exports; and the PLA would also favor military and technology exports under military-to-military cooperation with close allies such as Pakistan.

Second, economic factors and China's economic liberalization have had (and will continue to have) a mixed impact on its proliferation behavior. Macroeconomic considerations and the pace of economic growth have not strongly correlated with trends in missile exports. China's economic growth was particularly strong in 1992–94 and still strong though slowing in the middle and late 1990s, but its missile technology exports did not increase greatly in the late 1990s when growth slowed. Two structural and microeconomic firm-level factors also influence Beijing's willingness to adopt stronger export controls. On the one hand, liberalization structurally makes China more reliant on foreign technology and therefore more susceptible to foreign pressure to comply with the nonproliferation regime. On the other hand, privatization causes state-owned defense enterprises to emphasize profits and be more inclined to export potentially sensitive technologies. Moreover, as more firms privatize, and as government oversight of firms decreases, the challenges of monitoring their compliance with export control regulations increase considerably, especially for dual-use technologies.[61]

Third, strategic factors influence Beijing's compliance with the MTCR. Beijing may bargain for strategic concessions from Washington in exchange for formally joining the MTCR. In initial negotiations, Beijing sought restraints in U.S. arms and aircraft sales to Taiwan. In the late 1990s, U.S. missile defenses became a key concern for Beijing's leadership, which may seek American concessions on this issue before joining the MTCR. On a separate issue but illustrating the same dynamic, during the late 1990s at the Conference of Disarmament in Geneva, Beijing blocked fissile material cutoff treaty (FMCT) talks by linking these to space talks and U.S. missile defense initiatives in space.

This leads to a related point. On political grounds, Beijing appears to view nonproliferation as a bilateral U.S.-China issue rather than a commitment to a broader global regime. Although the causal connections are not clearly proven, trends indicate that when U.S.-Chinese relations improved (as in 1997–98 during reciprocal heads-of-state visits between the two countries), Beijing cooperated better with the nonproliferation regime. Conversely, when ties deteriorated (after the 1992 U.S. arms sales to Taiwan, and during 1995–96 tensions and the 1999 incident where NATO bombs hit the Chinese embassy in Belgrade), Beijing suspended or reversed its cooperation on nonproliferation issues. This logic suggests that in the future, increased political tensions with the United States may make Beijing more willing to export missiles or related technologies to U.S. adversaries.

In summary, the economic, ideological, and bureaucratic reasons for Beijing's rejecting the MTCR, while significant, are further supplemented by Beijing's political-strategic reasons to remain formally outside the regime. Beijing may restrain its missile-related exports for economic and strategic reasons—to take advantage of U.S. incentives such as satellite launch contracts, and to hinder regional powers from acquiring long-range missiles that could provoke extensive U.S. NMD and TMD initiatives. Yet it may not officially join the MTCR until it overcomes ideological and bureaucratic obstacles and obtains more significant strategic concessions from Washington.

NORTH KOREA

North Korea's missile program is reviewed in Chapter 7. Between 1987 and 1993, it exported 300 to 400 Scud missiles to Iran, Syria, and the United Arab Emirates. Thereafter, North Korea has probably not exported such a large number of ballistic missiles, but may have exported a few Nodong missiles or Nodong components to Iran and Pakistan in the mid-1990s. Unconfirmed press reports also indicate North Korean Scud transfers to, or discussions of transfers with, Zaire in 1994, Peru in 1995, and Vietnam in 1999.[62] Further, North Korea reportedly transferred twelve missile engines to Iran in November 1999.[63] It also sought to transfer chemical propulsion fuel items, and airlifted airframe or engine components and documents and manuals, to Iran in February and March 2001.[64]

North Korea's estimated revenues from selling 300 to 400 Scuds between 1987 and 1993 amounted to $1 billion. Its missile sales during 1994–2000, involving perhaps 50 Scuds to Syria, missile component transfers to Egypt, and 10 to 20 Nodongs or related components to Iran and Pakistan, were estimated at over $500 million (assuming $3 million per Scud, and $5–10 million per Nodong); it may have gained additional revenue from possible Scud transfers to Vietnam and Libya.

In several rounds of missile talks with Israel (in 1993) and the United States (from 1996 to 2000), Pyongyang offered to curb its missile exports for a compensation of $1 billion, but would not halt its indigenous missile development. In June 1998, it declared for the first time that it had exported and could continue to export missiles: "We will continue developing, testing and deploying missiles. . . . Our missile export is aimed at obtaining foreign money we need at present."[65] Thus North Korean missile sales may continue if U.S.-North Korean talks are unsuccessful, or may be halted if missile talks with the United States are successful.

MTCR MEETINGS, 1987–2002

The MTCR holds a plenary meeting every year. Intersessional consultations take place more frequently through point of contact (POC) meetings in Paris. Meetings of technical experts are held on an ad hoc basis. The MTCR has no secretariat, and the regime's working papers are distributed by France's foreign affairs ministry. MTCR meetings initially focused on bringing in new members (see Table 3.1), and then on addressing new issues and encouraging nonmembers to participate in the regime's activities.[66]

The MTCR was formally announced in April 1987; it then held meetings on September 8–9, 1988, in Rome, on December 5–6, 1989, in London, and on July 18–20, 1990, in Ottawa. Heightened concerns about missile proliferation spurred efforts to expand the regime. The first set of expansions through 1993

Table 3.1. MTCR Membership by Year

Year	Total Members	States Entering Regime in Each Year
1987	7	Canada, (West) Germany, France, Italy, Japan, U.K., U.S.
1989–90	15	Spain, Belgium, Luxembourg, Netherlands, Australia, Denmark, New Zealand, Norway
1991	18	Austria, Sweden, Finland
1992	22	Portugal, Switzerland, Ireland, Greece
1993	25	Iceland, Argentina, Hungary
1995	28	Russia, South Africa, Brazil
1997	29	Turkey
1998	32	Czech Republic, Poland, Ukraine
2001	33	South Korea

NOTE: MTCR nonmembers adhering to the regime include Israel (1991), China (statements from 1992 onward), and Romania (1993). China's adherence statements are different from those given by other states.

covered all members of treaties that involved technology sharing (NATO, EU, and the European Space Agency), because these formal treaties legally superseded informal policies like the MTCR. Therefore, an initial priority for the G-7 was to bring all European Union states into the MTCR before the removal of intra-EU trade barriers. Many European states were also NATO members who shared intelligence, or European Space Agency partners trading in launch vehicle technology, with the G-7 states.

Thus, new members Australia, Belgium, Netherlands, Luxembourg, and Spain attended the Ottawa MTCR meeting. A technical working group was established at this meeting, and member states examined each other's export control lists to check that they included all relevant missile technology.

At the fourth MTCR meeting, in Tokyo on March 19–20, 1991, Austria, Denmark, and Norway participated. MTCR members discussed expanding the regime to other European countries and Turkey, and agreed to extend the regime's objectives beyond nuclear proliferation to include stopping the spread of biological and chemical weapon delivery systems. Participants also agreed to include additional dual-use items in category II, which were added to seven sections of the control list; a technical experts meeting in May completed this process of updating the control list.

In November 1991, at their fifth meeting, in Washington, MTCR members discussed expanding the regime's scope to include all weapons of mass destruction, but without lowering range thresholds. They also adopted the updated and revised equipment and technology annex. Three weeks before this meeting, a delegation of representatives from Canada, France, Japan, and the United States visited Russia to discuss how it could participate in the MTCR. Recognizing that other countries were interested in joining the MTCR, participants evaluated criteria of admission such as a state's willingness to adopt and enforce controls, and an indication of having a nonproliferation policy such as through MTCR-like controls or membership in the NPT or London Suppliers Club. In general, states were interested in joining the regime for several reasons. First, they could prove their international standing and compliance with global nonproliferation norms. Second, they sought to avoid being targeted and used by arms traders as a transit point. This was especially relevant for states such as Ireland, Denmark, and New Zealand, which had no missile programs and no missile-relevant space industry. Third, there was a perception that MTCR membership would make it easier to acquire dual-use technologies, although this issue was subject to a case-by-case review.

At an April 1992 technical meeting, member states sought to determine how systems "intended" for (as opposed to simply "capable" of) WMD delivery would be controlled by the MTCR. Guidelines on this issue were agreed upon at the next MTCR meeting on June 29–July 2, 1992, in Oslo. In January 1993, the revised guidelines were adopted. Item 19 was earlier added to the MTCR annex to include complete rockets and unmanned air vehicles (UAVs) having a 300 km range, which could deliver chemical and biological payloads weighing less than 500 kg.

At the seventh MTCR plenary meeting, in Canberra on March 8–11, 1993, Iceland was accepted as the regime's twenty-third member. Participants agreed to implement stricter controls under item 20 of the Annex; this item restricted exports of item 19 subsystems (subsystems of 300 km range vehicles regardless of payload), as well as specially designed "production facilities" and "production equipment" for such systems.

On November 29–December 2, 1993, the eighth MTCR plenary meeting at Interlaken welcomed Argentina and Hungary as new members. The group encouraged less active members to take a more active diplomatic stand. Reflecting this position, MTCR members supplemented U.S. sanctions against China by jointly protesting China's missile transfers to Pakistan. At the ninth plenary session in Stockholm on October 4–6, 1994, the MTCR partners reacted favorably to Russia's petition for membership and also welcomed South Africa's steps to eliminate its missile program. The tenth MTCR meeting was held in 1995 in Bonn. At the eleventh plenary meeting on October 7–10, 1996, in Edinburgh, the regime expanded its focus from the behavior of members to that of non-members and also discussed the regional aspects of missile proliferation. On April 16, 1997, the MTCR marked its tenth anniversary. Its members expressed satisfaction that the regime had reduced the availability of missile-relevant equipment and technology and had lowered the global inventory of WMD-capable missiles.

In subsequent MTCR plenary meetings, the regime's members consistently expressed concern about proliferation in the Middle East, South Asia, and East Asia. At its twelfth meeting, in Tokyo on November 4–6, 1997, MTCR members jointly appealed to all states to support the regime and adopt its guidelines.[67] At the thirteenth, in Budapest on October 5–9, 1998, the Chair issued a statement of serious concern about North Korea's missile activities. MTCR partners also noted China's increased willingness to engage in a missile nonproliferation dialogue. They repeated their invitation in principle for Beijing to join the regime, and asked it to improve its export control system. Further, members resolved to make the MTCR's activities more transparent.

At the MTCR's fourteenth plenary meeting, in Noordwijk, the Netherlands, on October 11–15, 1999, members were alarmed that regional powers increasingly focused on longer range delivery systems, threatening countries both inside and outside the regions concerned, which could possibly set off a new arms race. They discussed possible new qualitative responses to emerging proliferation threats, and analyzed confidence- and security-building measures in the field of responsible missile behavior. Members also sought to increase outreach activities and encourage nonpartners to observe MTCR guidelines.

Finland hosted the fifteenth plenary session in Helsinki in October 2000, and Canada hosted the sixteenth in Ottawa in September 2001. At these meetings, MTCR members stressed two themes: they reaffirmed that missile proliferation was a global, not just a regional, security concern, and that export controls play a vital role in stemming it; and they continued their deliberations from previous years on a set of principles, commitments, confidence-building measures, and incentives that could constitute a code of conduct against missile proliferation. At the 2000 plenary meeting, members decided to engage non-MTCR states in seeking this broader multilateral instrument or Code of Conduct open to all states. The Ottawa meeting noted that the extensive contact with non-MTCR countries following the Helsinki plenary had resulted in an augmented draft Code of Conduct; it declared that the "universalization of the draft Code should take place through a transparent and inclusive negotiating process open to all states on the basis of equality."[68] France and Spain hosted these negotiating sessions in 2002, and the MTCR tightened its technology control list at its September 2002 plenary in Poland.

CURBING TECHNOLOGY TRANSFERS:
EUROPE, JAPAN, AND OTHER STATES

In the 1990s, the MTCR substantially curbed missile technology transfer to regional powers after several former and potential missile technology suppliers were brought into the regime. An initial priority for the G-7 was to bring all European Union states into the MTCR before the removal of intra-EU trade barriers. Many European states were also NATO members who shared intelligence, or European Space Agency partners trading in launch vehicle technology, with the G-7 states. European states generally supported the MTCR's principles, especially because of Europe's proximity to, and the consequent missile threat it faced from, North Africa and the Middle East.

The MTCR was enhanced after several European states joined the regime from 1990 to 1992. European governments passed stronger domestic laws against missile technology transfers and, more important, began strictly implementing these laws. For example, German firms had exported missile-related technology to Egypt, India, Brazil, and Argentina in the 1970s and 1980s, and were also involved in chemical transfers to Middle Eastern states. Bonn passed stricter chemical export controls in 1984 and 1989, and adopted strengthened export legislation on June 1, 1990. Under the new laws, the German government investigated fifty-nine firms for illegal cooperation with Iraq such as assisting in extending the range of Iraqi Scuds. In January 1993, German authorities halted a ship carrying machine parts (that could have been used for Scud production) to Syria. The vessel proceeded to Syria after the machine parts were removed and brought back to Germany.[69]

Other states also introduced and implemented stricter legislation. For example, in January 1994, Japanese police raided the Yokohama Machinery Trading Company suspected of selling spectrum analyzers to North Korea via China in 1989. In September 1990, the government of Denmark prosecuted a company that sought to export graphite cylinders to Libya. In 1990, the British government asked British Aerospace (BAe) to suspend its participation with the Cairo-based Arab-British Dynamics (ABD), which was developing Egyptian Scud-Bs; BAe complied and withdrew from Egypt within a year.

Besides the primary suppliers, a number of additional and potential suppliers joined the MTCR or adhered to its practices. Argentina, Brazil, and South Africa scrapped their missile programs and joined the MTCR. Israel retains its missile forces, but in October 1991 it pledged to adhere to MTCR guidelines. India and Pakistan have come under pressure to curb their missile and nuclear programs. For example, the G-7 states and Australia sent New Delhi separate but nearly identical notes in July 1993. They urged that New Delhi freeze the

Agni missile project, halt Prithvi missile deployment, scrap its fast-breeder nuclear programs, stop further fissile material production, and accept full-scope nuclear safeguards; a similar note was sent to Pakistan. On August 29–30, 1994, an MTCR delegation visited India and Pakistan to discuss their participation in the MTCR. Neither halted its missile program, but they have also not exported their indigenously produced missiles and missile technology.

In the 1990s, most major missile suppliers complied with the MTCR. Interstate cooperation was induced by a number of factors: power politics including sanctions and incentives, national interests, and an increasing awareness of the perils of missile proliferation.

SOURCES OF COOPERATION,
NONPROLIFERATION SANCTIONS, SPACE INCENTIVES

The most striking feature of the MTCR's operation is the significant role played by the United States (though other states also played vital roles in the regime). This U.S. role illustrates how powerful states secure cooperation in regimes. But power-based explanations must be supplemented by understanding the interests of states and their demand for a regime—factors that depend on knowledge of an issue.

The impetus for the MTCR's creation was a growing awareness of missile proliferation in the late 1970s and early 1980s. Increasing *knowledge* of the contribution of technology transfer to missile proliferation, and of the potential exacerbation of nuclear proliferation because of missile proliferation, led to an *interest* in a regime to control missile transfers. Washington then demanded tight restrictions over rocket and space technology transfers, and pressed for curbing missile and nuclear trade despite opposition from its allies because, as noted by Janne Nolan, avoiding "the long-term costs of proliferation are worth the short-term cost of incurring frictions with countries with whom we have relations."[70]

Moreover, because the initial MTCR members accepted norms against missile sales (they were not engaged in category I missile trade, though they were transferring rockets under European Space Agency auspices), they did not have to be coerced into joining the regime. The demand for the regime already existed, and the costs of creating it were low, especially because it was not market based. The MTCR does not supply economic public goods to its members, who therefore do not pay membership fees for participation. The economic costs are low while the nonproliferation benefits are great; this favorable cost-benefit calculation facilitated the regime's establishment and continuation. Social cost-benefit calculations also influenced national decisions on the MTCR. The desire to win prestige, respect, friendship, and social acceptance as responsible international actors had a bearing on the choice Brazil, Argentina, and South Africa made to join the MTCR.

But power considerations were not absent in the MTCR. The demand or enthusiasm for a regime does not guarantee consensus on its rules. States seek to bend the rules toward their self-interests. If these interests compromise the regime's objectives, coercion may be used to secure compliance from deviant members.

While the demand for a regime existed, states had not agreed on specific rules. The MTCR's rules permitted category II rocket technology transfers on a case-by-case basis. Moreover, France sought to transfer liquid-fuel engines to Brazil, and Russia sought to transfer cryogenic engines to India (these were category I items). These suppliers' expected marginal costs were probably less than the marginal benefit, and they were inclined to go ahead with the transfers. In these cases, a combination of U.S. incentives and sanctions secured their compliance with the stricter interpretation of the regime. It should be noted that sanctions may have domestic costs; however, MTCR-related sanctions hurt domestic lobbies mainly in the case of U.S. sanctions on China.[71]

U.S. missile sanctions, shown in Table 3.2, include those against Chinese firms for transfers to Pakistan (in 1991 and 1993, and in later years); against Russian firms for transfers to India (1992) and Iran (1999); against South Africa (1991); and against firms in North Korea, Iran, Syria, Egypt, and Pakistan (1992, 1996, 1997, 1998, 1999, 2000, 2001) for North Korean missile transfers to those states. It should be clarified that the latter sanctions did not cause the concerned regional power entities (who had little existing trade with the U.S.) to halt their technology transfers. And the sanctions on Russian and Chinese firms had mixed results; Speier (2001) notes that they mainly resulted in further negotiations that then caused their governments to more strongly curb technology transfers. Washington also offered incentives for states to comply with the MTCR. U.S. space policy requires that technology transfer agreements "will be conducted in a manner consistent with the MTCR," and that "international space launch trade agreements in which the U.S. is a party must be in conformity with U.S. obligations under arms control agreements, U.S. nonproliferation policies, U.S. technology transfer policies, and U.S. policies regarding observance of the Guidelines and Annex of the Missile Technology Control Regime (MTCR)."[72] The financial benefits from space agreements with Washington are a major incentive for countries to comply with the MTCR. The United States signed agreements with Russia, China, and Ukraine, giving them fifteen to twenty satellite launches in the 1990s (prices for a geostationary launch are typically $60–100 million).

During the 1990s, the MTCR's supply embargo tightened considerably as several new members entered (or remained outside but nevertheless complied with) the regime and adopted stricter national export control legislation. Thus a 2001

Table 3.2. U.S. Missile Nonproliferation Sanctions

Date	Parties / Firms	Category of Sanction
June 24, 1991	China (Great Wall Industries, Precision Machinery Import-Export Corporation), Pakistan (SUPARCO Space Commission)	II
September 17, 1991	South Africa (Armscor)	I
March 6, 1992	North Korea or Iran	I
May 6, 1992	Russia (Glavkosmos), India (ISRO)	I
June 23, 1992	Syria, North Korea	I
July 5, 1993	Possible Ukraine-Russia-China transfer	Determination
August 24, 1993	Pakistan, China	II
May 15, 1995	Unnamed parties, possible Russia-Brazil transfer	Determination
May 24, 1996	North Korea, Iran	II
June 16, 1996	Unnamed parties	Determination
August 6, 1997	North Korea	II
April 24, 1998	North Korea (Changgwang Corporation, Fourth Machine Industries Bureau), Pakistan (Khan laboratories)	I
July 1998	Several Russian firms	
January 1999	3 Russian firms, transaction with Iran	II
March 1999	3 Egyptian firms	II
April 6, 2000	1 North Korean and 4 Iranian firms	I
November 17, 2000	Iran, Pakistan (waived on China)	I / II
January 2, 2001	North Korea	
June 14, 2001	North Korea	
September 1, 2001	China (Metallurgical Equipment Corporation), Pakistan (National Defense Complex)	II
August 2002	North Korea (for prior transfers to Yemen)	

NOTE: In some cases, Washington made a determination of MTCR violations, but did not actually impose sanctions. Category I sanctions are for the transfer of complete missiles or complete subsystems, while Category II sanctions are for missile technology and component transfers.

SOURCES: Arms Control Association, "U.S. Missile Sanctions," factsheet, 2002; Richard Speier, Brian Chow, and S. Rae Starr, *Nonproliferation Sanctions* (Santa Monica: Rand, 2001).

crossnational comparison of export controls, measured on a 100 point scale (with 100 representing the most developed systems), ranked states as follows: U.S., Japan, U.K. (90 to 96), Russia (76), and China (65).[73] As a result of this tight supply embargo, technology transfers to regional powers were constrained, making it harder for those states to build ballistic missiles. But did regional powers halt missile activity when they were denied foreign technology? The following chapters study regional missile programs to answer that question.

4

Argentina, Brazil, South Africa: Curbed Missile Programs in the Southern Hemisphere

In July 1989 and November 1990, South Africa fired two-stage rockets from Overberg at Africa's southernmost tip toward Prince Edward Islands 1,450 km to the southeast. These rocket tests were part of a dual missile and space program that involved over a thousand personnel, but was dismantled before the country's transition to majority rule in 1994. Nelson Mandela's government took South Africa into the MTCR in 1995. That year, soon after President Fernando Cardoso's visit to Washington, Brazil also joined the MTCR. Brazil had first tested a one ton Sonda-1 rocket in 1964. Three decades later, in 1997 and 1999, it launched the more powerful 49 ton VLS rockets from the Alcantara equatorial station, inspiring commentators to declare: "Brazil races into space."[1] Brazil's political and technical elites aspired to use satellites for surveying the Amazon, patrolling Brazil's land borders and Atlantic coasts, monitoring natural resources, and forecasting agricultural harvests and the weather. Brazil's satellite launcher also gave it a medium-range missile capability, but Brazil renounced its missile ambitions when it entered the MTCR in 1995, and when it signed a nuclear safeguards agreement with Argentina in 1991. Buenos Aires had equally ambitious rocket aspirations. Its military regime had initiated the Condor-1 tactical missile program in 1977; its air force pressed ahead with a more powerful Condor-2 missile with little government oversight. When President Carlos Menem's administration finally restrained the project in the early 1990s, radical changes were necessary to assert civilian authority and curtail the program.

One or more of four factors—the MTCR's technology embargoes, a decrease in security threats, external political-economic pressure, and domestic politics— curbed missile activities in Argentina, Brazil, and South Africa. The MTCR's technology barriers considerably slowed and raised the costs of indigenous missile development. Simultaneously, decreased regional tensions reduced the security-related demand for missiles, while decreased prospects in the missile-export market or satellite-launch industry reduced the economic demand for those systems. In this situation of higher costs and a lower demand, international pressure (which was more effective because domestic economic liberalization required integration with international markets) attained the cessation of these missile programs.

ARGENTINA

The Rise and Fall of the Condor

Argentine military officers established a Condor-1 missile plan in 1977, but the project gained momentum only in the 1980s. The Condor-1 carried a 450 kg payload to 120 km and was derived from Argentina's Alcaran sounding rocket.

Argentina's two-stage Condor-2 was designed to carry a 500 kg payload to 1,000 km. It was modeled on the Pershing-2, with a solid-fuel first stage and a second stage similar to an upper-stage Ariane engine. Buenos Aires signed preliminary Condor-2 contracts in 1982 and more firmly established the program by 1984. The program received further formal approval through government decrees in 1984, 1985, and 1987.[2] In the late 1980s, the German firm Messerschmitt-Bolkow-Blohm (MBB) withdrew from the Condor project which still continued in collaboration with Egypt and Iraq (which provided much of the financing).[3]

The missile team constructed production facilities in Cordoba province (near Argentina's observatory and satellite ground station) around 1983–86. Over one hundred and fifty West European engineers and twenty firms (some already involved with the Condor-1 since 1979–81) worked on the Condor-2. MBB supplied the technology, missile design, integration and simulation assistance, and technical assistance for solid fuel motors; the Italian firm Snia-Bpd (Fiat-Avia) transferred solid propellant motors and guidance technology; and France's Sagem supplied guidance kits.

The MTCR significantly impeded the Condor project because it relied heavily on foreign suppliers; when foreign technology was cut off, the Condor program faltered. For example, the initial solid-liquid fuel combination could not be developed and the missile team then sought a new solid-fuel second stage, but this increased the project's cost and development time. Moreover, the missile team could not build a reentry vehicle or accurate guidance and control systems without foreign assistance. The Condor had advanced French inertial guidance and also sought more advanced terminal guidance systems, but the

MTCR blocked the transfer of such technology. A dummy missile test in 1988 revealed major technical problems. Despite these obstacles, the Condor team built over a dozen missile bodies and engines by 1990–91.

Argentina, Egypt, and Iraq invested approximately $4 billion on the Condor-2 from 1984 to 1991. Argentina spent roughly $800 million, and Iraq contributed most of the rest. An additional $1 billion was needed to complete the missile's development, and missile production would have required a further $8 million each for a series of 200 missiles, making the total cost at least $6.6 billion.[4] At this stage, Buenos Aires sought to suspend the project.

On April 22, 1990, Argentina's Defense Minister announced that the missile aspects of the Condor-2 had been halted, but added that the Condor was a satellite launch vehicle, effectively keeping the project alive. According to cabinet minister Domingo Cavallo, the Argentine government was searching for ways to involve the missile team in an unspecified international venture to preserve the country's advanced technological capabilities.[5] On May 28, 1991, Defense Minister Antonio Erman Gonzalez stated that the Condor-2 would be "deactivated, dismantled, reconverted and/or rendered unusable," partly meeting U.S. demands that the project be destroyed.[6] Yet Argentina kept open the possibility of using Condor components for "peaceful activities."[7]

The Menem government finally terminated the Condor-2 in 1992–93. In February 1992, it dismantled some Condor components. In April 1992, an MTCR delegation visited Argentina to assess its export control measures.[8] In January 1993, Argentina sent fourteen engines and seventeen missile bodies to Spain for recycling. Both states intended to cooperate technologically and convert the two-stage Condor missile into a three-stage satellite launcher (Spain itself had difficulties with its Capricornio launcher).[9] However, the venture was not pursued and Condor missile parts were then shipped to the United States. Argentina's MTCR membership was approved in March 1993. A shifting political environment—involving improvements in regional security, democratization, economic liberalization, and U.S. pressure—more thoroughly explains the key turning points behind the Condor's cessation in the early 1990s.

Security Considerations

Argentina's armed forces initially anticipated using short-range Condor-1 missiles in any conflict with Chile after the 1978 Beagle Channel dispute. Following the 1982 Falklands campaign, the Argentine military noted that the longer range Condor-2 could strike British bases in the Falklands.

Argentina's rivalry with Brazil also stimulated its nuclear and missile activity (though it should be clarified that neither state is known to have had specific intentions to deliver nuclear systems on missiles, and neither built nuclear weapons),[10] and when relations with Brazil improved, its nuclear and missile programs were scaled back.

Relations between Argentina and Brazil have been characterized not by military confrontation but by competitive technological rivalry. The two states had no major bilateral territorial or political disputes, but relations were historically tense. Analysts note that the 1970s were a "turbulent decade in Brazilian-Argentine relations characterized by intense and often shrill verbal warfare, keen politico-economic competition in adjacent countries . . . and atomic rivalry with ill-concealed military overtones."[11] Bilateral relations slightly improved in 1979–80 (following nuclear and economic cooperation agreements), but then cooled until 1985. Only after 1985 —when both Argentina and Brazil were democratic— did bilateral relations more significantly improve with the signing of nuclear and economic agreements. A November 1985 nuclear cooperation agreement was followed by more comprehensive nuclear security agreements in 1990 and 1991—agreements that were ratified by 1994.[12] On the economic front, Presidents Alfonsin and Sarney signed twenty accords including a customs union in December 1986. These led to the 1991 Mercosur free trade agreement, which became effective in 1995. This institutionalization and consolidation of economic and nuclear cooperation then enhanced prospects for missile nonproliferation in Latin America. In this relaxed security context, political-economic considerations related to democratization, economic liberalization, and external pressure from the United States resulted in the cessation of Argentina's missile activity.

Democratization and Civil-Military Relations

Argentina's 1983 democratic transition had no immediate impact on its missile program. The Condor project actually gained momentum under the first democratic administration. But democratization led to the improvements in regional security discussed above, which created the conditions for terminating Argentina's missile activity.

Democratic consolidation also reduced the military's role in Argentine politics, which further facilitated the Condor's cessation. Argentina's military budget decreased from 6 percent of GNP in the early 1980s to below 3 percent by 1990. Despite this, the air force maintained a hold over the Condor project, arguing that it brought in foreign exchange (from Iraq) and technology (from European firms). President Alfonsin also continued the Condor-2 project to appease the air force when he was overseeing the trial of military officers.

Argentina's next President, Carlos Menem, unsuccessfully battled his air force for control of the Condor in 1990 and early 1991. Menem gained some ground in mid-1991, when the civilian National Space Activities Committee (Conae) was designated to oversee the Condor project and all installations formerly under the air force National Space Research Commission. On October 23, 1991, Menem swore in Conae members and noted that Argentina's "space activities [should] always be carried out within a peaceful framework and with a social and scientific spirit to grant major well-being and knowledge to all countries."[13] In February 1992, ahead of Defense Secretary Cheney's visit to Argentina, the air force formally transferred control to Conae. Still, until mid-1992, the Menem government had "yet to act on a promise . . . to end an armed forces program to build a long-range ballistic missile."[14] It was only in 1993 that Argentina finally handed over Condor missile components to Spain, thereby effectively terminating the program.

Economic Liberalization and U.S. Pressure

Also influencing the scrapping of the Condor project were domestic economic constraints, economic reforms, and U.S. pressure. The latter two were considerably more influential than the former. In economic terms, the Condor was not bringing in foreign exchange because Iraqi financing halted in 1989. In 1990, the project required some $100 million in investment, but these funds were not available because of a national economic crisis. Economic growth rates were −1.8 percent (1988), −6.3 percent (1989), and 0.2 percent (1990). Noting the role of economic constraints, Defense Minister Romero stated on April 22, 1990, that the Condor program had been halted because of a political decision and because Argentina could not finance the project.

While the Condor project was frozen between 1990 and 1992 and a decision to terminate it was taken in 1991, this decision was not implemented until 1992–93 when Argentina had overcome some of its economic crisis (its economic growth rate was 8 percent in both 1991 and 1992). At this time, Argentina was susceptible to U.S. influence because the Menem government liberalized the economy to seek integration with world markets. It also pursued a pro-American foreign policy that was intended to bolster market confidence and facilitate foreign capital inflows required by reforms.

Argentina's changing foreign and economic policy and dependence on the United States made it more susceptible to U.S. pressure on the missile issue (despite official denials).[15] It was also given incentives by Washington to scrap its missile program. After it dismantled some Condor-2 components under the supervision of U.S. inspectors in February 1992, Argentina gained initial benefits when Defense Secretary Cheney announced weapons sales to Argentina (the Argentine military's requirement for U.S. technology actually increased U.S. leverage).[16] But to avoid further domestic political embarrassment for the Argentine government, the Condor missile prototypes were not destroyed in Argentina but shipped to Spain and then to the United States. This was part of an arrangement whereby Argentina would exchange the verified destruction of missiles for access to U.S. technology. Thus, under a February 12, 1993, memorandum of understanding, Argentina could buy advanced computer equipment, nuclear technology, and aeronautical guidance systems.

Several U.S. delegations visited Argentina in 1992–93 to discuss the Condor's destruction and to review Argentina's export control measures. On March 10, 1993, President Menem conceded that the transfer of Condor parts to Spain was for the benefit of the United States and that the transfer guaranteed termination of the project "which was useless for us anyway."[17] Controversy with the United States persisted when some Condor components remained unaccounted for, and Argentina hesitated to completely dismantle the Cordoba missile plant; Buenos Aires finally agreed to this step in mid-1993.[18]

The above arrangements did not find favor with domestic constituencies. The political left argued that Argentina was conceding sovereignty to the United States, and that some dual-use industrial equipment from the Condor project had civilian-economic applications.[19] Yet President Menem could override these objections because of the institutional stability of his presidency, as the opposition did not have power in Congress to derail the presidency.

Thus, Argentina scrapped the Condor by 1993, but powerful ideas about a sovereign right to space technology were still prevalent across its political spectrum. As a result, Argentina revived its space ambitions through a ten-year $700 million space plan approved by President Menem on November 28, 1994. The plan involved building satellites and satellite ground stations and reactivating the old Condor-2 facility at Falda del Carmen as the Teófilo Tabanera Space Center. In January 1996, a bilateral Argentine-Brazilian working group on space cooperation (that was created in 1989) held its fifth meeting to discuss a possible joint space launcher. In February 1996, Defense Minister Oscar Camilion stated that it had been "a mistake" for Brazil and Argentina not to have collaborated on space projects sooner. Camilion was also concerned that Argentina "fell further behind Brazil in the space sector" when it scrapped the Condor, and analysts noted that a joint Argentina-Brazil launcher would "end the animosity" that had been created in Argentina when Brazil retained its own VLS launcher while joining the MTCR.[20] In December 1998, President Menem approved a plan for Argentina's New Generation Space Vehicle (Vehículo Espacial de Nueva Generación, or VENG) to launch remote sensing and communications satellites. Yet, by 2002, the VENG had not advanced beyond the planning stage. Argentina's rocket ambitions remained grounded in the early years of the twenty-first century.

BRAZIL

Brazil's Missile, Rocket, and Space Programs

Brazil initiated three rocket programs beginning in the 1960s. Two of them—the sounding rocket program and the VLS space launcher (derived from the Sonda-4 sounding rocket)—continued despite being delayed by the MTCR's embargo. The third, a ballistic missile project, was curbed.

The Avibras Corporation and the Ministry of Aeronautics built the Sonda-1, Sonda-2, Sonda-3, and Sonda-4 sounding rockets. Each successive Sonda was an evolutionary refinement of the previous system; for example, the Sonda-3's second stage was the first stage of Sonda-2, and the Sonda-4's second stage used the first stage of Sonda-3. Sonda-4 (500 kg payload / 600 km altitude) began development in 1974 and was flight-tested in November 1984, November 1985, October 1987 (stage 2 failed to separate in this test), and April 1989. The Sonda-1–4 sounding rockets also formed the basis for Brazil's SS-07, SS-40, and SS-60 artillery rockets and SS-300 ballistic missile, respectively.

Brazil's ballistic missile programs were undertaken in the 1980s by two firms, Orbita and Avibras.[21] Orbita intended to build MB/EE-150, -350, -600, and -1000 missiles. Avibras financed the development of the 300 km range SS-300 missile, while a 1,000 km range SS-1000 missile was on the drawing board of the air force and ministry of aeronautics' Aerospace Technology Center (CTA).

Preliminary SS-300 engine tests were completed by December 1986, and flight tests were to take place eighteen months later. The missile was to be operational by 1990, but was never completed.[22] Brazil's missile projects were terminated after they encountered financial hardships. Avibras declared bankruptcy on January 5, 1990, partly because of Iraq's refusal to pay for artillery rockets. Its labor force was cut from 6,000 to 900, and all projects were suspended (although the artillery rocket projects were later revived). Engesa declared bankruptcy, and Orbita was closed down by Embraer in 1991.

Brazil's VLS program was part of a long-term "Complete Brazilian Space Mission" (the MECB) that was announced in 1979. The MECB had three components—satellites, a satellite launcher (the VLS), and a launch pad—and aimed to launch three satellites within a decade.[23] The VLS used four 8.4 ton S-43 motors (derived from the Sonda-4's first stage) for stage 1, one S-43 for stage 2, one 5.4 ton S40 for stage 3, and one 1 ton S44 for stage 4.

The VLS was originally to be completed by 1989 (and in 1989 it was anticipated that the first launch would be in 1992). By 1989, the VLS was barely halfway to completion; that year, two critical technology tests took place. First, the fourth Sonda-4 test on April 28, 1989, validated many technologies (the previous Sonda launch in October 1987 failed to achieve stage separation due to a defective relay).[24] Second, the VLS-R2, a three times reduced version of the VLS, was launched on May 8, 1989. This tested the separation system for the four first-stage engines by means of pneumatic pistons. The previous model, the VLS-R1, had a different configuration. The next VLS test was a vibration test of a full-scale rocket mock up. On April 2, 1993, the VS-40 that comprised the third and fourth VLS stages flew to an altitude of about 1,000 km. In October 1994, Brazil's Aeronautics and Space Institute (IAE) began constructing the VLS launch pad.

The VLS project had 670 employees and cost $300 million between 1980 and 1995.[25] Its major portions were complete by 1995, and the rocket was stored in a horizontal position until September 1997 while the guidance system was developed. Russia's transfer of microelectronics and carbon fiber technology for rocket motor cases, and Russian personnel training initiatives, enhanced the VLS program (in turn, Russian firms were interested in the Alcantara launch facility).[26] Russian technicians designed the inertial guidance, antirolling, and mechanical fin activation systems. The VLS was flight-tested in November 1997 and December 1999 (when the $7.5 million rocket carried the Saci-2 satellite to study the Earth's atmosphere and magnetic fields); both tests failed. In the first test, one first-stage booster did not ignite. In the second test, the rocket was destroyed after 200 seconds when the second stage failed to ignite.

Why was the VLS project delayed by nearly a decade? In general, four technical and economic reasons were behind the delays. First, several technicians moved to the private sector, resulting in the VLS program being understaffed. For example, some 150 employees and eight leading scientists left the project in 1988–89. Second, economic constraints and a 55 percent funding cut in 1989 caused further delays. Third, flaws in the VLS design caused engineering complications. The design using four engines required three times more steel than a single more powerful engine (such as France's 30–40 ton Viking engine).[27] Fourth, the MTCR's embargo hindered many aspects of the VLS project. Brazil faced few obstacles in solid-fuel propulsion systems because it already had experience with the Sonda-4 rockets. But the MTCR hindered the acquisition and development of inertial guidance and control components, liquid-fuel (Viking-type) propulsion systems, and ignition and stage separation technologies.[28]

Additional delays resulted from the prohibition on engineering services. In October 1989, the State Department granted a license to an American firm, Lindberg Engineering, to anneal eighteen VLS casings (that were made in Brazil and sent to the United States for treatment).[29] But in June 1990, when seven of the eighteen casings had been treated, the Department of Defense called for suspending the license. On September 21, 1990, a joint economic subcommittee of the United States Congress was informed that a decision had been made at a very high level of government to return the seven casings to Brazil and to ban any further work on the project.

Overall, the VLS program was delayed by five to eight years, and the costs of indigenously constructing infrastructure to overcome the MTCR embargo ran into millions of dollars. Once the MTCR embargo was lifted in 1995, the VLS project was completed more rapidly and VLS flight tests took place in late 1997 and 1999. If the embargo had remained, the VLS project would still have been completed (as evidenced by flight tests of reduced versions of the rocket in 1989 and 1993), but with further delays. Thus the MTCR embargo was the most important of four technical and economic factors that caused the delay in the VLS project. During this five to eight year period, broader political-economic considerations and security improvements significantly influenced Brazil's missile nonproliferation decision.

National Prestige, Civil-Military Relations, and Regional Security

Brazil's missile, space, and nuclear programs are part of a wider military-industrial complex and science and technology sector having dual civilian and military purposes. The advancement of these sectors has been linked with Brazil's economic and political development and its desire for technical autonomy and international status.[30] These prestige considerations, commercial reasons (for defense exports), and security motives sustained Brazil's missile and rocket activity. But domestic political-economic liberalization and improvements in regional security partly moderated Brazil's missile activity.

Brazil made a transition to democratic government in 1985. Brazil's missile program was not reversed but gained momentum under the first civilian government (1985 to 1990). Arms exports were an important revenue source and this made any Brazilian government less inclined to restrain the defense industry. Also, Brazil's military retained a constitutional role in foreign and defense policy after shaping the democratic transition process, and shielded military-industrial programs from civilian encroachment. Compared to Argentina, Brazil's military retained a much greater role in politics after the transition to democracy.[31]

Brazil's armed forces controlled substantial portions of science and technology activity and retained broad latitude in military-industry policy. For example, the military retained control of the Brazilian Space Activities Commission (COBAE). Civilian efforts to develop satellites (for natural resource survey and remote sensing) were delayed by the air force, which gave higher priority to a satellite launcher.[32] Under the Sarney administration, subsidies and funds were channeled toward the defense sector despite an economic deterioration, a budget crisis, and defense sector debts (by late 1989, Brazil's three leading defense contractors had a debt of over $1 billion).

The Collor administration struck a balance between imposing new restraints on the military and continuing to support the defense sector. Yet a number of obstacles remained to bringing the defense industry under firmer democratic control. For example, Brazil's Congress was unable to render independent judgments on military and industrial technological programs such as the VLS. As a result of this military control over defense projects, the democratic transition of 1985 did not substantially curb Brazil's military-dominated rocket projects.

Democratization, however, allowed for improvements in Argentine-Brazilian relations from 1985, which reduced the security-related demand for ballistic missiles. In these circumstances, U.S. pressure and domestic economic factors influenced Brazil's decision to scrap its missile programs but not its VLS satellite launch vehicle.

Economic Considerations and U.S. Pressure

Brazil has been vulnerable to U.S. influence because the United States is Brazil's major trading partner, accounting for 30 percent of Brazil's exports; Brazil's policy makers have unsuccessfully sought to reverse this dependence on the United States.[33] Brazil's economic vulnerability allowed Washington to extract concessions on its missile programs in the late 1980s.

Libya had been interested in Brazil's rocket programs since 1985. In January 1988, Libya's Director General for Armament Supplies visited Brazil at Engesa's invitation. The Libyans sought to buy the first batch of MB/EE-150 missiles, the Osorio battle tank, and artillery systems; they were also interested in the MB/EE-600 and MB/EE-1000 missiles. They offered to spend $1 billion on Brazilian arms, plus $400 million or more for five years to assist MB/EE missile programs.[34] The missile aspect of the Brazil-Libya transaction concerned Washington, which threatened to restrict Brazilian products from American markets. On January 22, 1988, U.S. Deputy Secretary of State John Whitehead demanded an explanation for the arms transaction from Brazil's ambassador to the United States, who responded, "The country's [economic] situation does not allow us to reject any deals [with Libya]."[35]

In Brasilia, Foreign Minister Roberto Abreu Sodre noted that American protests were "without effect" and of "no consequence," and that the weapons under discussion were purely "defensive."[36] Yet Brazil backed down because of the risks of economic and political losses if it continued to confront the United States.[37] In February 1988, it scrapped the Libyan contract even though negotiations were in an advanced stage. It thereby forfeited $1 billion at a critical time of economic distress and low defense sales, but was ensured of continued access to the U.S. export market. Orbita's missile program remained underfunded and was eventually halted.

While Brazil's ballistic missile programs thus collapsed, its democratic regime did not scrap the economically burdensome VLS program that showed no signs of economic returns and was also slowed by the MTCR's embargoes in the mid-1990s. This was because of strong military and bureaucratic internal pressures (discussed above) to continue the program, and weakening external pressure to scrap the project. External pressure on the VLS decreased when sections of the U.S. bureaucracy that favored closer relations with Brazil accepted the VLS as a civilian research effort for three reasons.

First, Brazil's political-economic importance gave it reverse leverage on the United States. Brazil represents a large economic market and is the most important political and economic player in Latin America, and Washington has therefore sought to maintain close ties with it. Second, Brazil had cooperated with the nonproliferation regime from the early 1990s. It signed the September 1991 Mendoza Declaration banning chemical weapon activity and also signed several nuclear safeguard arrangements including a December 1991 safeguards agreement with the IAEA; it hosted a visiting MTCR team in April 1992; and it drafted export control laws (which were sent to Congress in July 1995). Third, President Itamar Franco curbed the military's influence over Brazil's space program by transferring it to a civilian Brazilian Space Agency (AEB). AEB was established under a federal law sent to Congress in April 1993 and signed by the president on February 10, 1994; after COBAE's final meeting on September 16, 1994, its contract rights and obligations were transferred to AEB.[38]

Brazil formally joined the MTCR in October 1995. By joining the regime, Brazil sought not just to acquire technology and establish credibility for its space program, but to also be viewed as a responsible international actor and further its aspirations to join the UN Security Council.[39] Thereafter, AEB-NASA scientific cooperation expanded. In April 2000, Washington signed an agreement permitting U.S. launchers to operate from Alcantara, further boosting Brazil's space program.

SOUTH AFRICA

The Development and Decline of a Missile Program

South Africa's early rocket plans involved an Israeli-assisted project (that predated the 1977 international arms embargo on Pretoria) to launch reconnaissance satellites. This rocket was designed to place a 330 kg surveillance satellite in a 200 × 460 km orbit. In the 1980s, when South Africa's nuclear program gained momentum, its defense agency (Armscor) sought to use the rocket as a two-stage ballistic missile. Armscor began constructing the Overberg launch facility in 1983. South Africa's initial nuclear devices were glide bombs to be deployed on Buccaneer aircraft, and in the late 1980s, Pretoria sought to miniaturize nuclear warheads that could be carried on missiles. The Advena Central Laboratories for building two warheads per year and mating them to missiles were started in 1987 and completed in 1989.[40]

South Africa conducted three rocket flight tests in June 1989 (where only stage 1 was tested), July 5, 1989, and November 19, 1990.[41] Armscor noted that the rockets were intended to qualify the test range. On December 4, 1990, the UN General Assembly requested the Secretary General to report on South Africa's missile activities and to check allegations of Israeli assistance to the program.[42] U.S. satellite monitoring of South African missile tests suggested that the rocket plume was similar to that of Israel's Jericho-2 missile, and the testing equipment also resembled Israeli equipment.[43]

South Africa continued rocket activity even after it scrapped its nuclear program and signed the NPT in July 1991. Armscor was restructured and its defense subsidiaries were transferred to the civilian Denel Group (that comprised twenty-two firms) formed in April 1992. These firms pursued the rocket project at the Houwteq aerospace facility. The test range was at Overberg while the engine test facility was at Rooi Els, and the entire initiative involved about fifty companies and 1,300 to 1,500 personnel at its peak.[44]

South Africa's 23 ton RSA-3 launch vehicle had a 1.3 m diameter and 15 m length; the first and second stages each comprised a 10 ton solid-fuel engine, and the third stage was a 2 ton engine, similar to Israel's Shavit launcher. A follow-on RSA-4 was in the design stage but never built. It would have weighed 52 tons, with a 1.9 m diameter and 20 m length, comprising a 34 ton solid-fuel first stage, 15 ton solid-fuel second stage (essentially the 10 ton RSA-3 booster that was stretched by 50 percent), and 2 ton solid-fuel third stage.

After spending $55 million on the RSA-3, Denel announced its termination in late June 1993 on the grounds that it was uneconomic. This paved the way for an October 1994 U.S.–South African agreement to eliminate South Africa's missile program, and led to South Africa's accession to the MTCR in October 1995.

The impact of MTCR technology embargoes on South Africa's rocket program was moderate. South Africa had an established missile program (albeit acquired with Israeli assistance) in the 1980s, and overcame the MTCR's embargoes to test an intermediate-range ballistic missile. It required external assistance to upgrade this missile into a more capable satellite launcher in a cost-effective manner. This attempt to develop an advanced capability rocket was thwarted by the MTCR. But, given adequate time and a strong demand, South Africa could have built medium-range missiles or satellite launchers despite the MTCR, because it had an established industrial infrastructure. Security improve-

ments and U.S. political-economic pressure eventually halted Pretoria's rocket
program.

Regional Security and U.S. Pressure

South Africa's nuclear weapons program advanced in the 1980s because of a
deteriorating regional security environment (though other factors such as bureaucratic politics and the pressures of international isolation also influenced South
Africa's nuclear program). When the Namibia conflict was settled, Cuban troops
withdrew from Angola, and any Soviet-backed threat was removed, South
Africa's security environment improved. Pretoria then terminated its nuclear
weapons program and signed the NPT in 1991, but continued its rocket activity
for commercial reasons.

However, South Africa's commercial rocket aspirations could not proceed
rapidly because of the MTCR's technology blockade, and because an economic
reform policy made Pretoria susceptible to external pressure. U.S. efforts to halt
South Africa's missile program were spurred not solely by concerns about nuclear
nonproliferation (since Pretoria had already signed the NPT), but by the fear of
increased missile proliferation under a *democratic* African National Congress
regime (after a one-year interim administration in 1993–94, the transition to
majority rule formally took place in May 1994). On this issue, U.S. officials
noted that "the bottom line is that the ANC has historically maintained close
friendships with countries such as Libya, Cuba . . . [and other states] who must
not get access to South African missile technology."[45]

Washington first moved against Pretoria's missile program on September 27,
1991, when it announced missile-related sanctions against Armscor for receiving technology from Israel. These sanctions banned all contracts with, exports
to, and imports from Armscor and its subsidiaries. Foreign Minister Botha noted
that the sanctions had no immediate substantive impact, because the existing
UN arms embargo on South Africa was far more extensive than U.S. sanctions.
Yet Armscor executives privately complained that U.S. sanctions would damage the firm's search for overseas markets.[46]

After Prime Minister de Klerk called President Bush to protest the sanctions,
sections of Washington's bureaucracy sought to lift sanctions and allow South
Africa to keep its rocket program if it was safeguarded and not for military use.
However, ACDA and the Defense Department persuaded the Bush administration to maintain a firm nonproliferation line. The Defense Department had com-
missioned a study showing the unfeasibility and proliferation risks of new space
launch programs.[47] This study influenced Washington's policy of opposing South
Africa's dual-use rocket program during talks with Pretoria in 1992 and 1993.[48]

In early 1992, U.S. negotiators failed to obtain a South African commitment to join the MTCR.[49] In December 1992, U.S. negotiators held meetings at the South African foreign affairs department and at Denel. They informed South Africa that the West would prevent its development of space launchers and that without foreign technology its rocket program was not commercially viable. The State Department suggested that Pretoria finance the rocket privately. Pretoria took up the challenge, which eventually faltered.

The de Klerk government hesitated on terminating Denel's rocket program in 1992–93, and made several contradictory declarations on this issue. In March 1993, under pressure from the United States, the South African cabinet abandoned plans for a long-range solid fuel missile.[50] Yet on March 24, 1993, as part of his declaration of South Africa's prior nuclear weapons activities, President de Klerk stated that he preferred to continue with a space launch program. De Klerk noted that "we think that there is viability with regard to the satellite program and we would like that program to go ahead." He added that the termination of South Africa's nuclear program meant that any proliferation risk "has now fallen away, and we should be allowed to use the technology and technical expertise which we have."[51] On June 2, 1993, the Denel managing director stated that South Africa was drafting missile export legislation with the goal of joining the MTCR. Denel also anticipated that MTCR membership would help South Africa develop a satellite launching industry that could be worth $400 million annually.[52]

Ultimately, despite their resentment of U.S. pressure, South African officials recognized that several hundred million dollars still needed to be spent before their rocket program was technically viable. International Monetary Fund (IMF) officials expressed difficulty in approving new loans to Pretoria if it spent government funds on the rocket. Denel's project directors had unsuccessfully tried to find European satellite customers in 1992–93. A series of static rocket tests ending on March 2, 1993, also assessed South Africa's launch vehicle program. This was part of Denel's internal investigation which reached three conclusions on June 20, 1993: their rocket launcher was not commercially viable and would therefore be scrapped; Denel would continue space activity through a low-cost satellite (Greensat); and, the Overberg test range and the Hangklip test facility would not be shut down because international agreements might allow satellite support system tests or foreign rocket launches from the site.

Pretoria announced the termination of its rocket program in a June 30, 1993, statement at the UN.[53] It noted that this termination would cost jobs, but hoped for positive effects such as lesser world suspicion of South Africa and the lifting of sanctions on Denel and its affiliates. In a November 1993 agreement with Washington, South Africa undertook to restrict its missile-related imports and exports; its adherence to this agreement would enable the United States to recommend Pretoria's MTCR membership. After further discussions, the United States and South Africa signed a missile nonproliferation agreement on October 3, 1994. South Africa would abide by MTCR guidelines and terminate its category I rocket program. It could temporarily import space launchers for satellites (but this provision was not utilized because South Africa had no need for such a launcher and it could also not find commercial partners).[54] Simultaneously, South Africa received several hundred million dollars in U.S. and IMF aid. It also received $1 million in U.S. funding to destroy rocket motor cast pits and a motor testing facility.

In September 1995, South Africa's MTCR membership was approved when the group was satisfied with South African nonproliferation measures. Pretoria's foreign affairs ministry stated that MTCR membership could open up commercial opportunities for the country's defense-related industry and also strengthened its commitment to controlling weapons of mass destruction.[55] In February 1999, South Africa's space program achieved an important (but mainly symbolic) goal when its "Sunsat" scientific satellite with remote-sensing experiments was launched by a Delta-2 rocket. South Africa thus maintained its involvement in space while terminating its long-range rocket programs.

5

South Korea, Taiwan, Arab States: Restrained Regional Missile Programs

On September 26, 1978, at a South Korean military base, several antitank rockets, multiple-loaded rockets, and a new 180 km range ballistic missile zeroed in on their targets to the applause and cheers of a hundred viewers. Witnessing the missile display were President Park Chung Hee, his cabinet ministers, Korea's army chiefs, and General John Vessey, commander of U.S. forces in Korea. Seoul's ministry of defense proclaimed that South Korea had become "the seventh country in the world to produce the missile."[1] The *Korea Herald* boasted that Seoul's new missile was "powerful enough to overwhelm the North's Frog-7 [rocket]," adding that the missile's development "marks a gigantic leap forward in the national endeavor to establish a self-reliant defense posture" and that "the U.S. government decision last year to withdraw its forces from Korea has created the vital need for this country to accelerate the buildup of our defense industry."[2] Yet South Korea did not build much in the way of longer range missiles for the next twenty years.

Elsewhere in East Asia, another regional power's missile ambitions were also restrained. Lingering fears of a Chinese military invasion made deterrence a motive for Taiwan's repeated missile attempts. In 1974, an issue of *Overseas Scholars* published an advertisement from Taiwan's Chung Shan Institute of Science and Technology seeking seventy-seven missile-related specialists. In subsequent years, Taiwanese students sought missile training at the Massachusetts Institute of Technology. This program was soon canceled by the State Department, and Taiwan's ballistic missile ambitions remained grounded for the next quarter century.

In the Middle East, four national missile programs were similarly constrained. In an impressive display of rocketry, Nasser's military paraded three ballistic missiles at its July 25 Revolution Day celebrations in the 1960s. These missiles barely flew, and despite several further missile development attempts, Cairo could not build a medium-range missile during the next forty years. In March 1980, deep in the Libyan desert, a new rocket took off but failed to reach orbit; over the next two decades, European customs prevented critical technology shipments from reaching Libya and thwarted Muammar Qadaffi's missile programs. In 1991, Palestinians cheered as Saddam Hussein's forces fired dozens of missiles at Tel Aviv and Jerusalem; yet shortly thereafter, the UN Special Commission (UNSCOM) substantially dismantled Baghdad's missile arsenal. In 1998, during a regional crisis, Syria moved 36 Scuds to the Al-Samiyah base some 70 km from Turkey. These missiles had been bought from North Korea and were not built in Syria. That year, not counting missiles in Egypt or Iran, Israeli intelligence still assessed that between one to two thousand ballistic missiles could threaten their country by 2010 (380 to 950 in Iraq, 350 to 510 in Libya, and 400 to 460 in Syria).[3] These projections may or may not materialize. By 2002, neither Iraq nor Libya had advanced their missile plans, though Iraq had the capability for a substantial missile breakout.

South Korea, Taiwan, Egypt, Iraq, Syria, and Libya all embarked upon ambitious missile programs but were constrained from advancing these much beyond Scud-type missiles. U.S. leverage largely curbed the missile ambitions of technologically advanced South Korea; U.S. influence along with the MTCR's barriers checked the missile ambitions of technologically advanced Taiwan and technologically weaker Egypt; Iraq's missile activities were curbed by the UNSCOM regime; and technology embargoes alone were sufficient to delay Syria's and thwart Libya's missile programs.

SOUTH KOREA

South Korea built 180 km range NHK-1 and NHK-2 ballistic missiles from the mid-1970s, but was not permitted longer range missiles or a space launcher until it entered the MTCR in 2001, when it was allowed 300 km range missiles. Security threats from North Korea and domestic political pressures sustained Seoul's missile quest, but a U.S. security guarantee and U.S. political leverage moderated the scope of Seoul's missile activity.

The Historical Origins of a Missile Capability

South Korea began early missile development through a 1972 agreement with the United States to service American Hawk and Nike-Hercules surface-to-air missiles in Korea.[4] A U.S.-supervised maintenance facility was set up in Korea under a local firm, Gold Star Precision Industries Ltd. In 1975, South Korean personnel received training from the U.S. military and Raytheon to make missile improvements. Seoul also purchased a solid-fuel missile propellant mixer from a Lockheed plant in 1975, and some production equipment was shipped to South Korea in 1978.

These activities were part of an ambitious missile project within South Korea's Agency for Defense Development (ADD), the research arm of its defense ministry, that was established in 1970. In December 1971, President Park directed ADD to build a missile by 1976. This Nike-Hercules derived missile covered some 160 km in its first test on September 26, 1978. Seoul emphasized that this NHK-1 or "Paekkom" (White Bear) was an indigenously built missile that used new propellants, warheads, and guidance systems, though some of these technologies were obtained from the United States. Seoul then pledged to constrain itself to 180 km range missiles through a 1979 memorandum of understanding (MOU) with the United States. After President Park's assassination in October 1979, missile activity in South Korea decreased. Dozens of scientists, including missile research scientists, were dismissed from ADD in August 1980, and a further several hundred employees left ADD in December 1982.

From 1983–84, South Korea worked on the NHK-2 or "Hyonmu" missile (which was previously tested in October 1982 before its development was halted). While the NHK-1 used radar guidance that could be jammed, the NHK-2 used a British inertial guidance system that was not easily jammed. It also had a single stage booster motor instead of the four clustered motors of the NHK-1.[5] The NHK-2 was tested in September 1986 and deployed in 1987.

From 1995 onwards, South Korea sought to build longer range missiles. It argued that the North Korean capital, Pyongyang, was beyond the reach of U.S.-supplied 120 km range Lance and 37 km range Honest John missiles. South Korea first sought 300 km range systems (that would be MTCR-compliant) to target North Korea's capital and other major military and industrial centers from some strategic depth within South Korea. In July 1999, President Kim Dae Jung formally sought 500 km range missiles that could cover all of North Korean territory from secure bases deep inside South Korea. Korean analysts argued that a 300 km range missile "can reach Yongbyon and Shiniju, suspect sites in North Korea, but it cannot hit Chongjin and Najin, where there are many military installations."[6]

In addition to its missile activities, South Korea pursued restricted space activity that could provide the foundation for a more capable missile program. In June 1993 and September 1993, it launched single-stage KSR-1 sounding rockets to altitudes of 38 km and 48 km respectively. These were part of a six-year, $42 million project to build a two-stage, 2 ton version of the rockets to reach a 200 km altitude by 1996, and to then build a three-stage version to reach a 350 km altitude by 1999.[7] The first objective was achieved in July 1997, when South

Korea launched the 2 ton two-stage KSR-2. In 1996, Seoul announced a space plan to launch a 500–700 kg payload to a 600–800 km altitude orbit by 2009. In 1998, following North Korea's Taepodong test, Seoul advanced this schedule to seek a satellite launcher by 2005. In January 2000, Seoul reiterated its intentions to launch surveillance satellites and remove its dependence on foreign launchers within five years at a cost of $500 million to 1 billion. The South Korean rocket was expected to carry small satellites for mapping, coastline surveillance, and weather forecasting.

The MTCR was not specifically intended to halt South Korea's missile programs; even if it were, its impact would be marginal. South Korea's missile program initially benefited from external assistance by receiving the Nike-Hercules and U.S. technology transfer. Yet Seoul's missile activity would not be curbed without external assistance because South Korea's industrial base enables it to manufacture advanced missiles. South Korea's defense industry has a multi-billion dollar annual turnover, and several Korean firms produce missile-related goods. Political rather than technological constraints checked South Korea's missile programs.

Security Concerns, Regional Rivalry, Domestic Politics, and U.S. Influence

South Korea sought ballistic missiles primarily to counter a security threat from North Korea. The severity of the threat varied over time. By the 1980s and 1990s, South Korea had normalized ties with China (North Korea's main ally), and had substantial economic superiority over and bigger military budgets than North Korea, which mitigated the threat. Yet Pyongyang still had a 30 to 50 percent edge in military manpower and hardware such as tanks and artillery. Its consequent ability to overrun the South Korean capital, Seoul, which is only 50 km from the border, is a serious security concern for South Korea.[8] Pyongyang's nuclear, chemical, and missile activities in the 1990s were a further threat; and despite the successful June 2000 Korea summit, Pyongyang retained a substantial military capability. Seoul has stated that its missiles are a deterrent against North Korea, but has not elaborated on how conventionally armed missiles may provide deterrence (Seoul has signed the NPT and the CWC).

A security alliance with the United States restrains South Korea from developing a WMD and missile force to deter or defend against a North Korean military attack. Joseph Yager notes that "to the extent that U.S. defense policy builds South Korean confidence in the stability of the peace [against North Korea], it supports U.S. nonproliferation policy."[9] Washington used its strategic leverage to extract nonproliferation concessions from Seoul in four instances.

First, after indications of a U.S. military withdrawal from the Pacific in the 1970s, the Park government began a military modernization effort including a nuclear and missile program. The Ford and Carter administrations then used their *security* leverage (such as canceling troop withdrawal plans and threatening a military aid cut) to rein in Seoul's nuclear activity; Washington also used its *economic* leverage (the threat of halting foreign aid and loans) against South Korea for similar purposes in 1975–76. With less room for nuclear maneuver under the stricter institutional constraints of the NPT, Seoul's main option was to play its missile cards. Yet the Carter administration curbed Seoul's missile aspirations through its 1979 MOU. This agreement, signed between Korean Defense Minister No Chae-hyon and U.S. commander of forces in Korea John Wickham, prohibited Seoul from developing missiles with a range of more than 180 km (the distance between Seoul and Pyongyang). The agreement also banned South Korea from missile research and from acquiring missile components from a third country. It was signed to allow the transfer of Nike-Hercules technologies. The Chun Du Hwan government further restrained the NHK project and dismissed ADD scientists in the early 1980s, partly to cater to Washington.[10]

Domestic political influences on South Korea's missile activity should also be noted. In the 1970s, the South Korean military did not support an indigenous missile project because it hindered more important military priorities, and the missile project also diverted resources from other economic sectors.[11] Yet President Park advanced the NHK project, partly for prestige reasons. He sought missiles capable of striking Pyongyang in part because he resented North Korean superiority in missiles (North Korea's 55 km range Frog-5s and 70 km range Frog-7s could strike Seoul, while South Korea had longer 120 km range Lance missiles but these could not hit Pyongyang; North Korea still did not have 300 km range Scuds). Pressure to achieve results led to upheavals within the ADD, which exaggerated progress to maintain its position with Park. These origins of South Korea's missile program imply that it may have been more broadly debated under a politically liberalized regime. But, as discussed later, under a democratized regime and when resources were more easily available in the 1990s, although South Korea's missile program was widely debated, the debate concerned *expanding* rather than curbing missile and space projects.

Second, in 1983–84, South Korea resumed missile activity after North Korean agents bombed and killed seventeen members of President Hwan's entourage in October 1983 in Rangoon, and North Korea's 1984 Scud test. Seoul then developed the NHK-2 that was tested in September 1986 and deployed in 1987. But the Reagan administration convinced Seoul to restrict the missile's range to 180 km (instead of 250 km), and to limit deployment to a single twelve-missile unit. In return, Washington provided greater military aid to Seoul, and in November 1986 announced that it would reintroduce Lance missiles in Korea.

Third, in 1990, Seoul agreed to U.S. inspections of the NHK missiles to verify their 180 km range limit, and also pledged not to develop satellite launch vehicles. Washington urged Seoul to modify the 1979 MOU, inserting a clause that "South Korea will not try to develop any type of rocket system exceeding 180 km in range and 300 kg in warhead weight, regardless of its usage whether it is for military or commercial use or for scientific research."[12] In return, Seoul received U.S. technical cooperation for its NHK missiles.

Fourth, the Clinton administration reined in South Korea's missile activity in the middle and late 1990s. At this time, South Korea had security concerns over two issues. First, North Korea was expanding its nuclear activity (resulting in a nuclear crisis from 1992 to 1994) and increasing its missile activity (through its missile tests in 1993 and 1998). Second, the Clinton administration's talks with Pyongyang were perceived as possibly weakening U.S. ties with Seoul. In March 1994, Washington ordered Patriot batteries to South Korea to partly address Seoul's security concerns. Seoul nevertheless requested in June 1995 that the U.S.-ROK missile MOU be abandoned, and sought to build 300 km range missiles to counter North Korea's missile activity. Washington denied this request.

Domestic pressures under a democratic regime also influenced South Korean missile demands. In general, South Korean authoritarian regimes had a more militaristic foreign policy, and South Korea's democratization allowed some flexibility in reconciliation toward North Korea.[13] Yet, despite some inter-Korean reconciliation, the North Korean military threat remained significant in the 1990s. These threats were exaggerated under the pressures of democratic politics. Thus, during or ahead of U.S.-ROK missile meetings, editorials upped the ante. They noted that "it is unfair for the ROK, the first simulated target of a North Korean missile attack, to be bound by a 180 km range [limit on its missiles] when North Korea has already deployed 650 of remodeled Scud-B and C with a 500 km range. . . . In addition, we cannot help but worry about a possible situation where we may be bound in our space development projects. We hope the ongoing ROK-U.S. meeting will serve as momentum for correcting these perplexities and problems."[14] Under domestic pressure, South Korea's government repeatedly declared its desire to repeal the U.S.-ROK MOU. For example, in a July 1996 testimony at a National Assembly defense committee meeting, Defense Minister Yi Yang-ho stated that the government would seek to scrap the MOU during the third Korea-U.S. missile nonproliferation meeting. These remarks came after Representative Yim Pok-Chin of the opposition NCNP made the case that, upon subscribing to the MTCR, Seoul should not be bound by 180 km range limitations.[15]

The Clinton administration held twenty rounds of missile talks with South Korea between 1995 and 2001. Washington's delegation was mostly headed by Assistant Secretary of State for Nonproliferation Robert Einhorn; Seoul's delegation was (especially in the latter years) headed by the Director of South Korea's North American Affairs Bureau Song Min Soon. In the first four U.S.-ROK meetings in November 1995 (in Washington), June 1996 (Seoul), December 1996 (Washington), and July 1997 (Hawaii), the two sides exchanged information on U.S.-North Korea missile talks, discussed South Korean participation in the MTCR and Australia group, its ratification of the CWC (achieved in 1996), and the control of dual-use missile technology.[16] By the August 1998 round of negotiations, the two sides had moved closer on allowing Seoul to build 300 km range missiles, but could not agree on further issues.[17]

In 1999, Seoul upped the ante in several ways. First, on April 10, it launched a Hyonmu missile to a range of 40 km off its western coast (Washington may then have lodged a complaint that if fully fueled, the missile could have flown 296 km).[18] Second, on April 27, 1999, South Korea's Vice Defense Minister declared that Seoul would not limit the range and payload of its space projectiles.[19] Third, U.S. satellites detected a rocket motor test station in South Korea.[20] Fourth, and most significant, during a July 2 summit with President Clinton, President Kim publicly requested that South Korea be allowed a 500 km range missile (which was well beyond the 300 km range limits of prior discussions). Kim's announcement had several motives: it was a show of strength to his domestic critics; it indicated to Pyongyang that Seoul would match it in military terms; it signaled to Washington his willingness to develop an independent military capability; and it was a means to jump-start stalled missile talks. U.S.-ROK negotiations in 1999 remained deadlocked for several reasons. On the missile range issue, Washington had allowed Seoul to build 300 km range missiles; this would cater to South Korean domestic politics by appeasing pro-missile lobbies, but still conform to international nonproliferation standards of the MTCR. However, Washington would not permit longer range missiles. U.S. negotiators stressed that Seoul's security interests were better served through its strong alliance with the United States and a robust conventional deterrence that could be backed by 300 km range systems; in this context, the utility of 500 km range missiles was small, especially compared with the costs.[21] These costs included a reduced North Korean willingness to curb its missile program if Seoul expanded missile activity, plus increased expenditure on missiles that would reduce resources for South Korea's conventional forces, and increased suspicion from China, Japan, and Russia. On space issues, Washington allowed South Korea to develop space launchers and was prepared to assist Seoul in joining the MTCR (which could facilitate cooperation in space-launch activities),[22] but sought stricter monitoring of South Korea's space program.[23] A transparency issue concerning Seoul's missile program remained disputed: Seoul proposed providing Washington with materials and information on its missile program and deployments, while Washington sought to inspect manufacturing facilities and deployment sites.[24] The impasse was gradually resolved in 2000.

In July 2000, following missile talks with North Korea in Kuala Lumpur, Robert Einhorn traveled to Seoul to continue U.S.-ROK talks. By then, the missile range issue was resolved, as Washington agreed that South Korea could build missiles "to the extent to meet its security needs," and allowed 500 km range systems for research purposes; however, "five or so remaining technical issues which are quite important"—such as transparency and the mode of agreement— were unresolved.[25] Additional missile talks in September, October, and November 2000 finalized some of these issues, but the two sides still differed on the form of agreement. In a final January 11, 2001, round of negotiations, just before the Clinton administration left office, the form of agreement was resolved. It would be through Seoul's self-declared adoption of missile guidelines that were delivered to Washington, instead of a bilateral MOU that Washington had sought. Seoul then declared its missile policy on January 18, noting that "our government will be able to develop and possess missiles with enough range capabilities to meet our security needs."[26] Washington's missile talks with Seoul thus resulted in a negotiated settlement containing five main features.

First, South Korea could build and deploy 300 km range missiles with a 500 kg warhead. Second, South Korea could undertake limited activity with 500 km range systems; it could build these systems for research purposes, and could also use a tradeoff provision to develop 500 km range cruise missiles with a lighter 400 kg warhead. Third, South Korea could build satellite launchers without limits on their range and payload, but these could not use solid fuel. Fourth, Seoul's missile activities would be made transparent: Seoul would permit U.S. participation when it test-fired rockets for civilian purposes, and would inform Washington when it developed missiles for military purposes. Fifth, the form of the agreement was a missile declaration by Seoul that was delivered to Washington, and not a bilateral MOU between Seoul and Washington. Seoul also sent copies of its missile policy declaration to North Korea and other states. South Korea formally entered the MTCR in March 2001.

Thus, in the face of security concerns about (and prestige reasons to counter) nuclear and missile activity in North Korea, public opinion called for increases in South Korea's missile and dual-use space capability in the 1990s. Yet U.S. leverage, and Washington's sustained nonproliferation dialogue from 1995 to 2001, checked South Korea's missile aspirations. Eventually, despite some improvements in ties with North Korea in 2000, South Korea successfully bargained with Washington for a 300 km range missile and pressed on with a space program. While South Korea lacked core technologies for space launchers and would have to import crucial materials which were costly to develop, it still planned to launch satellite payloads of 100 kg by 2005, 200 kg by 2007, and 500–1,000 kg by 2010.[27]

TAIWAN

Taiwan initiated a missile program in the mid-1970s. Security threats from Beijing (intensified by the politics of democratization) sustained Taiwan's missile ambitions, but a U.S. security guarantee and U.S. leverage limited Taiwan to cruise missiles; Taiwan did not build medium-range ballistic missiles or space launchers despite domestic pressures to do so in the 1990s.

The Evolution of a Missile Capability

Beginning in the 1970s, Taiwan built several hundred Hsiung Feng (HF) antiship cruise missiles and Sky Bow surface-to-air missiles, but restricted its ballistic missile and space launcher aspirations. Taiwanese personnel initially sought missile training through a 1975 contract between the National Taiwan University and MIT to instruct fifteen students for two years in inertial navigation and guidance; the contract was terminated by Washington.[28] Taiwan's missile programs then continued at the Chung Shan Institute of Science and Technology (CIST). By the mid-1970s, CIST employed 2,000 professionals, half of them from universities and private industry.

Taiwan first developed the 100–130 km range "Green Bee" missile, resembling the Lance, which was displayed in 1981. It then planned to build the Sky Horse missile capable of reaching major cities in eastern China; a March 1980 testimony noted that Taiwan had allocated research resources for this 960 km range missile.[29] The Sky Horse was abandoned in 1981, partly under U.S. pressure, and partly because the CIST concentrated instead on the Sky Bow missiles.[30]

Beyond its missile program, Taiwan also embarked on a satellite launcher program that would borrow from and contribute to its missile research. In 1988–89, an economic advisory committee in the premier's office established a subcommittee to explore the development of civilian aircraft and space launchers, and announced plans "to launch an approximately 200-pound satellite within the next 5 years."[31] Yet high costs and technology transfer problems caused Taiwan to scrap its space launcher plans. In 1990, noting the MTCR's effects in raising the economic and political costs of rocket programs in other nations, Taiwan's policy makers decided not to develop satellite launchers, and instead restricted its space program to satellites.[32] That year, Taiwan authorized a 15 year $500 million budget for this space program. It established a strategic plan by August 1991 and a National Space Program Office under the National Science Council in 1992. Taiwan's space program operates a remote-sensing ground station that commenced operations in 1993, and seeks to build a communications satellite. A smaller Taiwanese satellite, the 400 kg Rocsat-1 with an experimental communications payload and an ocean imager, was launched on a Lockheed-Martin rocket in January 1999.

Despite being missile-capable, Taiwan confined its missile activity to short-range cruise missiles and surface-to-air missiles for three main reasons. First, technology embargoes deterred it from technologically more challenging satellite launchers. Second, economic considerations (the absence of any significant economic gains from a low capability launcher) also influenced this decision. Third, political factors such as security threats from China, U.S. leverage, and domestic pressures affected Taiwan's missile policy.

Security Considerations, Domestic Politics, and U.S. Influence

Taiwan has sought nuclear weapons and delivery systems to establish a deterrent or defense against a Chinese military attack. Despite an expanding Taiwan-China trade relationship, the 1995–96 missile crisis shattered any illusion that economic interdependence would replace military conflict as the central feature of their bilateral relations.[33]

Taiwan's modern conventional forces would make a military invasion by Beijing (which has only a limited seaborne invasion capability) costly, although Taiwan's military would eventually be overwhelmed by Chinese superiority in numbers.[34] Taiwan is also vulnerable to Chinese psychological and military pressure through a naval blockade and missile attacks (by 2001, Beijing had about 300 CSS-6 and CSS-7 missiles near Taiwan and was adding 50 missiles per year). Such Chinese action could cause economic panic (and create internal conflict) and damage assets and airfields and thereby soften Taiwan's ability to cope with an external attack.

Acquiring nuclear capabilities may or may not enhance Taiwan's deterrent. Any Taiwanese deterrent rests on the dubious assumption that Beijing must believe that Taiwan would initiate a nuclear exchange during an invasion, and that China would not strike first. But nuclear weapons have political and strategic value in enabling Taiwan to withstand Chinese nuclear blackmail. U.S. political and military ties with Taiwan address its security concerns, and implicitly deter Chinese military threats, thereby mitigating Taiwanese moves toward a nuclear and missile program. Four examples illustrate this dynamic.

First, Taiwan made nuclear moves in the 1970s following indications of a U.S. military withdrawal from the Pacific theater, but the Nixon and Ford administrations curbed these nuclear aspirations.[35] Second, Taiwan embarked on the Sky Horse missile project in the 1980s during a time of U.S.-Chinese normalization. However, the Sky Horse project was dropped under U.S. pressure in

1981, and then again in 1989. Third, in the early 1990s, the lack of scientific support during an internal debate, combined with pressure from the State Department, led Taiwan's policy makers to halt their dual-use space launcher program. Fourth, the Taiwanese military more actively pressed for a surface-to-surface missile in the mid-1990s, especially after Chinese missile tests in July–August 1995.[36] This crisis demonstrates the role of domestic pressures in proliferation, and the potential negative consequences of democratization for regional security. The Democratic Progressive Party (DPP)'s prom. nence in a democratic system allowed it to place the issue of independence high on the agenda (though DPP leader Chen Shui-ban adopted a moderate line when he assumed the presidency in 2000, and domestic groups also have an economic stake in ties with Beijing which makes them tone down the independence rhetoric). This increases tensions with Beijing and stimulates Taiwan's demand for missiles.

President Lee Teng-hui's steps toward an autonomous foreign policy in the mid-1990s (Lee could not back down on the issue because of the opposition DPP's pro-independence line) caused Beijing to respond with military exercises and missile launches in July 1995 and March 1996. This high-conflict environment made Taiwan's military and domestic groups call for a missile program. Supporting military demands, in 1996 a group of lawmakers (albeit not representing a majority view) argued for developing cruise missiles following reports that China had acquired cruise missiles from Russia. Lin Yu-fang, a New Party legislator who once headed Tamkang University's Institute of Strategic Studies, noted that Taiwan could upgrade the Hsiung Feng missiles to counter the Chinese threat (but at the same time, another legislator noted that for the mutual benefit of all Chinese, the two sides should not engage in an arms race).[37]

Thereafter, faced with an expanding Chinese tactical missile force in the 1990s, Taiwanese policy makers called for reviving the Sky Horse missile program. They argued that missiles capable of striking high-value Chinese coastal targets were more effective than air power or missile defenses (that could be overwhelmed by a growing Chinese missile arsenal) in deterring Beijing's use of force. Defense Minister Chiang Chung-ling also noted in the Legislative Yuan that "Undoubtedly, the best defense strategy is to attack. . . . The best defense measure is to destroy the [Chinese] M-class missiles before they are launched."[38] Taiwan may have deployed the HF-2 cruise missiles in their land-attack mode as early as 1994. In March 1999, Taiwan allocated $600 million for several short-range missile projects that included modifying the HF-2 to be capable of striking China's missile sites.[39] In December 1999 (in the months before the March 2000 presidential election), following news reports that China was deploying missiles across the Taiwan Strait, Taiwan's Vice President Lien Chan publicly called for a deterrent and missile force. Chan declared that "we must strengthen our naval and air power, and employ highly mobile naval and air power and the latent strike power of long-range surface-to-surface missiles to forge a foundation for a tactical strike force."[40]

Significant security reassurances from Washington in the late 1990s enabled Taiwan's government to counter strategic pressures for a missile-based deterrent. The 1995–96 Taiwan Strait crisis prompted the Clinton administration to send carrier battle groups to the Taiwan Strait. More important, it led to an intensive Pentagon study of Taiwan's defense needs, and Taiwan opened its military facilities to U.S. experts, who gained a better understanding of Taiwan's military requirements, allowing for deeper security cooperation between Washington and Taipei. In 2001, the Bush administration's $4 billion arms sale package (that included 8 submarines, 4 destroyers, and 12 Orion maritime patrol aircraft) further reassured Taiwan of Washington's strong defense commitment.

Thus, Taiwan's security concerns about countering Chinese missile activity, which are magnified (and sometimes exaggerated) by the turbulence of democratic politics, increase pressures for an indigenous ballistic missile program. A U.S. security guarantee, and Taiwan's security and economic dependence that gives Washington greater leverage, check Taiwan's nuclear and missile programs. Yet pressures for a missile-based deterrent increase during times of tension. Defense Minister (and former Air Force General) Tang Fei's December 1999 remarks, that "we want to research long-range surface-to-surface missiles," may accurately convey Taiwan's missile intentions and policies in the coming years.[41]

EGYPT

Egypt has made several missile development attempts since the late 1950s. Strategic considerations and prestige politics sustained Cairo's missile aspirations. MTCR embargoes and U.S. pressure curbed Egypt's medium-range missile ambitions, though Cairo continued its short-range missile programs and upgraded its Scuds during the 1990s.

Multiple Missile Projects

Egypt's first round of rocket activity took place in the late 1950s and 1960s. This caused (and was further stimulated by) a highly publicized launching of Israel's Shavit Shtayem sounding rocket in July 1961.[42] By 1962, Egypt had launched four single-stage sounding rockets. In addition, assisted by West German technicians, Cairo built the 370 km range Al Zafir and 600 km range Al Kahir missiles, each carrying 500–800 kg warheads. These programs failed, and Cairo then purchased Scuds from the Soviet Union.

Egypt's second round of missile development, in the 1980s, involved three projects—artillery rockets, the Condor program with Argentina and Iraq, and Scud activity. These projects were run by defense chief General Ghazhala. The Sakr 80 artillery rocket project began in 1983 in collaboration with the French firm SMPE. These rockets replaced, and could be fired from, Frog-7 launchers. Egypt joined the Condor program in 1984. This project was pursued at "Factory 17" outside Cairo, and the missile was called Badr-2000. It was halted in 1989.

Egypt also attempted to reverse engineer Scud-Bs with technology transfer from North Korea, German and Italian firms (involved with the Condor), a U.S.-based supplier, and the Arab-British Dynamics (ABD) firm. Egypt aimed to increase the Scud-B's range by 50 percent using an extended fuel tank. It sought 90 such Scuds by 1995. It received assistance from ABD at the Heliopolis factory (ABD had earlier worked on Scuds in the late 1970s when Egypt transferred these to North Korea, and Egyptian engineers received training in the United Kingdom in 1984).[43] However, because of this assistance, the British government influenced British Aerospace to withdraw from ABD by 1991. Cairo's missile efforts were further hindered by financial constraints and by the army's failure to release the Gebel Hamza test facility to ABD engineers. In late 1991, Cairo sought additional suppliers, and procured guidance units from Russia and other equipment from the former Soviet republics and Europe. In 1996–97, it received spare parts and technology from Russia, and North Korea delivered Scud components in March and April 1996.[44] By the late 1990s, the Center for Nonproliferation Studies estimated that Egypt had 100 Scud-Bs and 90 Project-T upgraded Scuds having a 450 km range with a 985 kg payload; Egypt was believed to be further developing Scud-Cs with North Korean assistance.[45]

Despite forty years of missile efforts, Cairo had essentially only upgraded its Scuds but had not built a more advanced missile although it received foreign technical assistance and had a modest defense industry. Egypt's defense industry builds jet engines, rockets, and other military equipment through the Arab Organization for Industrialization (AOI) and the National Organization for Defense Production (NODP).[46] One reason for Egypt's limited missile advancement was the MTCR's embargo. This embargo substantially halted foreign assistance that could have enabled Egypt to build the more advanced Condor missile. A second restraint on Egypt's missile programs was pressure from the United States.

The Demand for and U.S. Constraints on Egypt's Missiles

Egypt's missile demand arises from prestige politics and strategic considerations. On strategic security grounds, rivalry with Israel induced Egypt's early missile activity. Thus, President Nasser argued that Israel had tested the Shavit-2 rocket in July 1961, and that U.S. Hawk SAMs in Israel neutralized Cairo's bombers, and these developments influenced Cairo to "go to surface to surface missiles in order to have a deterrent capability against Israel."[47] Egypt's security-related demand for missiles against Israel was reduced when the two states normalized ties under the Camp David accords. However, prestige politics also influence Cairo's missile decision. The perception that it must have a formidable military machine to maintain leadership among Arab states partly drives Cairo's quest for modern weapons and missiles. For similar reasons, and stressing parity principles in Middle East politics, Cairo refuses to concede ground on weapons of mass destruction until the issue of Israel's WMD and missile program is addressed. Cairo has not signed the CWC and though it signed the NPT, it objected to the NPT's indefinite extension in 1995. As Foreign Minister Moussa noted: "giving Israel a waiver or an exemption from international nonproliferation norms will not make the Middle East, including Israel herself, safer or more secure. . . . the deep imbalance between her [Israel's] legal obligations and those of her neighbors in the field of arms control, in particular the NPT, prevent us from reaching a new framework for security."[48]

Egypt is also a missile technology exporter. It had transferred two Scuds to North Korea in 1976 or 1979–81. Further, in March 1999, three Egyptian firms—the Arab-British Dynamics, Helwan Machinery and Equipment Company, and the Kader Factory for Developed Industries—were sanctioned by the United States, presumably for their transactions with North Korea.[49] During a 1999 visit to Cairo, Defense Secretary William Cohen raised the issue of Egyptian-North Korean missile cooperation. U.S. leverage has been instrumental in checking Egypt's missile activities.[50]

Washington successfully halted one major Egyptian missile project in the late 1980s. In June 1988, two Egyptian embassy officials were arrested in the United States for conspiring with Abdel Kamel Helmy, an Egyptian-born rocket expert at the Jet Propulsion Laboratory in California. Helmy was charged with seeking to transfer rocket fuel chemicals, carbon phenol fabric that could be used for rocket nozzles and nose cones, and heat shields and other materials. Helmy's sentencing in 1989 embarrassed President Mubarak, and American pressure caused Mubarak to rein in the Condor project. General Ghazhala stepped down in 1989 and Egypt withdrew from the Condor project that year.[51]

Although it pressured Cairo on the Condor, Washington did not seek to curb Egypt's shorter range Scud-type missile activity. Four aspects of U.S. missile policy (which, in the 1990s, was more concerned with the international non-proliferation regime, in contrast to its concern with regional stability in the 1960s) explain this U.S. approach. First, in terms of the ranges of target missiles, Washington is more concerned with long-range missiles that gravely undermine the nonproliferation regime, and is less opposed to shorter range Scud-type missiles. Second, missile collaboration with states of concern (such as with Iraq in the Condor project) is a more serious threat. Third, missile programs are not seriously threatening when they are not directly linked with nuclear programs; although Egypt has not signed the CWC, it had signed the NPT. Fourth, Cairo has reverse leverage on Washington. It is a major U.S. partner in the Middle East, and Washington is also sensitive to Cairo's raising the issue of nuclear asymmetry in the region. These factors restrain Washington from pressing Cairo on Scud activity that is not of serious proliferation concern, especially because the (prestige-based) importance of the missile project for Egypt makes it prepared to confront the United States on the issue. For example, in 1991–92, a U.S. export control list removed Egypt (as well as Israel and other Middle Eastern States) from the listing of states or projects of concern. Moreover, during President Mubarak's March 2000 visit to Washington, the White House discussed Egypt's missile dealings with North Korea, but it also conceded some ground and Egypt was importing missile engines without much U.S. interference.[52]

Thus, Egypt's missile activity struck a balance in the 1990s. Egypt did not cross much beyond the Scud threshold, and Washington did not press Egypt to curb its short-range missile programs.

IRAQ

Iraq was the foremost Arab missile power in the 1980s. It purchased several hundred Soviet Scud-Bs, modified these into longer range Al-Husayn missiles, and collaborated with Egypt and Argentina in the Condor project. Iraq's missiles gave it a strategic capability against Iran and Israel and also enhanced its prestige among Arab states. The UNSCOM regime restricted Baghdad to 150 km range systems, but Iraq can make a substantial missile breakout in the coming years.

Iraq bought over 800 Scud-Bs through a 1973 contract with Moscow; missile deliveries continued through the early and mid-1980s. Iraq then modified the Scud-B by extending the fuel tank and decreasing the warhead weight to produce the 650 km range Al-Husayn missile. Initially, three Scud-Bs were cannibalized into two Al-Husayns, and eventually a 1:1 conversion was achieved by indigenously building the airframe and fuel tanks. The modification program took one and a half to two years and was complete by late 1987. Iraq benefited from foreign assistance, including technology from the Condor project and assistance from Brazilian and German firms that may have supplied turbopumps for rocket motors. Iraqi forces fired 160 Scuds on Iran between 1982 and 1987, and 190 Al-Husayns (135 on Tehran) in 1988. In the 1991 Gulf War, Iraq fired 38 missiles at Israel and 43 at Saudi Arabia and Bahrain. These missile campaigns demonstrated Iraq's multipurpose demand for unconventional weapons—ranging from tactical war-fighting and strategic deterrence against Iran, Israel, and the Allied Coalition, to maintaining prestige in the Arab world.

Ballistic missiles provided Iraq with a strategic deterrence against Israel. Saddam Hussein noted in June 1981, following Israel's strike on the Osirak nuclear reactor, that an Iraqi unconventional option would deter future Israeli attacks. Missiles also served a more immediate war-fighting purpose: missiles and chemical weapons helped Iraq to offset a larger Iranian military in the Iran-Iraq war. Thus, in 1986, after Iranian missile attacks on Baghdad, Iraq upgraded its Scuds into Al-Husayns that could reach Tehran (which was over 500 km from the border and beyond the range of the Scud-B). After the war with Iran, Saddam Hussein diverted resources back to the strategic or "Thunderstrike" option against Israel.[53] By the onset of the Gulf War, Iraq had built 28 missile launch sites in the western desert, and had 14 mobile launchers, 11 Scud-Bs, and 220 Al-Husayns. Some of these were strategic missiles to be armed with concrete warheads (for use against the Dimona reactor) or with chemical and biological warheads. During the Gulf War, Iraq first used the threat of striking Israel as a deterrent against Allied attacks, and then launched missiles on Israel in a political war-fighting mode seeking to disrupt the coalition. Missiles also had prestige value. Saddam Hussein had noted (in his June 1981 speech) that an unconventional deterrent would negate Israel's nuclear monopoly and technological edge against Arab states. Missiles thus became a prestige equalizer against Israel's military and technological superiority. Further, missile strikes on Israel enhanced Iraq's regional image by demonstrating that it was the primary Arab state with the capability and willingness to target Israel. The above reasoning suggests that in the long term, Iraq may continue to seek 600 km range missiles to balance Iran and Israel and to maintain prestige in the Arab world.

Iraq's missile activities were partly constrained by the MTCR, and further restricted by UN sanctions and the UNSCOM regime. Because Iraq relied on foreign assistance to extend the range of its Scuds, the MTCR should have substantially thwarted its missile activities. Yet on December 5, 1989, Iraq launched the first stage of a three-stage 48 ton Tammuz-1 satellite launcher that was built around five Al-Husayns. The Tammuz launch essentially failed, but it demonstrated that Iraq could build at least crude medium-range missiles despite the MTCR. In the 1990s, Iraq was constrained to 150 km range missiles under UN Security Council resolution 687 (which also covered Iraq's WMD programs). UNSCOM then destroyed some 60 Scuds and 45 chemical warheads, Iraq claimed to have unilaterally dismantled about 80 Scuds, and UNSCOM had accounted for 817 of Iraq's 819 Scud missiles by 1997, but this finding is disputed and Iraq may have hidden a dozen or more Scud and Al-Husayn missiles. In addition,

UN sanctions deprived Iraq of several billion dollars annually that could have been used for WMD activities (Iraq's GDP fell from $20 billion in 1989–90 to $7–10 billion in 1991–96, but revived to $20–24 billion in 1998–2000 after it resumed oil exports worth $4–10 billion annually).

In the 1990s, Iraq worked on the 150 km range liquid-fuel Al-Samoud, 50 km range liquid-fuel Ababil-50, and a 100 km range solid-fuel Ababil-100. These projects were pursued at the Ibn al Haytham center, and may have used upgraded SA-2 and scaled-down Scud engines. The projects give Baghdad a limited missile capability against Iran, and the staging of several Al-Samouds can produce a longer range missile. More important, Al-Samoud activity keeps Iraq's technicians and scientists actively working on missiles and allows for a future missile breakout. The Al-Samoud was tested in 1997 under the supervision of international inspectors. A U.S.-British December 1998 air strike on Iraq's missile production facilities then set back its missile program. Baghdad still conducted eight Al-Samoud tests between May 1999 and June 2000, though analysts reported that the program had technical problems: "They can't get the guidance to work right. They can't get the engines to work right. It's not close to going into production."[54] Iraq displayed four Al-Samouds and two Ababil-100s at the December 2000 Al Aqsa Cal parade.

Technological obstacles and international arms control constraints may hinder Iraq's missile program in the short term. The stabilization of regional security and normalization of ties with Iran, and the emergence of a new government that seeks greater political-economic integration with the West, may also moderate Iraq's demand for missiles and WMDs. However, if the international arms control regime falters (international inspectors had not visited Iraq since 1998), and if Iraq's demand for missiles remains high, then it has the capability of building medium- and long-range missiles.

SYRIA

When Iraq's WMD and missile programs were dismantled in the 1990s, Syria emerged with the most advanced Arab strategic capability. It obtained a few hundred Scuds and SS-21s, and while it is not known to have indigenously built missiles in the 1990s, it may subsequently have done so.

Syria sought missiles against Israel for both political and military reasons. Syrian policy makers had noted the widespread use of missiles in the Iran-Iraq war. They considered missiles to be cheaper, and possibly more reliable, than combat aircraft that had to be paid for in hard currency (especially after the collapse of the Soviet Union) and whose supply of spare parts was not assured. Missiles also enabled Syria to strike Israel's strategic rear and compensated for the weakness of its air force that was routed in 1982 over Lebanon. In the early

1990s, Foreign Minister Farouk al-Shara noted that Syria was "still in a state of war with Israel" and hence justified missile acquisitions to counter Israel's "many missiles" and "mass destruction weapons."[55] By the late 1990s, to counter Israel's superior conventional forces, Syria had integrated its strategic option (missiles and chemical weapons) into its war-fighting doctrine.

Syria obtained its modest-sized missile inventory from foreign suppliers. It purchased Scud-Bs from Moscow in 1974, ss-21s from Moscow in 1983, Scud-Cs from North Korea in 1991, and longer range North Korean Scud-Ds in 1999, and had acquired an estimated 300 or more missiles by 2000. However, Syria's attempts to buy longer range missiles and to manufacture its own missiles were not successful in the 1980s and 1990s. After the 1982 Lebanon conflict, Damascus planned to reverse engineer Scud-Bs and ss-21s when Moscow denied it the ss-23. Syria gave up these efforts due to technical difficulties. Syria then sought some eighty m-9 missiles from China under a May 1989 agreement, but Washington persuaded Beijing to halt this transaction. Thereafter, in late 1989 and early 1990, Syria turned to Pyongyang for Scud-Cs. It received these missiles from 1991 onward, tested them in July 1992, mid-1994, and mid-1996, and received Scud-Ds in 1999.

Syria's indigenous missile efforts progressed more slowly. Chinese and North Korean firms reportedly have assisted two Syrian missile facilities since 1990, and Syrian engineers received technical training in China. In June 1996, the China Precision Machinery Company shipped missile-related components to Syria's Scientific Studies and Research Center, which could assemble Scud-Cs from knock-down kits imported from North Korea.[56] In 1999, U.S. government reports noted that Damascus continued solid propellant motor development with Iranian help; it received foreign assistance for its liquid-propellant missile program, primarily from Russian entities, but also from firms in China and North Korea; and it persisted in efforts to assemble, probably with North Korean assistance, the Scud-C.[57] In 2002, Washington's National Intelligence Council (NIC) noted that "with considerable foreign assistance, Syria progressed to Scud production using primarily locally manufactured parts."[58] Though limited in range, these Scud missiles can still strike strategic targets in Israel from deep within Syria.

LIBYA

Libya's missile programs were probably influenced by Muammar Qadaffi's ambitions to boost Libya's regional status. They may also be intended to counter potential threats from Libya's neighbors and rivals Egypt and Algeria. Libya had several dozen Soviet-supplied Scuds and was also seeking North Korean Scuds, but it could not build its own missiles despite repeated attempts to do so.

Libya has made several missile purchase and missile development attempts since the 1970s, when it bought Scud-Bs from Moscow. Yet it had no pressing security missions for these missiles and transferred some to Iran in 1985. Libya's 1979–80 missile project with the German company Ortrag culminated in a failed March 1980 rocket launch.[59] Ortrag was then pressured to leave Libya, and although some of its engineers may have remained behind to assist Libyan missile activity, this activity was unsuccessful. Moreover, Libya was unable to purchase guidance systems through West European firms in the late 1980s.[60] Libyan attempts to acquire Brazilian missiles faltered in 1988. At that time, Libya probably sought missiles as a deterrent after the 1986 U.S. air strike on Libya.

Libya continued its missile efforts in the 1990s despite its economic weakness, which was exacerbated by UN sanctions from 1992 to 1999 (sanctions cost Libya some $24 billion in the four-year period 1993–96). Several news reports, if accurate, indicate Libya's persistent interest in ballistic missiles. In July 1991 and the spring of 1992, German and Dutch authorities seized furnaces bound for Libya.[61] In June 1993, Libya tried to obtain solid-fuel chemicals from Russia via Ukraine. In 1994, Washington protested to Cairo about Egyptian rocket specialists at Libya's Tarhuna missile center.[62] In 1997, Italian police confiscated a lathe (used to shape large metal cylinders) en route to Libya.[63] That year, Tehran may have agreed to assist Libya's missile efforts.[64] From March 1999, the China Precision Machinery Import-Export Company was reportedly helping Libya's Al-Fatah missile, and Chinese technicians were linked to this program from at least June 1998; it was also believed that China was training Libyan personnel to operate missiles, and providing Libya with a hypersonic wind tunnel.[65] In 2000, Libyan-bound machine parts were intercepted at Gatwick airport, and Serbian and Indian firms may have supplied dual-use technology to Libya.[66]

The above reports indicate Libya's strong interest in missiles to complement its obsolete Soviet-era Scuds and its aging air force. Yet Libya had not tested an indigenously produced missile by 2001; neither was it definitely known to have purchased missiles from suppliers such as Iran or North Korea.[67] Given money and ambition, Libya could eventually purchase or build a modest missile force, but it would require a missile more powerful than the Scud to strike Israel or NATO bases in Italy. Alternatively, noting the increased foreign investment it received after the lifting of UN sanctions, Libya may be willing to restrain its WMD and missile programs in exchange for continued and deeper political-economic integration with the world community.

LOOKING AHEAD

Iraq, Libya, and Syria did not substantially advance their indigenous missile programs during the 1990s. Yet they had not given up their missile ambitions. If their security and prestige related demand for missiles persists, then, with foreign technology and continuous indigenous efforts, they may buy or build modest quantities of Scud, Al-Husayn, and Nodong type missiles in the near term. Such missiles could target their primary regional adversaries. International observers remained divided about their ability to build longer range missiles. In February 2000, an International Institute for Strategic Studies official noted that Iraq and Libya "do not currently possess the means to manufacture modern rocketry capable of penetrating the conventional defenses of Britain or any other European nation."[68] Yet Germany's foreign intelligence agency (BND) noted that Iraq could have 3,000 km range missiles capable of hitting Western Europe within five years,[69] and Washington's NIC report of 2002 noted that if Iraq acquired Taepodong-2 engines, it could test an ICBM in five years, indicating that the threat from longer range Middle Eastern missiles remained real.

6

Israel, India, Pakistan: Medium-Range Missiles of Regional Nuclear Powers

On July 18, 1980, two thousand scientists and observers watched India's 17 ton SLV-3 rocket lift off from the Sriharikota complex on the Bay of Bengal. At an altitude of 300 km, it placed a 35 kg satellite in orbit. Prime Minister Indira Gandhi informed Parliament: "This is a notable achievement of India and Indian science. . . . The nation is proud of [Indian scientists] and wishes them further success."[1] But the Pakistan newspaper *Dawn* expressed concern that "the technological triumph should not be allowed to obscure the political and military aspects of the launching. The main impulse for the development of rocketry has been the urge to acquire a delivery system for deadly weapons of destruction."[2] Islamabad's suspicions were confirmed nine years later, when, on May 22, 1989, India's 14 ton Agni missile was fired from the Chandipur interim test range. The *Times of India* described the launch as "the biggest step forward in India's quest for a credible deterrent capability."[3] Prime Minister Rajiv Gandhi declared it "a major achievement in our continuing effort to safeguard the country's independence and security by self-reliant means."[4]

Islamabad gradually caught up with Delhi in the missile field. On February 5, 1989, Army Chief General Mirza Aslam Beg announced that Pakistan had attained a "landmark in indigenous arms production" by testing two missiles with ranges of 80 km and 300 km.[5] Beg added that "this indigenization is part of the process of building a strong deterrent capability so that the country was not made a victim of aggression."[6] Nine years later, on April 6, 1998, working from prefabricated sheds in stormy weather, Dr. A. Q. Khan's missile team flight-tested the intermediate-range Ghauri; the missile flew from Malute, near Jhelum in northeastern Pakistan, to an impact point near the southwestern city of Quetta.[7] Foreign Minister Gohar Ayub Khan emphatically declared that "in the missile race we have overtaken [India]"; he added that the Ghauri had "shattered the myth of India's strategic depth."[8]

One more stunning act would soon follow. On May 11 and 13, in a dramatic nuclear breakout that shook the world, Delhi conducted five nuclear tests; Prime Minister Atal Behari Vajpayee announced, "India is now a nuclear weapons state."[9] The *Times of India* ecstatically approved, carrying the headline: "India Joins Nuclear Club."[10] By the end of the month, Islamabad retaliated with six nuclear tests, and Prime Minister Nawaz Sharif asserted: "We have settled the score with India."[11]

South Asia's nuclear explosions resonated in the Middle East. Commentators raised concerns that "the Islamic bomb has become a reality."[12] Even if Pakistan's nuclear and missile technology is not transferred to other states, Israeli analysts were still "troubled by the prospect that the [South Asian nuclear] tests would encourage Iraq and Iran to acquire nuclear weapons."[13] Israel had already established a robust missile-based deterrent. In 1962–63, responding to Egyptian rocket activity, the Ben Gurion and Eshkol governments initiated a missile contract with France's Dassault corporation. By July 1968, sixteen tests of the 450 km range Jericho-1 were completed, and Israel Aircraft Industries (IAI) went on to develop the 1,400 km range Jericho-2 and the even longer range Shavit space launch vehicle.

Israel, India, and Pakistan built intermediate-range missiles to serve as nuclear delivery systems. The MTCR's technology barriers slowed and raised the costs of missile construction, especially for New Delhi and Islamabad. However, their governments pressed ahead with intermediate-range missiles. Prestige and bureaucratic politics influenced their missile policies, but these states also faced or perceived strong and long-term security threats. This high security-related demand caused their policy makers to withstand international pressures and seek missile-based nuclear deterrents.

ISRAEL

Security concerns prompted Israel to build a strategic missile force of 450 km range Jericho-1 and 1,400 km range Jericho-2 missiles beginning in the 1960s. U.S. pressure halted Israel's missile-related exports in 1991, but Washington did not press Israel on its strategic missile program.

The Evolution of a Medium-Range Missile

Since the 1960s, Israel has built artillery rockets, air-to-air missiles, ship-to-ship missiles, sounding rockets, and medium-range strategic missiles. Its missile activity takes place in three defense industries—the Armaments Development Authority (Rafael), Israel Aircraft Industries (IAI), and Israel Military Industries (IMO, or Ta'as).

Israel's strategic ballistic missile program was initiated after Egypt's 1962 display of a Frog-series artillery rocket greatly increased Israel's security concerns. The Ben Gurion government then solicited a missile feasibility study from France's Marcel Dassault in early September. Israeli scientists had argued for indigenous development and self-reliance, but the Eshkol government signed a missile agreement with Dassault in Tel Aviv on April 26, 1963.[14] This 7 ton 450 km range solid-fuel Marcel Dassault MD-620/660 missile was renamed the Jericho-1. Its first stage was tested on February 1, 1965; the complete missile with two stages was tested unsuccessfully on December 23, 1965, and successfully on March 16, 1966. By July 30, 1968, sixteen tests had been completed: ten were successful, three were partly successful, and three failed.[15] France transferred a few missiles to Israel but imposed an arms embargo during the 1967 war. Israel's defense industries then developed the missile without French assistance. In 1971, the New York Times reported that Israel was producing three to six Jericho missiles each month.[16] The Jericho was deployed in October 1973 after Israel discovered what it thought to be Soviet-manned Scud missiles in Egypt or Syria.[17]

Israel subsequently moved beyond the Jericho-1. In 1974 it requested but was denied the Pershing-1 from the United States. In 1977, then Defense Minister Weizman referred to a Jericho-1 successor as being possible but not "serious."[18] It was nearly a decade before the two-stage 1,400 km range Jericho-2 was flight-tested. Reports of the missile began appearing in 1985 and Israel conducted seven missile tests between 1986 and 1992, to ranges varying from 465 km (the 1986 test) to 1,300 km (the fourth test in 1989).[19]

The Jericho-2 forms the basis for the 20–30 ton Shavit rockets that launched satellites in 1988, 1990, 1995, 1998 (unsuccessfully), and 2002. The Shavit used 9 ton solid-fuel boosters (produced by Ta'as) for its first and second stages and had a smaller third stage (produced by Rafael); the Shavit-1 (launched in 1995 and 1998) had a stretched 13 ton first stage. The Leolink-1, intended for commercial launches from American sites, is a U.S.-built version of the Shavit with 13 ton first and second stages; a Leolink-2 has a larger first stage. The ranges of these satellite launchers are estimated to be between 2,400 km and 4,500 km.

The MTCR was not specifically intended to halt, and has had little impact on, Israel's missile development. By the time of the MTCR's advent, Israel's missile program was already in the advanced stage of flight-testing the Jericho-2. The regime has mainly curbed Israel's missile technology exports.

Security Motivations and U.S. Influence

Israel's rocket activities in the 1960s were a direct response to similar developments in Egypt. Israel's initial nuclear activities were not specifically intended to counter a neighbor's nuclear acquisition (there were no nuclear programs in the neighborhood, though Cairo had tried to expand its nuclear program in the early 1960s and had used chemical agents in the Yemen civil war). Instead, they were a deterrent against an existential threat created by conventional military asymmetries versus neighboring states and the lack of strategic depth; they also provided a "doomsday" option. As Prime Minister Ben Gurion noted in 1963, "If Nasser should break Israel's air force the war [against Israel] would be over in two days."[20]

Although the possibility of conventional war with neighboring states has receded since the 1970s, subsequent Israeli governments retained nuclear and missile forces as a deterrent against an unconventional threat, not just from nearby states but also from distant states. The gradual introduction of unconventional arms in the Middle East, the erosion of norms against their use in the Iran-Iraq war, and Iraq's missile attacks on Israeli cities in 1991, heightened Israel's security concerns. In the late 1990s, the missile and WMD programs of distant Iran and Iraq were seen as Israel's primary security threat.[21] Beyond their deterrent function, Israel's ballistic missiles can strike far-off targets without overflying Egypt or Jordan, and are therefore a useful military option because Israel cannot easily violate its neighbors' airspace without facing diplomatic repercussions.

The United States has strong security and economic ties with Israel, and has used these to halt Israel's missile-related *exports* but not its missile and nuclear programs.[22] On the nuclear issue, despite its potentially strong aid-based leverage over Israel, "Washington was not prepared to force an open breach over the nuclear issue; doing so could have cost the United States a valued strategic partner while probably aggravating the insecurities that drove Israel's nuclear program. . . . In these circumstances, the United States settled for the best it could get—an undeclared Israeli nuclear capability with a tacit understanding barring overt testing or deployment."[23] For similar reasons, Washington accepted Israel's missile program as a fait accompli. It also financed research and development of Israel's Arrow antimissile system. Moreover, Washington has not criticized Israel's space activity that is derived from its missile program. Thus the State Department did not condemn Israel's April 1990 Ofeq-2 satellite launch, but instead noted that Israel had declared that its satellite program was for peaceful purposes, and that "we [the United States] applaud and welcome the scientific and technological advancement which may result from this program."[24]

Washington has, however, used its leverage to halt Israel's missile-related transfers and make it comply with the MTCR. In the 1970s and 1980s, Israel transferred cruise missile and air-to-air missile technology to Iran, Taiwan, and China and ballistic missile technology to South Africa.[25] Israel was reluctant to participate in the MTCR, arguing that defense exports were a major revenue source, that other states such as China and Russia were not part of the MTCR, and that the MTCR was not preventing missile sales to Israel's neighbors. The Shamir government initially sought to adopt MTCR guidelines only from December 1992 after completing ongoing transactions such as upgrading guidance systems for Chinese missiles. Yet Washington insisted that Israel implement MTCR guidelines from December 1991. This was necessary for Washington to waive sanctions on Israel for missile-related transfers to South Africa (U.S. sanctions on South Africa were announced on September 27, 1991).[26] On October 3, 1991, Defense Minister Arens declared that Israel was adopting MTCR principles. Israel thus curbed missile technology transfers and adhered to the MTCR a year earlier than it desired due to U.S. pressure. In subsequent years, Israel largely adhered with its missile export restraints. It also signed the Comprehensive Test Ban Treaty (CTBT). However, in the late 1990s, anticipating WMD and missile threats from Iran and Iraq, Israel may have expanded its nuclear deterrent. In 1999–2000, it obtained three German-supplied submarines that could be equipped with cruise missiles to form the third leg of a nuclear triad.

INDIA

India built the SLV-3, ASLV, PSLV, and GSLV space launchers, and the 150–250 km range Prithvi and 1,000–2,000 km range Agni-1 and Agni-2 ballistic missiles (that were derived from the SLV-3), in the 1980s and 1990s. Strategic considerations as well as domestic pressures and prestige politics sustained Delhi's missile programs; MTCR embargoes, international political pressures, and the democratization of the India-Pakistan dyad in the 1990s did not cause Delhi to halt its nuclear and missile programs.

Space Launchers and Ballistic Missiles

India's missile and rocket activities can be differentiated into three historical and bureaucratic components—basic rocket research in the 1960s through several short-term ad hoc projects such as surface-to-air missile systems and sounding rockets, a more mature space program that gained momentum in the 1970s, and a ballistic missile program that began in the 1980s and absorbed technology from the first and second components (India's early rocket research and its space program). The basic rocket research in the 1960s involved three projects: an India-Swiss agreement ("Project Indigo") to develop surface-to-air missiles that was scrapped when Delhi opted for Soviet SA-2 missiles in 1962; a project of the Indian Space Research Organization (ISRO) involving sounding rocket activity (these rockets have not been used as ballistic missiles); and a project in 1963 dealing with experiments on rocket propellants at the Defense Research and Development Organization (DRDO) laboratory. In the 1970s, DRDO attempted to convert the SA-2 into a surface-to-surface missile under the "Devil" program. DRDO built two liquid-propulsion motors by 1974, but the project was canceled in 1978 after prototype failures.

While India's initial rocket projects stagnated in the 1970s, its space program gained momentum. ISRO's first chairman, Vikram Sarabhai, outlined a development plan in 1970, stating that "in a ten year time frame, one must acquire the capability not only of building telecommunication satellites such as INSAT-I but also of launching them into synchronous orbit. . . . [T]o begin with, we have set as a goal the development of a satellite launcher of the Scout type . . . [and] once the basic systems have been developed for this, and experience acquired in operating them, it is estimated that a five year period from 1975 to 1980 should be adequate for the second stage of development of larger boosters."[27] The Indian space program eventually lagged one to two decades behind Sarabhai's originally intended schedule.

ISRO built a four-stage 17 ton SLV-3 (centered around a 9 ton solid-fuel first stage) from the design of the U.S. Scout rocket. ISRO scientists ground-tested the stage engines in 1974–75, and flight-tested the complete vehicle in 1979 (this test failed), 1980, 1981, and 1983. ISRO's 41 ton ASLV (which used three of the SLV-3's 9 ton boosters) was flight tested four times between 1987 and 1994.

The second phase of India's space program involved two more advanced satellite launchers with specific missions. The PSLV is powered by two indigenously developed systems—a 130 ton solid-fuel booster and a 37 ton liquid-fuel engine named Vikas that is similar to the European Space Agency's Viking engine. The PSLV can launch a 1,000 kilogram payload—the Indian remote sensing (IRS) satellites—to an 800–900 kilometer altitude polar orbit. The same 37 ton and 130 ton engines are used on the geostationary satellite launch vehicle (GSLV), and supplemented with a Russian-supplied 12 ton cryogenic engine. These enable the GSLV to carry a heavier 2,500 kilogram payload (an INSAT-2 class communications satellite) to a higher 36,000 km GEO. The PSLV was launched six times between 1993 and 2001, and the GSLV first flew in 2001.

In addition to its space program, India embarked upon an organizationally distinct ballistic missile program in the 1980s. In 1982, a panel of scientists and armed force experts studied missile systems.[28] In 1983, DRDO began an Integrated Guided Missile Development Project (IGMDP) aimed at building five missiles— an antitank missile, two surface-to-air missiles, the 150–250 km range Prithvi missile, and the 1,000–2,000 km range Agni missile. By 1991, this missile program involved thirty-four institutions and R&D organizations, twenty-two public sector undertakings, ten ordnance factories, and nine private industries.[29] The

IGMDP was initially allocated a budget of Rs. 380 crore ($130 million) for its first decade and by 1994 had received over Rs. 780 crore ($275 million); it was allocated $55–70 million between 1992–97 and $125 million for 1997–2002.[30]

The Prithvi is a single-stage missile with two 3 ton thrust liquid-fuel engines (that are derived from the Devil project). Fourteen tests of the SS-150 (the 150 km range version of the missile) took place from February 1988 to June 1994. The SS-250 (the 250 km range version) was tested in January 1996, February 1997, June 2000, and March and December 2001. A naval Prithvi, the 8.56 m long 4 ton Dhanush missile with a 500 kg payload, was first fired (unsuccessfully) on April 11, 2000. The missile was again tested, apparently successfully, in September 2001.

India's 1,000–1,500 km range Agni-1 and 2,000 km range Agni-2 missiles are derived from the SLV-3. The Agni missiles and SLV-3 both use a 9 ton solid-fuel engine for their first stage. The Agni-1's second stage is a Prithvi-derived liquid-fuel system, while the Agni-2's second stage is a solid-fuel system built by ISRO. The Agni-1 was flight-tested in May 1989, May 1992, and February 1994, to a maximum range of 1,400 km; the missile weighed 19 tons in the 1994 test, which was 5 tons heavier than in the 1989 test because of additional fuel.[31] The Agni-2 first flew on April 11, 1999, when it reportedly covered 2,000 km in an eleven-minute flight from Wheeler Island. It was entirely solid-fuel, could be fired from a rail-based launcher, and had a superior navigation and guidance system. The missile was tested again in January 2001 "in its final operational configuration" from the Chandipur test range. Some analysts note that the Agni-2's further development could take a few years, because Indian scientists would prefer to conduct six to eight Agni-2 tests over five years to perfect its accuracy.[32] New Delhi also built a road-mobile, 12 ton, single-stage, 700 km range Agni (that was named Agni-1). It decided to build this missile in the backdrop of the 1999 Kargil crisis, and the missile was tested on January 25, 2002.

The Agni-1 and Agni-2 can barely reach China's main cities, Beijing and Shanghai, which are 2,500 km from Northeast India, 3,500 km from East India, and about 5,000 km from Central India's more secure launch locations. DRDO therefore plans to build a 3,000–5,000 km range Agni-3. It was considering adding a third stage to the Agni-1 and Agni-2 missiles or using components from ISRO's PSLV for such a new longer range missile.[33]

The MTCR's impact on Indian space and missile activities has been moderate. India benefited from foreign technology transfers in the 1960s and 1970s. For example, in the early 1970s, Germany's space agency transferred propulsion and guidance technologies, flight controls, material science, and wind tunnels to ISRO, and the SLV-3 was based on the design of the U.S. Scout.[34] MTCR technology embargoes delayed and increased the costs of India's space and rocket projects, but did not actually halt any project. From the mid-1970s, following India's 1974 nuclear test and the resulting supplier controls on the Indian nuclear program, ISRO expected technology embargoes, and short-listed one hundred technologies and products for indigenous development.[35]

When the IGMDP began in 1983, Indian scientists again anticipated forthcoming technology embargoes, and identified five critical components for indigenous development.[36] These were phase shifters for radar, impact diodes serving as high-frequency power sources, carbon composites for reentry vehicle heat shielding, sensors for guidance systems, and computerized fluid dynamic models. Moreover, Indian industry built many space and missile technologies after importing them was denied—these included shell catalysts for rocket fuel, magnesium plates for the Prithvi, radiation-hardened integrated circuits for satellites, and maraging steel for rocket motor casings.[37] This construction typically took five years and resulted in an approximately 10 percent increase in expenditures. India's 1996 Ministry of Defense annual report stated that the MTCR had delayed the Indian missile program. Following a September 1997 PSLV launch, India's prime minister publicly called for the removal of technology embargoes, an indication that these had affected India's space program. Yet Delhi's missile and space programs were in an advancing stage by the time of the MTCR; the regime only slowed, but could not halt, these programs.

Security Considerations, Prestige, and Domestic Politics

New Delhi sought a nuclear deterrent to counter a nuclear-armed China. Its nuclear program also counters and provokes a response in Pakistan's nuclear program. Yet the timing of advances and restraints in Delhi's nuclear and missile programs has not always corresponded to an increase or decrease in regional tensions, and instead has been influenced by bureaucratic, technological, and domestic political considerations.

India could not put aside nuclear weapons possibilities after its army was routed by China in 1962 and when Beijing tested a nuclear device in 1964. Delhi therefore remained out of the NPT in 1968, tested its first nuclear device in 1974, embarked on a more active nuclear program in 1988, and crossed the nuclear threshold through a series of nuclear tests in May 1998.[38] By 2000, it was estimated to have enough plutonium for 50 to 100 nuclear weapons.

India's ballistic missile program officially began in 1983 (although Delhi had a prior space program), several years after its nuclear program. The Agni IRBM was initially billed as a technology demonstrator in the early 1990s, when Delhi had not formally crossed the nuclear threshold. The Agni project was suspended by centrist Indian governments in 1996—when Delhi had begun normalizing ties with Beijing and the two states signed CBM agreements in 1993 and 1996. Citing an October 1996 Indian defense ministry report (that was written in August 1996), an Indian parliamentary committee stated in December 1996 that since all the objectives of the Agni technology demonstration project had been met, the project was being terminated. The committee added that the decision to produce a missile from Agni technology could be taken at an appropriate time consistent with the prevailing threat perception. The Agni was revived by India's BJP government after its May 1998 nuclear tests. Unlike its predecessors, this government perceived a strong security threat from Beijing.[39]

The democratic process has not significantly checked, but instead has unleashed pressures (through a vibrant press) against government restraint in, missile and nuclear activity. For example, Prime Minister Rao's government had restrained missile activity following the thirteenth Prithvi test in June 1994 (immediately after Rao's return from Washington); Prithvi tests were then halted until January 27, 1996, partly for technical reasons. Yet domestic lobbies argued that the Prithvi freeze was the result of U.S. pressure.[40] In another step toward moderation, on December 5, 1996, New Delhi suspended the Agni program. This decision was opposed by an All-Parliamentary Standing Committee on Defense, which, in April 1997, urged the Indian government to take the Agni program to its "logical conclusion"; the Indian press also routinely called for the government to reverse its decision.[41]

The goals and motivations of India's space activities have varied with time and political circumstances. In the 1960s, India's space program was intended to further a broad national policy of planned socioeconomic development through educational television, satellite communications, meteorology, and natural resource survey applications. India's leaders also recognized the military spinoffs from the space program, which was upgraded in 1972 following Delhi's perceptions of a Pakistan-China-U.S. convergence in the 1971 India-Pakistan war. Thus, soon after India's May 1974 nuclear test, ISRO's director Satish Dhawan stated in July 1974 before a parliamentary committee that India could produce medium-range missiles with locally developed solid fuels and guidance systems;[42] Dhawan was referring to the SLV-3, which was still some five years from its first flight. While the SLV-3 generated military spinoffs in the Agni missile (in part because it was light enough to be used as a mobile missile), India's more powerful launch vehicles, the PSLV and GSLV, are probably too heavy to have direct missile spinoffs. Instead, with India's economic liberalization in the 1990s, ISRO sought commercial opportunities for the PSLV. India's economic advancement and its consequent increased communications demand suggests that the GSLV may play an important role in the communications sector. Further, from a strategic perspective, the PSLV would be a useful launcher for reconnaissance satellites such as the Technology Experiment/Test Evaluation Satellite launched in October 2001.

PAKISTAN

Security threats from India sustained Islamabad's nuclear and missile programs that gained momentum in the 1980s and 1990s. MTCR embargoes, international pressures, and democratization in the 1990s did not halt Pakistan's missile activity. By the late 1990s, Pakistan had built several types of short- and medium-range missiles, such as the 100 km range Hatf-1, approximately 180 km range Hatf-2, 300 km range Hatf-3, 600–800 km range Hatf-4, and 1,000–1,500 km range Hatf-5.

Multiple Missile Programs

Pakistan's early rocket activity took place at its Space and Upper Atmospheric Research Commission (SUPARCO), which was formed in 1961–62. SUPARCO facilities include its headquarters and research center in Karachi; a satellite ground station near Islamabad; space applications and research centers at Lahore and Peshawar; a sounding rocket manufacturing plant (set up in 1968) in Karachi; and the Sonmiani Beach flight-test range 50 km west of Karachi. From the 1960s to mid-1980s, Pakistan launched over two hundred domestic and foreign (U.S. Nike-Cajun and French Sud-Aviation and CNEA) sounding rockets and pursued remote sensing space activity, but is not known to have built ballistic missiles.

On March 5, 1989—a year after Delhi's Prithvi test—Islamabad announced that it had tested the 80 km range Hatf-1 and 300 km range Hatf-2 missiles.[43] These are believed to be derived from Dauphin and Eridan sounding rockets. They initially had a large circular error probability, and may have originally been training aids rather than effective weapon systems. But Islamabad subsequently modified these systems and improved their accuracy and payload capacity; it launched an upgraded combat-capable Hatf-1 on February 7, 2000, to a range of 100 km. It also launched a 180 km range Abdali missile (which it called Hatf-2) in May 2002. This missile may be a modified version of the original Hatf-2, or may be a new missile that replaced the earlier Hatf-2. Describing Pakistan's early missile activity, General Mirza Beg, Pakistan's chief of army staff until 1991, noted that for the period until 1991:

> Efforts to improve Hatf-1 continued and Hatf-2, with a range of 250 km and a payload of 500 kg, was produced in 1989. This was a free-flight rocket, with an inertial guidance system. . . . Hatf-3 was a major breakthrough, which had a 600 km range and a payload of 500 kg, and a proper terminal guidance system, with an

accuracy of 0.1 percent, as the circular error probability, at 600 km. The main features of this missile were that it was a two-stage rocket with a warhead separation, a terminal guidance system, and five different varieties of warheads. The most difficult part of the missile was its guidance system which was developed with the help of Pakistani engineers and scientists working in Pakistan and abroad.[44]

To supplement the Hatf-1 and Hatf-2, Islamabad received an estimated thirty-four of the 250–300 km range M-11 missiles from China in 1991–92. Beijing initially shipped a training M-11 and launcher to Pakistan in 1990 or 1991 (as a result of which U.S. sanctions were imposed on Beijing and Islamabad in June 1991). Beijing subsequently transferred about thirty-four M-11s that were unloaded at Karachi in November 1992 (and resulted in renewed U.S. sanctions in August 1993).[45] These missiles were reportedly stored at the Sargodha air base and defense complex. Other sources of foreign assistance to Pakistan were German firms that transferred missile testing equipment (in 1989) and furnace equipment (in the mid-1980s). In 1992, a British scholar had seen reports of a "Hatf-3 Technical Training manual."[46] This reference to the Hatf-3 ties in with the M-11. In May 2002, Pakistan announced the first test of an indigenously built 290 km range Ghaznavi missile, which it also called Hatf-3. This missile's range is similar to that of the M-11, and the missile may have been an M-11 that was manufactured in Pakistan.

Islamabad's indigenous missile activity slowed between 1989 and 1997, as no missile tests were reported in this period. However, Pakistan was undertaking two key longer range missile programs—the 600–800 km range Shaheen (Hatf-4) and the 1,000 km range Ghauri (Hatf-5). In July 1997 (after domestic pressure for a response to June 1997 press reports of India's Prithvi deployment), Islamabad announced the test of an 800 km range Hatf missile. It remains unclear whether any test took place, and if so, whether it was a ground test or a flight test, and whether it was a ballistic missile or a SUPARCO rocket.[47] On June 4, 1997, addressing the Naval War College, Pakistan's army chief stated that in the absence of reassurances Pakistan would have no option but to go ahead with the development of its indigenous capability.[48]

Pakistan first tested the Ghauri-1 missile on April 6, 1998, and then tested an upgraded Ghauri-2 on April 14, 1999, and May 25, 2002. The missile was reported to cover 700 km in its first test and 1,100 km in the second.[49] The liquid-fuel single-stage Ghauri resembles the Nodong. It was developed at the Khan Research Laboratories (KRL) at Kahuta, headed by Dr. A. Q. Khan, who also supervised the Kahuta nuclear complex for uranium enrichment. The Ghauri program was initiated in the early to middle 1990s. Prime Minister Sharif stated, "I can say with full authority this program is indigenous since I am engaged with it since 1991,"[50] in the years after India's 1989 Agni test. Benazir Bhutto declared that the Ghauri missile program was furthered by her government (that held office in 1993–96). Bhutto noted, "Several army chiefs and other key figures know my contribution to [the] missile program," adding that the missile "was to be tested on August 14, 1997 as a gift to the nation on the eve of [the] 50th anniversary of the country's independence."[51] Pakistani officials visited North Korea in 1992.[52] Jane's Defence Weekly notes that Prime Minister Bhutto visited North Korea in December 1993, a North Korean foreign ministry delegation traveled to Iran and Pakistan in April 1994, another North Korean delegation traveled to Pakistan in September 1994, and a North Korean military delegation toured Pakistan's missile production sites in late November 1995.[53] It adds that this delegation may have finalized an agreement to supply major components including Nodong fuel tanks and rocket engines. These items were produced by North Korea's Fourth Machine Industry Bureau and delivered to Pakistan's Khan Research Laboratories early in 1996 by the Changgwang Sinyong Corporation (also known as the North Korean Mining Development Trading Corporation); these organizations were sanctioned by Washington on April 24, 1998.

As noted above, a Ghauri test may have been initially scheduled for August 1997, but this did not take place; in January 1998, press reports noted that the Ghauri would be displayed or tested on March 23, but this also did not occur.[54] Other reports noted that "Washington had indirectly been hinting at [sanctions] since early February when it was first conveyed Pakistan's likely testing of the Ghauri missile."[55] Still other reports noted that Washington had urged a delay in the Ghauri test, but "had the latest test-firing been put back by six months as desired by [the] U.S. government . . . Pakistan would have come under tremendous pressure. This point would have been top of the agenda during the visits of the U.S. Army Chief and President Clinton. It would have been too difficult for Pakistan not to oblige."[56]

The design of the Ghauri deserves some clarification. David Wright notes that the Ghauri is structurally an 85 percent reduced version of the Nodong. Given a fuel mass of 13 tons and a total weight of 16 tons, it would have a 1,100 km range with a 700 kg payload or a 1,500 km range with a 200 kg payload.[57] A. Q. Khan subsequently provided more details on the Ghauri program, noting the interaction between the civilian and military leadership and the defense-science enclave: "Prime Minister Nawaz Sharif, Army Chief General Jehangir Karamat and the team of nuclear scientists deserve high accolade for the development of Ghauri."[58] The army chief called attention to the Ghauri being part of a larger national security research program, stating that "achievements like missile development were the result of years of dedicated teamwork and the missile test was a necessary step in the overall research and development effort."[59]

The Ghauri may form the basis for a two-stage missile, with a range of 2,000 km. Analysts note that the addition of a Hatf-1 stage to the Ghauri-1/2 would produce a missile with a 1,500–2,000 km range (with a 700 kg or 200 kg payload, respectively), similar to the Taepodong-1.

Pakistan also built solid-fuel Shaheen missiles through its National Defense Complex (NDC). These are the 600–800 km range Shaheen-1 (that resembles the Chinese M-9) and 1,500–2,500 km range Shaheen-2. One report notes that the NDC was established in 1993 and the Shaheen program was initiated in 1995; components for the missile were developed at SUPARCO facilities and at existing industries in Pakistan, and were brought to the NDC for quality control checks and then integrated with the Shaheen missile.[60] On August 25, 1996, the *Washington Post* reported that Pakistan was "building a medium-range missile factory using blueprints and equipment supplied by China," and this "partially completed factory, said by U.S. officials to be located in a suburb of the northern city of Rawalpindi, near Islamabad, is expected to be capable in a year or two of producing most of the major components of a missile modeled after the Chinese-designed M-11. Some officials believe the factory will produce precise duplicates of the missile."[61] This factory at Tarnawa was reportedly similar to an M-11 facility in central China, and engineers from the China Precision Machinery Import-Export Corporation visited the Rawalpindi site (this report may have been referring either to M-11s or to M-9s). Two years later, in a June 1998 interview, Dr. S. M. Mand of the Pakistan Atomic Energy Commission noted that he was also director of the NDC which had "developed this [Shaheen-1] missile within two-and-a-half years and at present it is in the production stage. Its ground testing is almost complete and whenever the government gives the go-ahead, we will begin flight testing."[62]

The Shaheen-1 missile was flight-tested on April 15, 1999, from the Sonmiani naval area. A year later, the missile (or its successor, the Shaheen-2) was displayed at the Pakistan Day parade on March 23, 2000. *Jane's* notes that the 9 ton Shaheen-1 is 12 m long and 1 m in diameter. The two-stage Shaheen-2 is 17 m long, 1.4 m in diameter, and weighs 25 tons; it incorporates advances in staging technology, reentry technology, and guidance and control systems, but possibly received Chinese assistance for specialized steel and solid fuel.[63]

Pakistan's missile activity was considerably delayed by the MTCR and no missile tests were reported from 1989 to 1997. U.S. sanctions were also imposed in 1991 and 1993 to curb Chinese technical assistance to Pakistan's missile program. Yet Islamabad's missile activity did not cease; with external (North Korean and Chinese) technical assistance, it built new medium-range missiles that were tested in 1998 and 1999. Without this external assistance, would Pakistan's missile activity have been halted? A complete embargo would have delayed

Pakistan's missile activity and pushed back its missile tests from the late 1990s to early in the next decade, because Islamabad would have required a few additional years to build vital missile components such as engines and airframes. Yet, because Islamabad had two missile teams and a modest defense industrial complex, it could ultimately have built these systems and advanced its missile program despite any foreign technology blockade.

Security Considerations

Pakistan's primary security concerns stem from its rivalry with India. A detailed discussion of the India–Pakistan conflict is beyond the scope of this study, but Islamabad fought and lost wars against Delhi in 1948, 1965, and 1971. Islamabad then sought a nuclear option to counter security threats from Delhi for three reasons. First, Islamabad's confidence in its allies (China and the U.S.) decreased because of their inability and perceived unreliability to provide timely and sufficient military assistance. Second, Islamabad's limited economic capabilities could not support a strong conventional deterrent. Third, Islamabad's nuclear deterrent not only balances India's nuclear arsenal but also offsets India's superior conventional forces.

Echoing the need for a nuclear program, Foreign Minister Zulfiqar Ali Bhutto argued in 1969: "If Pakistan restricts or suspends her nuclear program, it would . . . enable India to blackmail Pakistan with her nuclear advantage."[64] Islamabad's nuclear program was accelerated after its defeat in the 1971 war and India's 1974 nuclear test. In 1990, President Bush failed to certify that Islamabad was not engaged in nuclear weapons activity. Islamabad announced six nuclear tests in May 1998, and it is estimated to have some twenty or more nuclear weapons.

Islamabad sought intermediate-range missiles as nuclear delivery systems to enhance its deterrent in the 1990s. Its strategic environment had deteriorated because a strategic partner—the United States—had sanctioned and terminated military aid to Pakistan in 1990 (though another ally, China, continued its assistance during the 1990s), and due to missile activity in India. Pakistani officials and analysts made several points on the need for missiles in the 1990s. First, ballistic missiles compensated for the range limitations and vulnerability of Pakistan's air force,[65] as well as the uncertainty about augmenting this air force. Islamabad sought Chinese M-11s in 1991–92 after Washington's nonproliferation sanctions blocked the delivery of additional F-16s. Moreover, ballistic missiles were considered cheaper than the alternative of purchasing forty French Mirage fighters (though in 1996, Islamabad paid $120 million for forty used Mirage IIIs and Vs at $3 million each).

Second, short-range Hatf-1, Hatf-2, and M-11 missiles could not target India's major cities. While Pakistan's key economic and population areas are within 50 to 250 km of the Indian border, India's major cities New Delhi and Bombay are 350 km and 600 km, respectively, from the border. Islamabad therefore sought the 1,000 km range Ghauri and 600–800 km range Shaheen-1 that can reach most of North and West India, and the 2,000 km range Shaheen-2 that can strike East and South India.

Third, a series of arms purchases and deployments by Delhi in the mid-1990s appeared to neutralize Islamabad's deterrence and necessitated a missile response to reestablish a credible deterrence. For example, although Pakistan's F-16s provided a modest nuclear delivery capability, "ever since su-30's induction in the IAF [Indian Air Force] in 1996 Pakistan's non-conventional response had lost its credibility because the delivery system, the F-16s, no longer enjoyed unchallenged superiority."[66] Moreover, Delhi's interest in an antiballistic missile capability in the mid-1990s compounded Islamabad's security threat perceptions.

Fourth, prospects for missile controls receded by the mid-1990s as New Delhi repeatedly rejected restraints unless they were linked with corresponding steps by China. Islamabad argued that in 1993, Delhi rejected a South Asia missile control initiative proposed by Washington, while Pakistan supported it by proposing a zero missile zone. In 1995–96, when Delhi may have started serial production of the Prithvi, "Pakistani demarches in important capitals met with concern. But muted western calls for restraint elicited no indication that Delhi was prepared to forswear testing, production or deployment."[67]

Reports that New Delhi had deployed the Prithvi in May 1997 accelerated Islamabad's missile decisions. Islamabad then noted that its "reaction time" to a preemptive launch of the Prithvi was now "less than three minutes" and "the operationalization of the Prithvi missiles marked a qualitative change in the strategic landscape."[68] Thus, Islamabad's decisions on medium-range missiles were probably taken in the early and mid-1990s, and influenced by India's 1988 Prithvi and 1989 Agni tests. Thereafter, 1993–96 press reports of Prithvi production and 1997 reports of Prithvi deployment further advanced Islamabad's missile decisions. At this time, democratic governments headed by Prime Ministers Benazir Bhutto and Nawaz Sharif did not rein in Islamabad's missile activity.

Democratization, Civil-Military Relations, and Missile Proliferation in South Asia

How have domestic politics and democratization influenced proliferation in South Asia? In Latin America, democratization decreased the influence of the military (which was the primary driver of nuclear and missile programs) and also resulted in a "democratic peace" that reduced the security-related demand for nuclear and missile programs. But democratization did not curb missile and nuclear activity in the subcontinent for a number of reasons.

At the monadic (national government) level, nuclear and missile programs in India were initiated and sustained by democratic governments. India's military plays virtually no role in nuclear and missile development, which is instead in the hands of a strategic scientific enclave that has direct access to the civilian leadership. Pakistan's nuclear and missile activity was undertaken under both military and civilian regimes. Two civilian prime ministers—Zulfiqar Ali Bhutto and Nawaz Sharif—actually sought to strengthen their hands versus the military by controlling the national nuclear program (but the military remained dominant in defense and security policy).[69] Civil society has also not exerted a moderating influence on missile proliferation. The press debate in a democratic India mostly called for accelerated missile activity; similarly, in Pakistan, commentators argued for a strong response to India's Prithvi missile deployment in June 1997.[70]

At the dyadic level, although the democratization of neighboring states generally improves regional security and thus moderates proliferation, this was not the case in the subcontinent. Proliferation increased after the democratization of the India-Pakistan dyad (after Pakistan made a transition to democracy in 1988) for three reasons.

First, despite a transition, democracy was not consolidated in Pakistan. The more strongly pronuclear military and the president (who had and used the power to dismiss the prime minister), rather than the civilian leadership, remained in control of key national security decisions. Pakistan's military viewed itself as the last bastion of stability and security: "the military, with its institutionalized decision making and capability for structured response, was a powerful stabilizing and deterrent factor in an exploitable internal and external environment."[71] The military was not categorically opposed to arms control, and it acquiesced to a freeze in fissile material production in the 1980s, which was necessary to avert U.S. sanctions that would have cut off military aid. Yet it still opposed excessive nuclear and missile restraints that threatened its corporate interests or that weakened Pakistan's military position versus India.

Thus, during Pakistan's first democratic regime (Benazir Bhutto's government from 1988 to 1990), while President Ghulam Ishaq Khan and General Aslam Beg allowed Bhutto to represent Pakistan to the world, they dominated national security issues such as the nuclear program and relations with India. Bhutto was not fully informed about key elements of Pakistan's foreign and security policy. Bhutto made concessions to the military on Afghanistan and on not compromising the nuclear and missile programs, and agreed not to make unilateral reductions in defense expenditure. The military also felt that the Nawaz Sharif government (in power from 1990 to 1993) was not doing enough to revive weapons procurement from the United States that was halted under Pressler Amendment legislation in October 1990. Moreover, because South Asia's regional security environment did not improve (and a nuclear and missile race continued), this regional insecurity increased the military's relevance to political decision making.[72]

Further, during Pakistan's initial transition to democracy in the late 1980s and early 1990s, Delhi's decision makers were reluctant to consider Pakistan as a democratic state. This Indian perception precluded the possibility that a basic premise of the democratic peace—that peace arises because both states view each other as democratic and therefore less inclined to war—could operate in the subcontinent in the early 1990s.

The second reason for continued nuclearization was that democratization in South Asia was followed by (but did not directly cause) a deterioration in interstate relations because of the Kashmir insurgency. Domestic pressures to support the insurgency did not allow Islamabad to back down, and Delhi accused Islamabad of furthering the insurgency. In such a charged atmosphere, the possibilities of constraining Pakistan's nuclear and missile programs (which were beyond strict civilian control in the first place) became even more remote.

Third, even though democratic governments in India and Pakistan were at times inclined to move toward cooperation, a sustained dialogue between the same set of governments was precluded because of the rapid succession of unstable, short-term governments between 1989 and 1991. Several years later, in February 1999, India and Pakistan appeared to be reconciling when Prime Ministers Vajpayee and Sharif signed the Lahore accords (but their nuclear and missile programs were far advanced by this stage). However, these initiatives were set back by a limited war in the summer of 1999 and subsequent tense relations. Thus the theoretical promise of a democratic peace was not realized in the subcontinent in the 1990s. Democratization did not bring about the normalization of India-Pakistan relations, which remained tense, and consequently these South Asian states did not curb their missile and nuclear programs.

Political-Economic Influences,
International Leverage, and Prospects for Restraints

Delhi pursued an extensive economic liberalization program in the 1990s; Islamabad also opted for economic reforms at this time. The success of economic reforms depends on greater levels of trade, aid, and investment from the West. This would enable the West to have leverage on these South Asian states similar to its influence on Argentina, Brazil, and South Africa.[73] Could this situation curb further proliferation in the subcontinent? Two points should be noted on this issue.

Security concerns are significantly greater in the subcontinent than in Latin America. These security concerns have not allowed possible tradeoffs on nuclear restraint in exchange for economic incentives. Delhi and Islamabad both conducted nuclear tests in May 1998 despite being aware of the economic sanctions that would follow. Further, geostrategic equations in South Asia are not a bilateral India-Pakistan issue, but also involve China; the pacific influences of democratization do not extend to the China-India dyad.

In addition, because systemic and domestic political-economic pressures appear at a different stage of proliferation—in the 1990s, India's and Pakistan's missile programs were in an advanced stage and not in their initial stages as in Argentina and Brazil—a similar outcome, namely the elimination of missile programs, is harder to attain. Instead, South Asia's nuclear and missile programs may simply be capped but not eliminated under external pressure.

This situation is reflected in Washington's nonproliferation policies for South Asia. In April 1993, the Clinton administration's report to Congress noted that its goals were to "cap, then reduce over time, and finally eliminate weapons of mass destruction and their means of delivery from the region." This emphasis on capping was a departure from the earlier goal of focusing exclusively on the elimination of nuclear programs by having Delhi and Islamabad sign the NPT. And in 1998, Washington conceded further ground by mainly seeking only the nondeployment of missiles instead of missile elimination or the cessation of missile tests.[74] Deputy Secretary of State Strobe Talbott's 1998–99 nonproliferation dialogue with New Delhi and Islamabad sought their "demonstrating prudence and restraint in the development, flight testing, and storage of ballistic missiles and nuclear-capable aircraft."[75] Although Delhi agreed to a nuclear test moratorium, it would not accept qualitative and quantitative limits on its nuclear and missile development. In February 2001, defense minister George Fernandes told Parliament: "The government has decided to induct the [Agni-2] missile system based on security needs."[76] Delhi had thus firmly established its military IRBM program.

This discussion highlights the significance of timing and the stages of proliferation. Because proliferation is too advanced to be quickly rolled back, political-economic pressures on New Delhi and Islamabad may only *restrain the advancement of* but not reverse their missile and nuclear programs. Any strategic restraint regime could thus focus not on a complete nuclear rollback, but on more feasible steps such as persuading New Delhi and Islamabad to control their technology exports, adopt missile test notifications and restraints, accept nondeployment or nonweaponization of missiles, and accept bans on long-range missiles. Such a strategic restraint regime, and broader strategic and political-economic considerations, may constrain Islamabad and New Delhi from further advancing their missile programs, though Delhi remained under domestic pressure to build long-range missiles.

In September 2000, the Indian press carried the headline: "ICBMs Any Day, Says Kalam."[77] Missile scientist Abdul Kalam (who later became India's president) had declared that his team could build an intercontinental ballistic missile. In May 2001, *Defense News* indicated that Delhi could test a 5,000 km range Surya or Agni-IV and a 12,000 km range Surya-II or Agni-V. However, an Indian cabinet minister rejected these reports on the Surya, declaring, "There is no such intention, no such project."[78] Delhi had no immediate strategic need for an ICBM. Moreover, because any public declaration on an ICBM could damage relations with Washington (with whom Delhi sought better political ties, more scientific and technological cooperation, increased trade and investment, and the lifting of Washington's nonproliferation sanctions), Prime Minister Vajpayee's government did not publicly endorse any ICBM program. Thus, as India entered the twenty-first century, political-economic considerations had at least temporarily restrained it from following the five major nuclear powers on the road to ICBMs.

North Korea and Iran:
Emerging Missile Threats

O n July 22, 1998, a Shehab-3 rocket lifted off from the Iranian desert, flew toward the southeast, and detonated 100 seconds into its flight. The *Jerusalem Post* reported ominously, "Iran has joined the long-range missile club," adding that this development was "one of the toughest challenges in the history of the state [of Israel], and we are taking it seriously."[1] Iran's former president Hashemi Rafsanjani noted defensively that Tehran's missile program had "started from scratch" in response to Iraqi missile attacks on Iranian cities, and missiles then became vital to Iran's national security.[2] The *Tehran Times* stated that the Shehab-3 test "aimed at demonstrating Iran's determination that it was not ready to accept the hegemony of others."[3] Yet hostile slogans against Israel were painted on the Shehab-3, and Iran's defense minister subsequently announced plans for longer range Shehab-4 and Shehab-5 rockets. These could strike Europe and the United States.

Five years earlier, in May 1993, Iranian observers watched four North Korean missiles being fired into the Sea of Japan. One of these was the Nodong, from which the Shehab-3 was derived. The Nodong also formed the first stage of the longer range Taepodong-1. On August 31, 1998, North Korea stunned the world by launching this rocket over Japan and into the Pacific. The following year, Pyongyang was also preparing to launch the more powerful Taepodong-2, making it the first hostile country to threaten the United States since China began deploying ICBMs in the early 1980s.

How did North Korea and Iran build long-range missiles? What motivated their missile programs, and can international diplomacy and technology barriers contain their missile activities?

NORTH KOREA

North Korea built several hundred 300 km range Scud-B and 600 km range Scud-C missiles in the 1980s and 1990s; it also built more than one hundred of the 1,000 km range Nodong (tested in 1993), a few of the 2,000 km range Taepodong-1 (tested in 1998), and the 4,000–6,000 km range Taepodong-2 (that had not flown as of 2002). Pyongyang pursued a missile program due to security considerations (to enhance its WMD-based deterrent), as well as with commercial motivations (to acquire revenue from missile exports) and political objectives (as a bargaining chip to secure economic aid and political recognition from the West). U.S. missile talks beginning in 1996 did not halt Pyongyang's missile activity, but economic liberalization, improvements in regional security, and international engagement may restrain Pyongyang's missile advances.

The Development of a Long-Range Missile Capability

North Korea's missile program first involved low-technology surface-to-air missiles, cruise missiles, and artillery rockets in the 1960s and 1970s and then moved on to produce more capable liquid-fuel Scuds, Nodongs, and Taepodongs in the 1980s and 1990s. In the first phase of missile activity,[4] it purchased several low-technology systems: Russian SA-2s in 1962–63, SSC-2b Samlet coastal-defense cruise missiles in 1965, SS-N-2 Styx antiship missiles in 1967–68, and about fifty of the 55 km range Frog-5 artillery rockets in 1968 (it later obtained twenty-five to fifty of the 70 km range Frog-7s from Egypt in 1975–76). Further, under a September 1971 military cooperation agreement with Beijing, North Korea obtained the HQ-1 (the Chinese version of the SA-2), HQ-2 (an upgraded HQ-1), and HY-1 (the Silkworm, which is China's version of the Styx) systems, and it reverse engineered and domestically produced some of these systems.

North Korea also established an indigenous manufacturing capability. Premier Kim Il Sung set up the Hamhung Military Academy for weapons development in 1965. Its First Department, or the Department of Missile Engines, studied German V-1 and V-2 and Soviet Frog designs. By the late 1970s, North Korea had developed better missile facilities such as the 125 Factory in Pyongyang, a military research facility at Sanum-dong (25 km north of Pyongyang), and the Musadan-ri launch station. The Guided Missile Division of the Academy of Defense Sciences, and the Fourth Machine Industry Bureau of the Second Economic Committee, undertook North Korea's missile program.[5]

From 1975, Pyongyang tried to build three rockets and missiles—Frog-5, -6, and -7 artillery rockets (concentrating on the maintenance of these systems); a surface-to-surface version of the HQ-2 (the system had a 150–200 km range with a 190 kg warhead); and the 500–1,000 km range DF-61 in collaboration with China (North Korean personnel gained technical experience before this project was scrapped in 1978). This missile activity followed and further stimulated Seoul's development of the NHK-1 missile that was tested in September 1978. In addition, to overcome difficulties in designing missiles, Pyongyang sought assistance from Egypt, which transferred a few R-17E (Scud-B) missiles to North Korea and signed technology cooperation agreements with it in the period 1979–81.

North Korea built five ballistic missiles—the Scud-B, Scud-C, Nodong, Taepodong-1, and Taepodong-2—in its second phase of missile development. It first worked on the R-17E in 1982 and 1983, and tested three Scud-A prototypes in April and September 1984 (three other tests failed), and then slightly modified its Scud prototypes, extending the range from 280 km to 320–340 km and improving guidance systems. The resulting 6 ton, 11.3 m long, 0.9 m diameter Hwasong 5 (Scud-B) missile began small-scale production in 1985 followed by greater production in 1986. Iranian interest and funding supported North Korea's missile activities.

Pyongyang began work on the 500 km range Hwasong 6 (Scud-C), which was a modified Hwasong 5, in 1987–88. The missile's range was extended by reducing the warhead weight from 1 ton to 770 kg, and lightening the airframe using Soviet-imported stainless steel. Small-scale production began in 1989, and North Korea conducted five Hwasong 6 flight tests—one each in June 1990 and July 1991, and three in late May 1993; one of these missiles traveled 100 km and the other two fell short of that distance.[6] North Korea exported an estimated 300 to 400 Scuds to the UAE (25 Scud-Bs, 1989), Iran (Scud-B, 1987–88; Scud-C, 1991–92), and Syria (Scud-C, 1991–93; Scud-D, 1999–2000),[7] at an estimated price of $1 to 3 million per missile.

North Korea began developing the 1,000 km range Nodong missile while it worked on the Scud-C in 1988. U.S. intelligence detected a Nodong prototype on a launch pad in May 1990. Early reports indicated that the Nodong was built around a cluster of four Scud motors.[8] But others argue that the Nodong is a scaled up Scud-C by a factor of 150 percent, to attain a missile that is 16–17 m long with a 1.23–1.3 m diameter and weighing 15–16 tons.[9] While airframe production proceeded quickly, engine and guidance system development was harder. Russian engineers formerly with the Makayev design bureau helped upgrade the North Korean produced Isayev 9D21 engine.[10] The Nodong was tested on May 29, 1993, to a range of 500 km.

From 1993 to mid-1998, no additional North Korean missile tests took place. Yet press reports indicate that test preparations were being made in April–June 1994, and again in October 1996. Nuclear talks with the United States in 1993–94 probably restrained Pyongyang from missile testing. However, other sporadic North Korean missile activity was reported in the period 1994–98. In February 1994, North Korea conducted a static liquid-fuel engine test.[11] It obtained access to Syrian SS-21s and the DR-3 Reys UAV in 1994. North Korea also tested cruise missiles (that may have been upgraded Silkworms) on May 31 and June 2, 1994, March 1995, and May 1997.

North Korea also exported Nodong missiles or related technology beginning in 1993. It initially hesitated on an Iranian request for the Nodong, but then transferred related design and technology. It also supplied the Nodong design and components (and possibly a few complete missiles) to Pakistan, from which Pakistan built the Ghauri missile. In April 1994, a North Korean foreign ministry delegation traveled to Iran and Pakistan, and several further North Korean delegations visited Pakistan in 1994–96.

Pakistan's Ghauri and Iran's Shehab-3 tests provided information on the Nodong's flight parameters (the Ghauri covered a range of 700–1,000 km, further than the distance of the May 1993 Nodong test). This may have allowed North Korea to skip additional testing for the Nodong as well as for the longer range Taepodong.

North Korea began developing the multistage Taepodong series missiles in the late 1980s or early 1990s. The two-stage 27 m long Taepodong-1 has an estimated 1,500–2,200 km range with a 1 ton warhead. It is designed around a Nodong first stage and a Scud second stage, and is used as both a ballistic missile and satellite launcher.

On August 31, 1998, North Korea launched a three-stage version of the Taepodong-1. The first stage separated after 95 seconds and landed 253 km from the launching station; the second stage separated in 266 seconds and impacted 1,646 km from the launch station; and the third stage attempted to place a satellite in orbit 27 seconds after the separation of the second stage.[12]

North Korea developed a more powerful 4,000 to 6,000 km range two-stage Taepodong-2 missile in the 1990s. This missile was seen near its launch pad in July 1999 and may also form the basis for Iran's Shehab-5. The Federation of American Scientists notes that the missile has a 60 ton first stage (either derived from China's 2,500–3,500 km range CSS-2, or from four Nodong thrust chambers) and a 15 ton second stage (derived from the Nodong).[13] With a third stage, this missile could have a longer range and reach the United States.

The MTCR's technology embargoes slowed North Korea's missile programs, but despite these embargoes, and with foreign assistance, North Korea made impressive strides in missile development. North Korea's macroeconomic and industrial capability is, in relative terms, much smaller than that of other regional powers in this study. Yet it still had a large heavy industry (until its economic decline in the 1990s) that was acquired as a part of the *juche* ideology of economic self-reliance. This industrial base supported Pyongyang's missile advancement. North Korea also demonstrated that a state with few technical and economic resources can attain significant missile capability through a focused effort.

Security Considerations

North Korea has historically had security concerns about four issues: U.S. military forces in South Korea and decades of confrontation with Washington; its economic decline relative to South Korea; perceptions of reduced support from its allies Russia and China; and its diplomatic isolation from the West. These concerns are likely to have influenced its missile activity in the 1960s and 1970s, and again in the 1980s and 1990s. In turn, this missile and WMD activity and militarization was a security concern for North Korea's neighbors.[14]

In the 1960s and 1970s, North Korea's missile activity was part of an overarching quest for security through an independent military capability; this self-sufficiency theme of the *juche* ideology was intended to reduce North Korea's dependence on its two uncertain allies, Moscow and Beijing. Two factors contributed to Pyongyang's insecurity syndrome at this time. First, South Korea's economic performance and military expenditures caught up with the North's, although the absolute size of North Korea's army remained larger.[15] Second, North Korea's confidence in its two major allies China and Russia decreased because of incidents such as strained relations with Khrushchev, Moscow's nonsupportive stance in the Pueblo incident, Beijing's post-1966 tensions with Pyongyang, and its later normalization of ties with Washington. Beyond security concerns, Pyongyang's missile activity was driven by prestige reasons and the desire to match and upstage South Korea's nuclear and missile programs that had advanced in the mid-1970s. (From a South Korean perspective, North Korean militarization and signs of a U.S. military withdrawal caused Seoul to increase its defense modernization and missile and nuclear activity.)[16] Despite these security concerns, Pyongyang still did not view the situation as an entirely losing game. Kim Il Sung expressed confidence about his regime in December 1977, and (especially after indications of a U.S. military withdrawal and President Park's assassination in 1979) also anticipated a declining rather than a rising South Korea.[17] North Korea eventually acquired and built thousands of SAMs, cruise missiles, and artillery rockets. Its SAMs were intended to defend against the superior U.S. and South Korean air force; antiship cruise missiles were intended to battle the U.S. navy; and artillery rockets were intended to bombard the city of Seoul.

North Korea's missile programs (that complemented its nuclear and WMD activity) in the 1980s and 1990s served as a deterrent against external military threats that arose for two reasons. First, North Korea's economic decline in the 1990s placed it in a much weaker position versus South Korea, which had also undertaken military modernization in the 1980s. Second, North Korea again became uncertain about its allies China and Russia, who both gradually rejected socialism, increased their economic and diplomatic ties with South Korea, and could not provide Pyongyang with substantial economic aid. As a result, despite receiving Soviet arms in the 1980s, North Korea's ties with Moscow deteriorated,[18] and relations with Beijing also cooled.[19] Given these security concerns, Pyongyang increasingly relied on unconventional weapons to level the playing field versus South Korea, Japan, and the United States.

North Korea thus intended to use its unconventional weapons for strategic deterrence. Medium-range missiles would enable Pyongyang to deliver WMDs against American military targets in South Korea and Japan (which had long been Korea's historical adversary). Pyongyang anticipated that the threat of such strikes would reduce Washington's willingness to intervene in any Korean conflict. As far back as the 1960s, Premier Kim noted: "If war breaks out, the US and Japan will also be involved. In order to prevent their involvement, we have to be able to produce rockets which fly as far as Japan. Therefore it is the mandate of the Military Academy to nurture those personnel which are able to develop mid- and long-range missiles."[20] Pyongyang could also use WMDs for war fighting in a "one-blow, nonstop attack" to quickly overrun South Korea.[21]

In parallel with its missile program, North Korea built a nuclear infrastructure beginning in the 1960s (albeit for a combination of energy-related, prestige-driven, and security reasons). It may have extracted plutonium for one or two warheads before its plutonium program was frozen through the 1994 Agreed Framework. Yet North Korea's missile program advanced in the 1990s because of continued security concerns, economic considerations, and its diplomatic isolation from the West.

Political and Economic Influences

Economic and political-economic factors influenced North Korea's WMD and missile activity in three ways. First, North Korea's economic decline probably decreased its defense and missile budgets and slowed the pace of its missile program; North Korea's economy contracted from 1990 to 1998 and it also faced widespread famine. Yet it maintains a large military budget, which has historically been about 25 percent of its GNP; at 1997 prices, its military expenditure was $6 billion or 23 percent of GNP in 1985, and $2 billion or 14 percent of GNP in 1998. This enabled Pyongyang to continue missile activity (if only slowly) in the 1990s despite its economic decline. Moreover, missile export revenues (estimated at $1 to $2 billion since 1987) partly offset North Korea's economic problems.

Second, Pyongyang's economic decline caused security concerns (discussed above) by resulting in an inability to maintain a conventional balance versus South Korea. North Korea sought to redress the issue through its unconventional (nuclear, chemical, and missile) forces.

Third, because of its autarkic economic policy and a U.S. economic embargo since the Korean War, North Korea has almost no economic ties with the United States or the West (except through Japan). It is thus not structurally dependent on the United States and the West, which consequently have less leverage on Pyongyang. But to stem its economic decline, Pyongyang may opt for economic liberalization and seek greater foreign trade and investment from the West. This may give the international community leverage on Pyongyang's nuclear and missile program.

Kim Jong Il pursued a limited economic opening in the mid-1990s through measures such as the Rajin-Sonbong Free Trade Economic Zone and the nuclear Agreed Framework (that involved foreign technology and $5 billion in foreign capital). However, North Korean leaders were reluctant to pursue deeper liberalization. They assumed that limited reforms and foreign investment could revive their economy and boost the government's legitimacy, and reaffirmed that despite limited reforms, *juche* (self-sufficiency and autarky) dominated their economic policy.[22] Echoing similar themes, the Perry report in 1999 noted that, "Wrapped in an overriding sense of vulnerability, the DPRK regime has promoted an intense devotion to self-sufficiency, sovereignty, and self-defense as the touchstones for all rhetoric and policy. The DPRK views efforts by outsiders to promote democratic and market reforms in its country as an attempt to undermine the regime. It strongly controls foreign influence and contact, even when they offer relief from the regime's severe economic problems. The DPRK appears to value improved relations with U.S., *especially* including relief from the extensive economic sanctions the U.S. has long imposed."[23]

Beyond its limited economic opening to acquire aid from the West, Pyongyang also pursued a diplomatic opening with the West and engaged in missile talks with the United States.

Israeli and U.S. Missile Talks with North Korea

North Korea's missile sales prompted American and Israeli diplomacy to halt these activities. In a January 1993 meeting in Pyongyang, Israel offered to establish diplomatic ties and provide North Korea with several hundred million dollars in investment and technical assistance. Discussions covered the possible Israeli purchase of a gold mine near Unsan if North Korea curbed missile exports; the North Koreans reportedly asked for $1 billion, including thousands of trucks.[24]

After Pyongyang's March 1993 threat to withdraw from the NPT, Washington persuaded Israel to break off talks, and North Korea tested Scud and Nodong missiles on May 29–30, 1993. In early June, Israel's foreign minister, Shimon Peres, was persuaded by Secretary of State Warren Christopher and South Korea's foreign minister to cancel an impending trip to Pyongyang; Peres then dispatched a foreign ministry representative to meet North Korean officials. During Israeli–North Korean discussions in Beijing on June 24, 1993, Israel explored economic and agricultural assistance if North Korea halted missile exports to Iran and Syria. A third round of talks was held on August 11 at Israel's embassy in Beijing. Immediately thereafter, Washington objected that Israel's talks with Pyongyang could undermine ongoing U.S. nuclear diplomacy with Pyongyang. Israel then suspended missile discussions with North Korea.

U.S.–North Korean missile talks may be viewed against the background of broader political relations between the two states. The 1994 nuclear agreement was also a road map aimed at improving relations. From 1995 to 1998, U.S. efforts focused largely on food aid (totaling $400 million through the World Food Program) to prevent starvation and provide stability in North Korea. Following Pyongyang's August 1998 missile test and the subsequent review of U.S. policy by William Perry, Washington focused more sharply on halting Pyongyang's long-range missile program. Missile talks had actually begun two years earlier.

The Clinton administration pursued several rounds of missile talks with Pyongyang between April 1996 and December 2000. The talks initially made little headway but acquired considerable momentum in late 2000. In the first missile talks on April 20–21, 1996, Washington offered to lift sanctions if North Korea curbed its missile development and sales; these initial talks were characterized as useful and a good beginning.[25] Subsequently, leaks in the U.S. press on North Korea's missile technology transfers and U.S. sanctions against Pyongyang made it harder for the Clinton administration to continue the dialogue.[26] Pyongyang noted that if such "groundless news reports" continued, it would boycott missile talks. Thereafter, in October 1996, North Korea prepared for missile tests, reflecting a toughening stand. The State Department noted that any missile tests "would be destabilizing [and] harmful to our efforts to provide stability in the Korean peninsula, and the United States would be very much opposed to this."[27] North Korea responded that the missile test issue "belongs to our sovereignty and no one else is entitled to or has any ground to meddle with it. . . . [W]e may test fire the missile any time we think fit."[28]

A second round of U.S.–North Korean missile talks was held in June 1997. Washington's goal was to cover missile exports and missile development, and to halt North Korea's biological and chemical weapons programs. Pyongyang sought to deal more comprehensively with military-security issues such as a U.S.-DPRK peace treaty, the removal of U.S. missiles and military forces from South Korea, and the initiation of regular U.S.-DPRK meetings.[29]

A follow-up session scheduled for August 27, 1997, was called off after two North Korean diplomats defected to the United States; Pyongyang again prepared for missile tests in September 1997. In March 1998 it agreed to further talks but these were delayed for several months. In May 1998, Pyongyang refused inspections of a suspected nuclear site, and threatened to revive its nuclear program if the 1994 Agreed Framework's implementation was delayed. On June 16, 1998, Pyongyang declared for the first time that it had exported and could continue to export missiles: "We will continue developing, testing and deploying missiles. . . . [O]ur missile export is aimed at obtaining foreign money we need at present."[30] Leon Sigal notes that the statement was also significant because it went beyond only *exports* to cover *development*. Pyongyang had noted: "The discontinuation of our missile development is a matter which can be discussed after a peace agreement is signed between the D.P.R.K. and the United States and the U.S. military threat [is] completely removed."[31] Yet no further discussions took place in the coming months. North Korea tested the Taepodong-1 on August 31. Japan responded by suspending its aid that helped implement the 1994 Agreed Framework.

Despite international discord over the nuclear and missile issue in mid-1998, the third round of U.S.–North Korean missile talks was held in New York on October 1, 1998. As in previous talks, Pyongyang sought financial compensation for lost missile revenues, but added that Washington was already obligated to ease sanctions under the Agreed Framework, which called on both sides to "move toward full normalization of political and economic relations."[32] The failure to reach agreement was apparent as chief DPRK negotiator Han Chang-On stated, "We disagreed in almost all matters," and added that a missile "is a tool to defend a country and is a natural independent right of a sovereign state. Nobody can negotiate on this. So there has been sincere exchange of opinions in the talks but there is no agreement"; Han also noted that the DPRK would continue to launch satellites "for peaceful use."[33]

A fourth round of missile talks was held on March 29–30, 1999. U.S. negotiator Robert Einhorn declared: "We had frank discussions. . . . but I can't say we have made any breakthrough."[34] Pyongyang suggested that it could halt missile exports in exchange for $1 billion annually for three years. A few weeks earlier, on March 16, 1999, Pyongyang had allowed multiple inspections of the Kumchang-ni nuclear site and obtained several hundred tons of food aid.

In May 1999, William Perry met senior North Korean leaders (but not the head of state) in Pyongyang as part of a review of U.S. policy. In late June and July 1999, the diplomatic dialogue was set back, and tests of North Korea's Taepodong-2 missile appeared imminent.[35] Intense diplomacy then caused Pyongyang to back down. A June 20 G-8 statement and a July 27 joint statement by the foreign ministers of the United States, South Korea, and Japan cautioned Pyongyang against missile tests. A tentative deal was reached during the September 7–12, 1999, talks in Berlin between U.S. Ambassador Charles Kartman and DPRK Vice Foreign Minister Kim Gye Gwan. Washington announced on September 17 that it would lift trade sanctions (though foreign aid sanctions remained); Pyongyang announced on September 24 that it would not test missiles as long as a dialogue continued.

A fifth round of missile talks was held in Kuala Lumpur on July 10–12, 2000, between Jang Chang Chon, head of Pyongyang's bureau on United States affairs, and Robert Einhorn. Pyongyang restated its offer to halt missile exports for $1 billion. Einhorn noted that the North Koreans should not be compensated for not conducting activities they should not be conducting in the first place, and that Pyongyang stood to gain far more from a better security environment and normalized relations with Washington.[36]

The missile dialogue gained considerable momentum in the second half of 2000. Russia's President Vladimir Putin visited Pyongyang in July 2000, and noted that North Korea could curb its long-range missile program if other states launched its satellites. On August 28, 2000, Washington's special adviser on North Korean affairs Wendy Sherman traveled to Moscow to confirm the missile proposal. Washington and Pyongyang had further missile talks on September 27 in New York. On October 9–12, 2000, North Korea's military chief, Vice Marshal Cho Myong Rok, visited Washington and furthered the dialogue. Later that month, Secretary of State Madeleine Albright met Kim Jong Il in Pyongyang, and Kim made important missile concessions (discussed below). A seventh round of missile talks was held in Kuala Lumpur in November 2000. Robert Einhorn characterized the discussions with his North Korean counterpart Jang Chang Chon as "detailed, constructive, and very substantive" but added that "significant issues remain to be explored and resolved."[37]

Based on these talks, Washington prepared a draft missile agreement with technical notes. Wendy Sherman was prepared to take this draft to North Korea in December to clear any final barriers. If Pyongyang accepted it, then President Clinton could have visited North Korea and signed a missile deal. But time ran out on the Clinton administration; because election results were being recounted in December, Washington's bureaucracy decided that U.S. negotiators should not visit North Korea and therefore no missile agreement materialized. Summing up the issue, Wendy Sherman noted that a "deal with North Korea . . . came tantalizingly close for President Bill Clinton in his final days in office. That agreement, when completed, would both halt North Korea's exports of missiles and related technology and stop further production, deployment and testing of long-range missiles."[38]

These two key points are worth clarifying. First, Pyongyang offered to halt exports of missiles, missile components, technology, and training, which meant that it would probably annul existing contracts with other states. Second, it agreed not to produce, test, or deploy missiles with a range of more than 300 miles (500 km) (i.e., ranges beyond those of Scud-C missiles). In exchange, Pyongyang sought a U.S. willingness to provide satellite launches (Marshal Cho had affirmed this proposal in Washington in October), and also sought economic compensation. Pyongyang dropped its earlier demand to be paid a billion dollars in cash, but sought a billion dollars of food, coal, or other commodities for its stricken economy; Washington considered providing several hundred million dollars a year in food aid. Details of the satellite launch mechanism were also not specified.

Three more important obstacles remained.[39] First, Washington wanted Pyongyang to restrict itself to 180 mile (300 km) range missiles that fell within MTCR guidelines (William Perry had noted these range limits during his 1999 talks in Pyongyang). This meant that Pyongyang would have to stop building Scud-Cs and longer range missiles, though it could presumably still build and deploy Scud-Bs. Second, Secretary of Defense William Cohen and the Joint Chiefs of Staff wanted Pyongyang to destroy its existing missile stocks (of Scud-C, Nodong, and Taepodong missiles) which threatened Japan and American troops in South Korea, although some U.S. officials would have settled for a promise to negotiate this in the future. Third, verification issues remained unresolved. Pyongyang would not permit intrusive inspections and wanted Washington to monitor compliance through satellites and other technical means; Washington wanted stronger verification provisions and also sought a North Korean declaration on the numbers and types of missiles in its arsenal.

Thus, by late 2000, intense negotiations had moved North Korea and the United States closer to a missile understanding, but still not close enough to facilitate a U.S. presidential visit to North Korea. Yet Washington had achieved one key restraint through North Korea's missile test freeze, which had several nonproliferation benefits. North Korea could not, in the absence of testing, confirm the reliability of upgrades to its Taepodong-1 (whose August 1998 test was only a partial success). It would also have less confidence in the untested Taepodong-2, thus slowing that missile's development. Moreover, since missile tests are a marketing tool (to demonstrate the missile's viability to potential clients), the absence of testing potentially dampened North Korean missile exports. However, the test moratorium was easily reversible. Further, North Korea could confidently build missile hardware and components that had been previously tested (in the Nodong, Ghauri, and Shehab tests), and simply wait for future tests to integrate these with other components when reviving its missile program.

In 2001, the Bush administration froze the dialogue, and Pyongyang threatened to revive missile tests; it may also have exported missile-related items to Iran in early 2001.[40] In May 2001, Pyongyang informed a visiting EU delegation that it would extend its missile test freeze until 2003, but would not unilaterally halt missile exports, which it considered to be regular trade. In June, the Bush administration sought to cover all military issues including Pyongyang's conventional forces in any resumed dialogue. In late June 2001, Pyongyang ground tested a missile engine; it was unclear whether this involved a Taepodong-1 or Taepodong-2 engine. In 2002, Pyongyang extended its missile test moratorium but also admitted to a uranium-based nuclear program.

Assessment:
International Incentives, Domestic Politics, and Regional Security

Several rounds of U.S. missile talks with North Korea moderated but did not halt its missile activities. In the long run, any deal on North Korea's missile program would probably involve incentives and account for broader military security issues, and would also be influenced by domestic politics.

First, incentives have partly moderated North Korean behavior. Analysts and policy makers Leon Sigal, Jongchul Park, William Perry, and Selig Harrison have studied and advocated various types of economic incentives (sometimes in combination with security assurances) to deal with Pyongyang.[41] Sigal points out that North Korea responded positively to cooperative international gestures in the 1994 nuclear agreement.[42] Park, a senior official in the South Korean reunification ministry, noted that two stages of dialogue may be undertaken with Pyongyang.[43] A first step would require North Korea to halt its missile technology exports and join the MTCR. In return, Washington could partly lift economic sanctions, permit U.S. firms to invest in North Korea, approve ship and aircraft visitation, and allow remittances to North Korea via U.S. banks (the September 1999 U.S. sanctions waiver included most of these measures). As a second step, in exchange for a halt to North Korea's missile, biological, and chemical programs, Washington could open trade and investment, remove North Korea from the list of terrorist states, offer it most-favored nation (MFN) status, support Pyongyang's admission into the IMF, World Bank, and Asian Development Bank, and support loans to Pyongyang by these international financial institutions.

Second, an improved security environment and diplomatic engagement (that includes better ties with South Korea, the United States, and Japan, as well as with China and Russia) could increase prospects for a missile deal with Pyongyang. North Korea's relations with South Korea improved in the late 1990s. Upon assuming office in February 1998, South Korean President Kim Dae Jung initiated a "sunshine policy" under which Seoul assured Pyongyang that it does not seek the isolation, destabilization, and absorption of North Korea, and that it would separate humanitarian aid from politics. South Korea and North Korea held their first summit in June 2000, and agreed to work toward reconciliation and reunification. This successful summit was viewed as a historic breakthrough but was only the first step toward any deeper reconciliation. South Korea's military modernization continued, and the United States retained a strong military presence in South Korea. (In 2000, Pyongyang moderated its earlier policy by not calling for a U.S. military withdrawal, but it backtracked on this issue in 2001.)

North Korea also sought to normalize relations with the West from 1999. Beyond its talks with Washington, it established ties with Australia, the Philippines, most EU states, and three G-7 states—Britain, Italy, and Canada. Pyongyang's opening to the West was motivated by the desire for economic aid. It resumed talks with Japan, and although difficult differences remained to be resolved, Japan resumed its economic aid that had been frozen since Pyongyang's August 1998 missile test.

At the same time, Pyongyang's ties with long-standing allies Russia and China, which were strained during the 1990s, improved. Kim Jong Il visited Beijing ahead of the Korea summit, and again in January 2001 (in part to examine Beijing's economic reform model). Russian President Vladimir Putin visited North Korea in July 2000, and Kim Jong Il visited Moscow in August 2001. These ventures eased North Korea's diplomatic isolation and thus addressed some of its security concerns. However, more fundamental security issues such as the conventional force balance and inter-Korean rapprochement remained to be addressed.

Third, internal politics will also influence Pyongyang's missile bargaining. By 2001, after seven years in power, Kim Jong Il's domestic position was more consolidated. Moreover, although its economy remained weak and required comprehensive restructuring, the worst phase of North Korea's economic crisis may have ended. A leadership that was secure and had slowed the economic decline was in a better position to bargain effectively and to explore economic openness. The Korean Workers Party and the military also generally supported economic reforms (and Kim had increased the military-dominated National Defense Council's political power). However, conservative sections of the military and party could still thwart rapid economic reforms or excessive concessions by reformists on their missile program.[44]

Further, viewed in historical perspective, Joseph Bermudez notes that "during the past forty-five years, the DPRK has developed such [unconventional] weapons with determination. . . . These nuclear, biological, and chemical capabilities are managed by a leadership that views such weapons as necessary for national survival."[45] Thus, even if North Korea gives up its long-range missiles, it could retain Scuds, cruise missiles, artillery, and aircraft for WMD delivery and war fighting until its security concerns are more comprehensively addressed.

North Korea's bargaining behavior should also be noted. Scott Snyder points out that Pyongyang often does not respond in a reciprocal manner. It instead uses crisis diplomacy and brinkmanship (the mixing of aggressive and provocative tactics including unconditional demands, deadlines, and walking out of talks) to gain leverage in international negotiations.[46] Even after agreements are signed, North Korea challenges their interpretation, which raises difficulties during the implementation phase, and gives rise to a continuous cycle of negotiations.

U.S. and South Korean (or any broader international) dialogue with Pyongyang that addresses its security concerns and offers meaningful incentives may generate reciprocal missile concessions. North Korea may seek firmer military-security assurances before completely eliminating its missile forces and accepting strict restraints on missile research and development. In the interim, it may limit itself to Scuds and curb its missile exports in exchange for political-economic concessions. It may not test and build long-range rockets if other states launch its satellites. However, if the diplomatic dialogue breaks down, then North Korea's missile program could expand and it could build and export intermediate-range Nodong and Taepodong-1 missiles on a large scale. It could also accelerate development of the 4,000–6,000 km range two-stage Taepodong-2, which, with a third stage, can strike the United States.

IRAN

Iran pursued a missile program in the 1990s for defense and security reasons. Its limited technological capability and the MTCR's embargo prevented rapid advances in this missile program. However, by the late 1990s, Iran had acquired about 200 Chinese 150 km range CSS-8 missiles; an estimated 300 North Korean or indigenously built 300 km range Scud-Bs (or Shehab-1s); 100 North Korean 600 km range Scud-Cs (or Shehab-2s); and a few 1,300 km range Shehab-3 missiles (an Iranian-built version of the North Korean Nodong). Iran's 2,000 km (or greater) range Shehab-4 was under construction but not flight-tested by 2002, and a longer range Shehab-5 was probably still in the design phase. Iran's partial political and economic liberalization in the 1990s did not reduce the scope of its missile activity; foreign political-economic and diplomatic leverage on Iran was also negligible and did not restrain its missile programs. Deeper internal liberalization, international engagement, and the stabilization of the regional security environment may restrain Iran's missile activity in the coming years.

Technical Capability and the Evolution of a Missile Program

Iran built or acquired three types of progressively more sophisticated missiles in the 1980s and 1990s—cruise missiles and artillery rockets, Scud missiles, and intermediate-range missiles. It purchased antiship cruise missiles from China and built solid-fuel artillery rockets. These included the 40–50 km range Oghab (derived from China's Type-83 rocket) in 1985, the 120 km range Mushak-120 in 1986–87, and the 160 km range Mushak-160 that was flight tested in July 1988. The first two systems were used in the Iran-Iraq war. Writing in 1998, Aaron Karp noted: "Iran's greatest strength is manufacturing small-diameter solid motors, best suited for use in unguided artillery rockets. . . . Despite their significant tactical potential, even the largest artillery rockets, however, will not serve Iranian strategic priorities."[47]

Iran's short-range ballistic missile activities involved the 1989 purchase of Chinese CSS-8 / M-7 missiles, the purchase of North Korean Scuds in the 1980s, and indigenous assembly or development of Scuds. Iran sought North Korean Scuds during its war with Iraq. On October 26, 1983, Iranian officials, including Defense Minister Colonel Mohammed Salimi, returned from a three-day visit to North Korea where they may have arranged to finance North Korea's Scud development.[48] In 1985, then Speaker of Parliament Ali Akbar Hashemi Rafsanjani led Iranian delegations to North Korea, Libya, China, and Syria to seek Scuds and other missile assistance.[49] Iran purchased HN-5A SAMs from North Korea, and obtained assistance for a factory to assemble North Korean Scuds. In June 1987, Iran concluded a $500 million arms agreement with North Korea for Scud-Bs and HY-2 Silkworms. It received about a hundred Scud-Bs and twelve transporter launchers (TELS) between August 1987 and February 1988, and a further twenty Scud-Bs in early 1990. Iran may also have manufactured Scud-Bs. In April 1988, senior defense official Colonel Rahimi stated that "we have also succeeded in manufacturing missiles with a range of 324 km,"[50] and reports indicated that Iran began assembling Scud-Bs in 1988.

In October 1989, Iran Revolutionary Guards Corps (IRGC) commander Mohsen Rezai visited Pyongyang and may have discussed expanding the Isfahan missile complex and buying the Scud-C.[51] A November 1990 North Korean delegation visiting Tehran may have finalized Scud-C sales to Iran. Iran received about sixty Scud-Cs from early 1991 to 1992, and tested the missile in May 1991; it also obtained five to ten Scud-C launchers (including four launchers delivered in 1995).[52]

Iran moved beyond Scuds to build intermediate-range Shehab-3 and Shehab-4 missiles. In 1993, several Iranian delegations visited North Korea. On December 25, 1993, U.S. officials noted that North Korea had delayed transfers to Iran for unstated reasons (which could have included diplomacy surrounding nuclear inspections, production problems, or final arrangement problems with Iran), and Israel's *Ha'aretz* carried a similar report on January 4, 1994.[53] Iran probably then turned to Russia for missile technology.

The Shehab-3 has an estimated range of 800 miles (1,300 km) with a 750 kg warhead. In an August 2, 1998, statement, General Mohammad Bagher Qalibaf, head of the Revolutionary Guards air wing, noted that the Shehab-3 was a 53 foot long missile traveling at a speed of 4,300 miles per hour (1.9 km/second) and carrying a 1 ton payload to an altitude of 820,000 feet (250 km);[54] while the 1.9 km/second velocity is that for a 400 km range system, the 250 km apogee is that for a 1,000 km range system.

The Shehab-3 is derived from the Nodong but may have some differences. Iran is believed to have built (with varying degrees of foreign assistance) the fuel tanks, warhead, and body sections, and imported the guidance and motor systems from North Korea. Russian companies and technicians may have helped in designing an engine for the missile, but did not have success in integrating Russian flight control and other subsystems.[55] On December 15, 1997, satellite reconnaissance of the Shahid Hemmat Industrial Group detected the heat signature of an engine test, which was the sixth such test in 1997.

Iran flight-tested the Shehab-3 on July 22, 1998. The missile did not cover its full range and exploded or was detonated about 100 seconds into the flight, either because of a mishap or because the technical team was satisfied with its performance and detonated it by remote control.[56] On July 16, 2000, a second Shehab-3 test was apparently a success. During the third Shehab-3 test in September 2000, the missile exploded shortly after launch. Tehran noted that this missile was a solid-fuel Shebab-3D (which would be different from the liquid-fuel Shehab-3; the Federation of American Scientists clarified that the missile probably had a solid-fuel second stage), and was intended to launch communication satellites.[57] The reference to communication satellites ties in with Iran's Shehab-4 project.

Iran's Shehab-4 is reportedly based on the RD-214 engine that powered Russia's ss-4. The 1950s vintage 30–40 ton liquid-fuel ss-4 had a 2,000 km range with a 1.4 ton warhead or greater ranges with lighter warheads, and also formed the first stage for satellite launchers. In February 1999, Defense Minister Ali Shamkhani announced that Iran would test a motor for a Shehab-4 satellite launcher. He noted that this rocket "has no military use and will not be produced on a large scale," because Iran already had "the deterrent capability it wanted with the Shahab-3 missile"; he added that an earlier engine test had mechanical problems.[58] Iran's interest in a longer range Shehab-5 remains unclear. It could build such a long-range multistage missile using an ss-4 / Shehab-4 (or Taepodong-2) first stage and a Shehab-3 second stage.

A combination of domestic capability and foreign technical assistance furthered Iran's missile programs. In terms of foreign assistance, reports note that China's Great Wall Industry provided missile testing and telemetry equipment, while Russian assistance took three forms—the transfer of materials and components, transfer of manufacturing and testing equipment, and training and know-how.[59] Russian firms assisted in the wind-tunnel testing of nose cones, the design of guidance and propulsion systems, and a solid-fuel project.[60] The German government traced several Iranian efforts to buy dual-use components such as gyroscopes and targeting systems from German firms in 1996–97. In April 2000, Washington sanctioned North Korea's Changgwang Sinyong Corporation and four Iranian entities—the Ministry of Defense and Armed Forces Logistics, the Aerospace Industries Organization, the Shahid Hemmat Industrial Group, and the Sanam Industries Group—for the transfer of major systems and subsystems such as rocket stages, guidance systems, or production facilities.

Iran's missile development is also supported by a modest defense industry. Anthony Cordesman notes that Iran has 240 state-owned arms plants under the Ministry of Defense, the Defense Industries Organization (DIO), the Revolutionary Guards, and the Reconstruction Jihad Ministry, as well as 12,000 privately owned workshops.[61] The DIO (which manages Iran's aircraft industry and some of its electronics industry) oversees Iran's missile activities based at the Shahid Hemmat Industrial Group northeast of Tehran and the Sanam Industries Group. Iran's missile infrastructure includes two assembly plants, a design center, a test range, and smaller design and refit facilities.

Overall, the MTCR delayed Iran's intermediate-range missile programs for several years. Further delays would have resulted if Russian, Chinese, and North Korean firms had more completely curbed their missile-related training and technology exports to Iran. Yet Iran tested medium-range missiles from 1998 onward, demonstrating that it could develop these missiles (albeit with a low production rate and poor guidance systems) thereafter without significant foreign assistance.

Security Motivations

Iran sought ballistic missiles after its cities were subject to a sustained missile assault from Iraq, and Tehran could not adequately respond because of an international arms embargo. Security concerns about its regional neighbors and from the international environment also drive Iran's missile activity. Regionally, Iraq's weapons of mass destruction and missile programs are Iran's primary security threat, although those Iraqi programs were curbed by the UNSCOM regime in the 1990s. In addition, Russia, Turkey, and Pakistan compete with Iran for influence in Afghanistan and Central Asia, while Saudi Arabia and the United States (and its military forces) are Iran's competitors in the Gulf. Internationally, Iran viewed the post–Cold War international system, where the United States was the primary actor and weaker states had reduced leverage, to be a hostile environment.[62] Adding to Tehran's insecurity syndrome is the fact that Washington influenced the World Bank and its Western allies to block aid and investment to Iran, and also influenced Russia, China, Argentina, and India to halt nuclear and missile technology transfers to Iran.

Acquiring nuclear and missile programs may not directly tackle many of the above security concerns. But a nuclear and missile force could reduce Iran's reliance on more expensive conventional weapons. Scud and Shehab-3 missiles would be sufficient for Iran to counter Iraq. The Shehab-3 can strategically counter (but thereby be a security threat to) a nuclear Israel, and may also be intended to deter an Israeli attack against Iran's unconventional facilities. Reflecting this intention, Defense Minister Shamkhani stated: "Thanks to this deterrent punch [of the Shehab-3] Israeli leaders have sharply reduced their threats and hostile language against Iran."[63] Former Revolutionary Guards commander Mohsen Rezai similarly noted that "if Israel directs one missile against our territories, we will retaliate with 10 missiles. We have the capability of making such a retaliation and they are aware of this. Therefore, we don't think that they are considering any military confrontation with us."[64] The Shehab-4 could provide a capability against Turkey and Europe. Finally, conservative Iranian groups opposing the U.S. military presence in the Persian Gulf may seek ICBMs that can strike the United States. Overall, Iran's unconventional force doctrine has two components. Its defensive deterrence and second-strike aspect is preferred by the civilian leadership and the military; its offensive first-strike aspect is preferred by the Revolutionary Guards.[65] In the 1990s, Iran undertook several military exercises involving unconventional operations.

Domestic Politics and Political-Economic Influences

How do domestic politics influence Iran's missile activity? In particular, are reformist coalitions that place a greater emphasis on economic liberalization more inclined to curb Iran's WMD and missile activity? Iran undertook gradual and limited political-economic liberalization in the 1990s, and also partly moderated its foreign policy, but did not decrease its nuclear and missile activities in the corresponding period. Indeed, during the Khomeini-dominated revolutionary regime between 1979 and 1989, characterized by political conservatism and autarkic economic policies, Tehran disavowed and was not extensively pursuing nuclear activity (partly because it had fewer resources to allocate to a nuclear program). Further, Iran did not extensively use chemical weapons in the Iran-Iraq war (it did so in only a few isolated instances).

In the post-Khomeini era, President Rafsanjani pursued limited political and economic liberalization, opting for pragmatism instead of an ideological-revolutionary approach to foreign and economic policy. Economic reforms, privatization, and foreign assistance were intended to repair a war-damaged economy. The new (foreign capital dependent) approach to economic development could not be implemented without a changed foreign policy, because only a moderation in foreign policy could bring in external creditors. At this time, tentative signs of normalization with Iran's neighbors and with the West were discernible. Iran stayed neutral and did not oppose Coalition actions against Iraq in 1990–91, and also influenced Hezbollah to release Western hostages in Lebanon. As a result, Iran's international image improved, the U.S. ban on Iranian oil imports was relaxed, and Washington released $270 million for military equipment undelivered to Iran after the 1979 revolution. By 1992–93, the United States was Iran's sixth largest supplier of goods, and Iran drew closer to the European Union. Moreover, Iran's economy benefited from debt rescheduling and foreign investment.

Yet Iran's limited political-economic liberalization in the early and mid-1990s coincided with modest arms purchases and nuclear and missile activity. Iran acquired T-72 tanks from Russia and Poland, Kilo-class submarines and Mig-29 and Su-24 aircraft from Russia, and two hundred C-801 and twenty-five to fifty C-802 antiship cruise missiles from China.[66] Further, Iran's missile program, previously restricted to Scud type missiles, advanced to the level of medium-range Shehab-3 missiles.

Three institutional and geopolitical factors explain why Iran's limited political-economic liberalization did not moderate its military and WMD programs in the 1990s; they also provide clues to whether liberalization could restrain proliferation in the future. First, on geopolitical grounds, Iran's post-1989 political-economic liberalization coincided with a postwar military reconstruction effort. Tehran sought not only to replace or rebuild its military inventory destroyed in the Iran-Iraq war, but also to upgrade its obsolete major weapons systems. Thus, while Iran's defense spending somewhat decreased (a decrease required for economic reforms), it still acquired modern conventional forces and embarked upon nuclear and missile activity.

Second, liberalizing reformist groups lacked the institutional power to influence strategic weapons programs. To begin with, the reformist-conservative dichotomy must be clarified: "reformists" are simply the reformist sections of the clerical establishment that has a monopoly over political power. More important, the reformist president and parliament do not make Iran's foreign and security policy. These are dominated by the Supreme Leader and the security forces—institutions that are controlled by conservatives. Further, the armed forces and the Revolutionary Guards (with whom President Rafsanjani maintained, while President Khatami lacked, strong ties) dominate weapons procurement. The Revolutionary Guards have had first choice among certain arms such as missiles and Kilo-class submarines. The Revolutionary Guards ordered the Scud-C delivered by North Korea in 1991, and the Revolutionary Guards commander led the 1994 Iranian delegation to North Korea that may have discussed the Nodong missile.[67] Indeed, control over Iran's ballistic missiles strengthens the prestige and status of the Revolutionary Guards.

Third, even if reformists had the institutional capacity to moderate Iran's missile and nuclear programs, they may not seek to completely curb those programs for security reasons. As a result of Iraq's military technology superiority in the Iran-Iraq war, much of Iran's political spectrum agrees on the need for a professional and technologically modern military.

The proposition that conservative groups are more supportive of a nuclear and missile program than reformist groups needs further clarification. There is some (but only some) empirical evidence supporting this proposition. For example, the conservative inclination for a WMD program can be seen in the remarks of Revolutionary Guards Commander Yahya Rahim Safavi in April 1998, when he questioned the utility of international nuclear and chemical arms control regimes.[68] Such remarks suggest that hard-line groups place little stock in and are willing to ignore international arms control regimes and obligations; and these hard-line factions have considerable influence on Iran's WMD decisions. Conversely, pragmatist groups that prefer reintegration with the international community would be less willing to violate international control commitments and treaty obligations; and Iran's foreign ministry favors international arms control commitments.[69] To take another example, a leadership change in the Atomic Energy Organization of Iran (AEOI) in 1997 was accompanied by some opposition in the Iranian parliament to the costs of the Bushehr nuclear project; this was a sign that liberalizing-reformist sections of parliament were not averse to restraining Iran's nuclear activity.[70] Liberal-reformist groups also noted that South Asia's nuclear tests weakened India's and Pakistan's international standing and were not an example to follow. In contrast, hard-line domestic groups urged Iran to join the nuclear club, more for reasons of prestige and less out of concern about any security threat from a nuclear-armed Pakistan.[71] To take a third example, in February 2000, Iran's newly elected reformist parliamentarians held out the possibility of rapprochement with the United States if it took practical steps toward conciliation.[72]

However, a point of counterevidence should be noted. Even some reformists are not opposed to WMD activity; for example, Ayatollah Mohajerani, a liberal Minister of Culture and Islamic Guidance in the Khatami administration, had in October 1992 called for nuclear weapons to counter Israel's nuclear capabilities. Michael Eisenstadt points out that pragmatists are nevertheless Persian nationalists seeking a strong Iran, and may not be averse to a nuclear program, especially under compelling security considerations.[73]

On balance, security concerns drive Iran's missile and nuclear programs, but under stable security conditions, political-economic considerations can have some influence on those programs. Thus, does deeper internal liberalization offer prospects for strengthening Iran's ties with the West and the United States? Would the economic benefits of such closer ties bolster reformists, and also increase Iran's political-economic dependence on the West that in turn increases international leverage on Iran? Can both these factors cause positive nonproliferation outcomes?

U.S.-Iranian Relations and International Engagement

U.S.-Iranian relations were strained after Iran's 1979 revolution and the hostage crisis, and Washington imposed economic sanctions and broke off diplomatic ties with Tehran. Trade increased between 1990 and 1993 after a partial sanctions relaxation, but the Clinton administration and Congress then again tightened sanctions and prohibited U.S. oil investments in Iran, drastically curbing trade. These sanctions were intended to dissuade foreign investment in Iran's energy sector and deprive it of resources to fund terrorist groups and expand its military capabilities. Washington also persuaded the EU and Japan to block World Bank loans and bilateral credits to Iran.

The U.S. economic embargo hurt an already weak Iranian economy, and therefore Iran had fewer resources for its military and WMD programs. Thus, sanctions hurt Tehran in the world capital market and (when combined with domestic factors which account for much of Iran's economic distress) infuenced Iran's hard currency military expenditures to decrease by half between 1992 and 1994.[74] Further, Washington's 1995–96 sanctions may have reduced Iran's foreign exchange receipts by $2 billion (or 10 percent of all such receipts). While sanctions increased economic constraints and may have slowed Iran's WMD and missile programs, they did not actually halt this activity.

The absence of economic ties also decreased Tehran's dependence on the United States, which in turn reduced Washington's leverage on Tehran. Echoing this view in January 1998, President Khatami stated that U.S. sanctions had reduced Iran's dependence on Washington so that "today we feel no need for ties with the United States."[75] Clarifying this statement, Gary Sick noted that although Iranian leaders such as President Khatami accept that U.S. oil and gas technology would boost Iran's energy development, Iran diversified its sources of technology by importing items from European firms. If, as suggested above, Iran finds alternative suppliers and therefore does not need ties with Washington, there are few incentives that Washington can offer Tehran to curb its missile program. Policy makers and analysts consequently called for relaxing the U.S. trade boycott in order to have some influence in Tehran.[76]

Although official diplomatic and economic ties remained banned, U.S.-Iranian hostility has gradually decreased since 1997. President Khatami's January 7, 1998, CNN speech called for cultural exchanges to break the wall of mistrust. In June 1998, Secretary of State Madeleine Albright offered to explore new confidence-building measures and develop a road map to better relations, but added that Washington's embargo would remain because Iran continued to support terrorism, committed human rights violations, and pursued missile and nuclear programs. These concerns and Iran's opposition to the Middle East peace process led others to make similar arguments.[77] In February 2000, following liberal-reformist victories in Iran's parliamentary elections, Washington made positive speeches but still did not lift sanctions. In addition, Washington found it difficult to locate the appropriate Iranian groups for a diplomatic dialogue.

Tehran also continued to rebuff Washington, in part because reformists could not easily support closer ties with the United States. The Iranian revolution was inspired by the desire to rid Iran of its dependence on the West, and thus the Iranian polity remained sensitive to foreign influences and rapprochement with the United States. Direct U.S.-Iranian talks on security issues (similar to U.S.–North Korean nuclear and missile talks) are politically difficult for Tehran because they could generate a backlash from Iran's hard-liners, and therefore engagement may have to be initially pursued through unofficial channels. As Geoffrey Kemp notes, "Until the political crisis in Iran between reformists and conservatives is more muted, however, no significant change in U.S.-Iranian relations can be expected."[78] If Washington does engage Tehran, either for geostrategic reasons (the two sides had partially common interests against the Taliban in Afghanistan, and also had a common adversary in Iraq), or because of Iran's domestic liberalization that enables such engagement, then resumed U.S. ties might have three consequences that could moderate Tehran's missile program.

First, the lifting of sanctions can strengthen liberalizing groups such as the Khatami presidency against hard-line domestic opponents. The *New York Times* noted that as a result of a May 1998 U.S. sanctions waiver, "Khatami may now be able to portray the removal of the barrier to the big energy investment as the first significant fruit of his policies of increased openness."[79] While the lifting of sanctions alone will not solve Iran's economic problems or guarantee further democracy, it will boost public support for reformist factions. Such public support can help a liberalizing government gain greater institutional power. If the influence of hard-liners is reduced, reformists would be in a better position to take more concrete steps toward meeting U.S. concerns.[80]

Second, the lifting of sanctions would encourage Tehran to undertake structural economic reform.[81] A consequently liberalized economy that is dependent on external financial support increases the international community's leverage on Tehran.

Third, U.S. ties and international engagement would reduce Iran's concerns about a military threat from American forces in the Gulf. Such engagement would diminish threat perceptions and moderate the conflict-prone worldview that dominates strategic thinking in Iran.[82] This in turn would alleviate some of the domestic pressure for a WMD program. Such engagement may be pursued in parallel with Tehran's own desire for normalization with its regional neighbors and the West. This desire was manifest in President Khatami's visits to Saudi Arabia, Syria, and Qatar in 1999 (the first by an Iranian head of state to the Arab world in twenty years), and to Italy and the Vatican, France, and Germany in 1999–2000.

International engagement that strengthens liberalizing groups in Iran may still not moderate Iran's missile activity, for a number of reasons. Reformist groups may continue to face institutional constraints in foreign policy making. Liberalizers may also not totally oppose Iran's nuclear and missile activity, because there is a general recognition across Iran's political spectrum about the necessity for modernized defense forces to counter regional threats.

Yet Iran faced a threatening regional environment in the 1980s but pursued only limited WMD activity. Later, it signed the Chemical Weapons Convention in 1997, an indication of its support for internationally recognized WMD restraints (though groups in Iran were still suspected of pursuing a secret chemical program). And Iranian officials have occasionally suggested that Iran could restrain its missile program.[83] Indeed, Scud or Nodong-class missiles would be sufficient for Iran to counter threats from Iraq and other regional powers. This suggests that if Iran's geopolitical environment stabilizes (for example, if it is integrated into the international community, and if the most threatening WMD programs such as those in Iraq are constrained by the nonproliferation regime), then Iran could limit its missile ambitions. It may then be willing to rely on short-range missiles to supplement strengthened conventional forces for its national security.

Tehran's missile program is likely to mature despite the MTCR's embargoes. Technology barriers alone are unlikely to halt this program, but can restrain it to Shehab-3 (and perhaps Shehab-4) systems for several years. Those missiles lack accurate guidance and cannot strike much farther than the Middle East or Southern and Central Europe. In this period, engagement could influence Tehran's

WMD program in three ways. Engagement could decrease Tehran's insecurity syndrome, thus reducing its security need for missiles; it could strengthen liberalizing groups within Iran who may give priority to economic restructuring and ties with the West in exchange for concessions on their WMD programs; and it could, especially in the middle term, create a situation of structural dependency, which allows the West further leverage on Tehran's nuclear and missile activity. But in the absence of significant political engagement or improvements in regional security, Iran could proceed to develop a mature missile force.

ASSESSING REGIONAL MISSILE PROGRAMS

The MTCR's technology barriers slow down but do not entirely halt target missile programs. National missile decisions are ultimately influenced by security considerations and political-economic conditions. Improvements in regional security or a security umbrella from an external power, combined with domestic political-economic liberalization and interdependence with the United States, curbed missile programs in Argentina, Brazil, South Africa, South Korea, and Taiwan. In the absence of regional security improvements, India, Pakistan, Iran, and North Korea were less influenced by external pressure and continued their missile activity. But international engagement with these countries could enhance prospects for constraining their missile programs.

In the long term, however, the political, economic, and security factors that curb proliferation may diminish over time and under a changed international system. As regional powers diversify their economies and exports, and consequently if their degree of interdependence with the United States decreases, they will become less subject to U.S. influence. American power preponderance in the international system may also decrease. Further, a number of states that curbed their missile and space aspirations in the early 1990s have been reviving them since the late 1990s, or could do so in the future. This desire for missile programs could arise either out of renewed security concerns, or to seek profits from missile exports or space programs. In a future international system characterized by declining U.S. leverage on regional powers, U.S. pressure alone may not be able to check such renewed missile aspirations. In this situation, could the missile nonproliferation regime curb proliferation? The following chapter analyzes the institutional components of the regime to answer that question.

8

Toward a Treaty Regime: Five Institutional Options to Tackle Missile Proliferation

In November 2002 at The Hague, ninety-three countries adopted and signed an International Code of Conduct for missiles. The Code had gained precedence over another missile nonproliferation initiative, a global control system (GCS) for missiles that was discussed during 2000–2001 at meetings in Moscow. The GCS and Code of Conduct contained important confidence-building measures (CBMS). They called upon states to increase the transparency of their missile programs and provide notification of rocket launches. In a third missile initiative, a UN experts group examined ways to curb missile proliferation. And in a further initiative, the United States and Russia signed agreements for a joint data exchange center (JDEC). When established, the JDEC would provide information on U.S. and Russian rocket launches and preclude a false missile attack warning. Can the MTCR's technology barriers, along with confidence-building measures of the Code of Conduct and JDEC, restrain missile proliferation? Would an NPT type treaty be necessary if the MTCR and missile confidence-building measures are not sufficient to contain missile proliferation? These questions are explored in this chapter.

The first section of this chapter assesses how well the MTCR has tackled the two issues that fall within its scope: restricting missile technology transfers and thwarting missile development in target states. The second section analyzes whether the MTCR's supply embargo can be retained in the long term; it examines national perspectives on the MTCR, and the regime's consolidation and future prospects. The third section explores the need for a broader missile nonproliferation regime because of increasing trends in missile proliferation, the possible revival of missile sales, and the limitations of ad hoc missile elimination measures. The fourth section examines five policy initiatives and institutional options to strengthen the missile nonproliferation regime: regional missile free zones, global intermediate-range missile bans, flight-test bans, verification mechanisms, and space service initiatives.

ASSESSING THE MTCR, 1987–2002

Missile Exports and Technology Transfers

In its first fifteen years, the MTCR substantially halted missile sales and technology transfers. On the issue of missile sales, two major missile exporters, Russia and China, are not known to have exported ballistic missiles since the early 1990s. The third major exporter, North Korea, reduced the quantity but perhaps not the quality of its missile sales in the middle and late 1990s. The missile regime also moderately controlled technology transfers. Major suppliers such as West European states, Russia, and China adopted and implemented strengthened export controls, although Russian and Chinese firms nevertheless supplied some dual-use industrial technology to regional powers. Moreover, the MTCR raised international awareness of missile proliferation, and it provided states with a structure and technological guidelines to deal with missile proliferation.

The MTCR's technical parameters also expanded to prohibit the transfer of a wider category of missiles and related technologies. In 1987, the MTCR covered only nuclear capable missiles, which were defined as missiles capable of delivering a 500 kg payload over a 300 km range. By 1993 the regime covered any missile system intended for WMD delivery regardless of its payload weight.

Further, in the mid-1990s, the MTCR tightened its supply embargo by covering the transshipment of missile technology. U.S. attempts to interdict North Korean vessels carrying Scud missiles to Iran and Syria were successful in 1991, but failed in 1992. In January 1993, German authorities halted a ship carrying machine parts to Syria. In late 1996 at Zurich airport, Swiss officials intercepted missile parts en route from North Korea and China to Egypt.[1] The 1996 MTCR plenary examined controls by states that might unknowingly contribute to proliferation through transshipment facilities such as ports. Transshipment and export control seminars were also added to the MTCR's outreach activities. These included a 1997 Asian Export Control Seminar in Tokyo, subsequent Export Control Seminars in 1998 in Berlin and Neuchatel (Switzerland), and transshipment workshops in Washington, London, and Switzerland, attended by Cyprus, Hong Kong, Jordan, Malta, South Korea, Singapore, and the United Arab Emirates, in 1996–97.

In addition to expansions in the regime's scope, the MTCR's domain greatly increased. By 2002, the regime had thirty-three members plus additional adherents, reflecting wider international acceptance of the regime's prohibitions against missile technology transfers.

Target Missile Programs and MTCR Effects

As a result of its tight technology embargo, the MTCR restrained many target programs. Nine out of fourteen target states did not build medium-range missiles in the 1990s, but this observation warrants closer examination on three issues—changes in regime effectiveness over time, three positive outcomes, and several types of effects on target programs.

The MTCR's effectiveness has varied with time. In the regime's first three years (1987–90), few target states had curbed their missile activity. Over the next five years (1990–95), many target missile programs were curbed: South Africa, Argentina, Taiwan, South Korea, and Egypt restrained or scrapped their missile aspirations. Yet in the late 1990s, though some missile-seeking states remained thwarted from advancing their missile programs (Libya, Iraq, Syria), no additional state curbed its missile program. Instead, key regional powers (North Korea, Iran, Pakistan) that were previously constrained to short-range missiles tested more powerful medium-range missiles in 1998. Thus the MTCR's influence on target programs somewhat decreased since the mid-1990s.

Moreover, variations in the MTCR's impact are only partly correlated with the number of suppliers in the regime. In the late 1980s, many key suppliers remained outside the MTCR, and many target programs were continuing. By the mid-1990s, more suppliers joined the regime, and many target missile programs were curbed. Yet in the late 1990s, although further suppliers joined the MTCR, no additional target missile programs were curbed.

The MTCR has had three positive or semipositive outcomes. First, the regime thwarted missile activity among technologically very weak states; its technology barriers were substantially responsible for thwarting missile development in Libya and Syria in the 1990s (though Syria eventually built Scuds thereafter). Second, the MTCR was part of a process that curbed missile activity in technologically more capable states such as South Korea, Taiwan, Argentina, Brazil, South Africa, and Egypt. Although technology embargoes did not completely halt target missile programs, they did hinder and delay them. Some programs (those in Argentina, Egypt, Brazil, and South Africa) were even more vulnerable because they employed sophisticated high-performance technologies that increased their reliance on foreign suppliers.[2] But given adequate demand-pulls, these states may still have proceeded with more feasible lower technology programs. They ultimately constrained their missile programs because of political considerations. Third, while the MTCR could not prevent some technologically weaker states—Pakistan, North Korea, and Iran—from advancing their missile projects in the 1990s, it still had a modest impact on these states. It delayed them from rapidly advancing to a higher category of missiles—from 100–300 km range systems to 1,000 km range Nodong class missiles for Iran and Pakistan; and from single-stage Nodong class to multiple-stage 2,000 km range Taepodong-1 class missiles for North Korea. These states took five to seven years (between the early and late 1990s) for such advances, and technology embargoes accounted for some of the delays.

While the MTCR generally delayed, hindered, and raised the costs of target missile programs, its actual effects varied across countries. The specific type of effect and missile component that was hindered (airframes and missile bodies, engines, rocket stages, rocket fuel, guidance and control systems and electronics, reentry heat shields and nose cones, test equipment, machine tools, and manufacturing equipment), varied from case to case. Several such effects are worth noting.

Some target states *could not build* particular missile subsystems without foreign technological assistance. The Condor project encountered obstacles in liquid propulsion, guidance and control, and reentry systems (and Brazil also could not develop liquid propulsion). The MTCR successfully blocked these projects.

Some states were *psychologically deterred* rather than technologically blocked by the MTCR. These states did not encounter actual technological obstacles, but they factored the anticipated high costs of MTCR embargoes in decisions to constrain rocket activity. Thus, South Africa was deterred from advancing its IRBM into a satellite launcher, while Taiwan was deterred from even starting a dual-use space rocket program.

Despite (or because of) MTCR hindrances, some states *indigenously built* missile systems. They either anticipated MTCR embargoes and did not seek to import these systems, or they built these systems after importing them was denied. India built radar phase shifters, guidance sensors, carbon composites for reentry heat shielding, fuel shell catalysts, magnesium plates, and maraging steel.

States circumvented the MTCR to *import items* from non-MTCR states or dual-use items and construction equipment; these efforts were successful in some cases and failed in others because the attempted transfers were halted. Egypt sought guidance systems and carbon for reentry nose cones, and collaborated with North Korea in its Scud upgrades; Iraq sought turbopumps and gyroscopes; Syria may have sought assistance for a solid-fuel plant and missile assembly facilities; Libya reportedly attempted to acquire solid fuel, furnaces, lathes and machine parts, and wind tunnels; North Korea is believed to have imported stainless steel, control systems, and transport vehicles, and received assistance in upgrading engines; Iran sought (and in some cases received) motors and rocket stages, guidance systems, wind tunnels, gyroscopes, and production facilities; Pakistan is believed to have sought or imported engines, fuel tanks, test equipment, and manufacturing equipment.

The *category of technology* sought by regional powers has varied with time. By the late 1990s, regional powers had difficulties acquiring MTCR category I *complete subsystems* (airframes, engines), and category II *subsystem components* (steel for airframes, chemicals for rocket fuel). They therefore had to start missile activity from an even more basic level: they increasingly sought the *manufacturing equipment* to build subsystems and subsystem components. Even here, they have not always been able to procure advanced equipment from the West, and therefore sought less advanced equipment from other states. Thus a 2001 congressional report notes: "Increasingly rigorous and effective export controls and cooperation among supplier countries have led the other foreign WMD programs to look elsewhere for many controlled dual-use goods. Machine tools, spare parts for dual-use equipment, and widely available materials, scientific equipment, and specialty metals were the most common items sought."[3] In summary, the MTCR has had a varied and mixed impact on target missile programs.

Curbing the Range, Pace, and Size of Target Missile Programs

The MTCR's technology embargoes can further constrain target states' missile activity in three ways. First, they will delay the development of even longer range missiles. Iran and Pakistan could be restrained to their 1,000–1,500 km range single-stage missiles or 2,000–3,000 km range two-stage upgrades to those missiles for about five years. North Korea could be restricted to the Taepodong-1 and Taepodong-2 type missiles for these years. In terms of missile development time, regional powers typically take five years to build a short-range missile, and five to seven additional years to advance to intermediate-range missiles. For example, North Korea required nine years to progress from the 300 km range Scud (1984) to the 1,000 km range Nodong (1993). It then took five more years to test the multiple-stage 2,000 km range Taepodong-1 (1998), and a prototype 4,000–6,000 km range Taepodong-2 was also ready by 1999–2000. Both Iran and Pakistan possibly began to develop Nodong infrastructure and components in 1993–94 and tested these missiles in 1998. India took fourteen years to progress from the 1,500 km range multiple stage SLV-3 (1979) to an 8,000 km range PSLV (1993). The Rumsfeld Commission noted: "With the external help now readily available, a nation with a well-developed, Scud-based ballistic missile infrastructure would be able to achieve first flight of a long range missile, up to and including intercontinental ballistic missile (ICBM) range (greater than 5,500 km), within about five years of deciding to do so."[4]

Second, during this time frame, technology embargoes could restrain a target state's production capacity. For example, they can hinder North Korea from building more than about two Taepodong-2 missiles annually. The historical record from the 1980s and 1990s is that regional powers can annually build 50 to 100 short-range Scud type missiles (this was North Korea's Scud production rate) or 10 to 20 medium-range missiles (this was North Korea's estimated Nodong production in the 1990s, and is India's planned Agni-2 production rate). Yet they may annually build only one or two intercontinental-range systems such as the 130 ton booster used on India's PSLV (that had six launches in eight years between 1993 and 2001). Third, technology embargoes can hinder regional powers from developing more sophisticated guidance and maneuvering systems. This implies that, since missile inaccuracy increases with distance and long range missiles are therefore less accurate, regional power ICBMs without advanced guidance systems may entirely miss a target city when fired from halfway across the planet.

Ultimately, these three constraining effects will progressively diminish over time, and regional powers could build five to ten or more ICBMs annually in the period around or after 2010. On this issue, it is worth comparing the above missile production capabilities with those of China, the United States, and Russia when they began their missile programs in the 1950s and 1960s (when their GDP levels were still greater than regional powers' 1990s GDP levels).[5] Following its first IRBM test in the early 1960s, China deployed about five IRBMs annually for five years, and ten IRBMs annually thereafter. Beijing's ICBM type rockets—the CZ-2 space launcher and its DF-5 ICBM equivalent—were tested in 1975 and 1980, respectively. Beijing then built about five to ten such rockets annually, of which one was used as a space launcher and two were deployed as ICBMs. The Soviet Union and United States both tested ICBMs in 1957–58, just four years after their first IRBM tests. They initially built a few tens of ICBMs annually. By the middle and late 1960s, they deployed 50 to 100, and then up to 300, ICBMs annually. Beyond these comparative statistics, regional power missile programs would more rapidly advance when they acquire new technologies (such as computer assisted design) and better trained manpower, if they focus on simple rather than sophisticated technologies, and if their governments allocate more resources to missile programs.

Thus technology barriers can limit the quality as well as the quantity of target missile programs, but they cannot prevent regional powers from eventually acquiring small forces of intermediate- and long-range missiles. Technology controls alone cannot stop missile proliferation because virtually all missile technology can be commercially obtained or developed by a country with an airframe industry, chemicals such as nitric acid and hydrazine, and the ability to repair jet and turboprop engines.[6] If a state has strong motivations and the necessary capital from oil or mineral revenues to develop missiles, it could do so either independently or by pooling resources with other states. Indeed, the missile trade among regional powers dates back to the 1970s, when Egypt transferred Scud missiles to North Korea. The Argentina-Egypt-Iraq Condor project, Israeli support for South Africa's rocket program, and Brazilian assistance to Iraq and Iran are other examples of missile cooperation among regional powers. Cooperative weapons programs have many advantages: they enable states to get the most from scarce technological resources; they create opportunities to broaden national technological and scientific sectors; and they foster diplomatic relationships which strengthen technological and political bonds between states.[7] Thus regional powers can, in time, overcome technological obstacles and build medium- and long-range missiles.

REGIME CONSOLIDATION

Although technology embargoes are not sufficient to halt missile proliferation, they remain necessary to at least slow the pace of target missile programs. Therefore, MTCR members must maintain technology embargoes if the regime is to be even partially successful. An examination of national perspectives on technology controls and the MTCR, and an analysis of the three components of regimes—power, interests, and knowledge—can usefully indicate whether states will comply with the MTCR in the middle term.

International Perspectives on Technology Controls

The technology sharing approach in arms control, which had its intellectual roots in the 1954 Atoms for Peace initiative and in NPT Article IV, was prevalent in the 1960s and 1970s. Yet by the 1980s, it was increasingly challenged by the technology denial and supply-side approaches. The supply-side approach acquired greater international acceptance partly because of increased proliferation concerns after the Gulf War. This acceptance is reflected at the 1997 NPT Preparatory Conference where several countries, including former targets of technology embargoes such as South Africa, as well as Australia, Japan, and Canada, endorsed the EU view that export controls were an obligation complementary to NPT safeguards. Developing countries nevertheless have reservations on technology embargoes, and analysts have noted that "for restraints to be perceived as legitimate and thus effective, they must be the result of difficult but more comprehensive deliberations that result in restraints that the major powers observe along with the lesser powers."[8]

Further, analysts have challenged the legality of the MTCR's actions in impeding space activity; they argue that regimes cannot "ignore the sovereign right of [a state] to launch objects into outer space through its own means, unless a new universal international treaty establishes otherwise."[9] In practice, despite their reservations about excessive technology denials, MTCR members and at least some other suppliers have largely conformed with the regime's prescriptions against technology transfers.

International Perspectives on the MTCR: Regional Powers, China, Russia

In the 1980s and 1990s, although many states were supportive of the MTCR and acknowledged its legitimacy, some were concerned about enforcement through coercion (U.S. sanctions), and emphasized that the MTCR should not impinge on national sovereignty, the national right to space technology, and national security. The views of several states on the MTCR's technology barriers, and on missile proliferation in general, are discussed below.

In Argentina, domestic groups stressed a national sovereign right to dual-use technology and opposed President Menem's 1992–93 decision to scrap the Condor program. Argentina's opposition argued that MTCR membership "must be achieved without accepting the precondition of destroying our country's ability to possess [dual-use] components and limitations that are incompatible with sovereignty."[10] Given these strong domestic pressures, Argentina revived its space launcher aspirations in the late 1990s.

In Brazil, a similar theme about sovereign rights to space technology is manifest. When joining the MTCR, Brazilian officials stated that the regime would not limit their national space program or harm international cooperation in such programs. To extract greater domestic support, they added the benefits of signing the MTCR: it would show the international community that Brazil was contributing to nonproliferation, and would be a step toward obtaining sensitive space technology.[11]

In South Korea, some analysts have echoed North-South structural conflict themes, arguing, "The MTCR passes for an instrument of an exclusive 'nobles club' in that the 5 big nuclear powers can enjoy their vested rights to the already-developed missiles and even make them improved."[12] However, at a policy level, the Korean government supported and joined the MTCR. Yet, under domestic pressure, it still sought missiles beyond MTCR limits rather than reliance on the United States to counter foreign threats, and successfully bargained for 300–500 km range missiles and a space program when joining the MTCR. Taiwan's polity echoed somewhat similar themes—a need for national action (rather than dependence on the United States) to counter a neighbor's missile force. Taiwanese legislators did not challenge the MTCR, but called for cruise missiles and ballistic missiles to counter similar missiles in China.

North Korea had both practical and ideological reservations about the MTCR. On practical grounds, it sought financial compensation in exchange for halting its missile program. On ideological grounds, it echoed North-South issues and concerns that other states are not criticized for missile activities. For example, in response to Russian criticism of its 1998 Taepodong test, North Korea noted that it had simply launched a satellite, and that in similar cases, the United States, Russia, and other countries do not provide prior warning. It added that "the world cannot be divided into countries with the right to produce missiles and threaten others, and countries that are denied this right."[13]

In India, issues of sovereignty and great-power aspirations have been two sources of opposition to the MTCR. Some analysts argued that the Indian missile program "shows that this country means to retain its sovereign decision on national security matters."[14] Bureaucrats and government officials routinely declared that "no country can exert pressure on us," and that defense industry programs such as the Prithvi missile "established confidence that we can [build such projects] irrespective of the technology control regimes."[15] In response, the government is hard pressed to show restraint and frequently declares in Parliament that it is not succumbing to U.S. pressure. In practice, New Delhi had shown some missile restraint, for example by not testing Agni missiles from 1994 to 1999. Further, Indian analysts made occasional statements favoring a global INF arrangement.[16] This short-term restraint was overtaken by political events. The BJP government's 1998 nuclear decision caused the revival of the Agni program by 1999.

Although it has not halted its missile program, New Delhi has conformed with the MTCR's norms against technology exports. It is not known to have exported rocket technologies to states of concern. It also halted a North Korean vessel suspected of carrying a missile-relevant cargo to Pakistan in June 1999. But in a different context, ad hoc statements against the MTCR by India's leading missile scientist raised concerns that Delhi could reverse its export control commitments in the middle term.[17]

In Pakistan, three views on the MTCR have been prominent. First, Islamabad sought the MTCR's support to curb India's missile activities, which implies acceptance of the regime, at least to deal with missile programs in other states. Islamabad raised the issue of New Delhi's missile advances with MTCR members, but "despite the fact that there was an international protest over its missile program, New Delhi test fired its missiles."[18] Second, Islamabad opposed the MTCR's restrictions on its own missile activity; Washington's MTCR-related sanctions have drawn heavy criticism. U.S. sanctions were described as "unacceptable" and "galling," especially because "Pakistan has stood by the U.S. as a 100 percent ally in the last half century."[19] Islamabad expressed concern that "the U.S. is also exerting pressure on its allies; this is why Japan refused to give a $400 million loan to Pakistan."[20] It called Washington's November 2000 missile sanctions "unwarranted and unjustified."[21] Third, Pakistan is not known to have exported missile technology, but a visit by Saudi Arabia's defense minister to Pakistan's missile facilities in 1999 raised concerns about this issue.[22]

Further views on the MTCR and missile proliferation can be examined in the context of UN Resolution 54/54 F (December 1999). This resolution noted that UN members were "Convinced of the need for a comprehensive approach towards missiles, in a balanced and non-discriminatory manner," and requested "the Secretary-General to seek the views of all member states on the issue of missiles in all its aspects, and to submit a report to the General Assembly at its fifty-fifth session."[23] Seven states (India, Japan, Jordan, Qatar, the U.K., Iran, Bangladesh) submitted their views by August 2000, and nine additional states (Belarus, Bolivia, El Salvador, Mexico, Russian Federation, Saudi Arabia, Sweden [on behalf of the European Union], China, and Pakistan) responded by August 2001.[24] Most of these states recognized that missile proliferation was an international concern, but noted that it was linked to national and regional security considerations, and also observed the potential peaceful uses of space rocket technology. Many states further noted the absence of missile nonproliferation treaties similar to the NPT, CWC, and BWC. The Swedish (and EU) statement noted "an urgent need for the development of globally accepted norms in support of ballistic missile non-proliferation." The U.K. noted that states should "examine how to promote restraint and roll-back" in their missile programs. It added that "Making development of satellite launch vehicles more transparent would be a first step towards addressing more contentious issues" about the dual civil-military use of space launchers. National views on the MTCR also varied. Pakistan noted that the MTCR was not an "equitable framework" and added that "it is essential that the MTCR be replaced by a comprehensive multilateral dialogue" on missile nonproliferation. In contrast, Japan noted that the MTCR "plays a key role" in halting missile proliferation, and its statement did not seek treaty bans (though at a March 2001 workshop for Asian states, Tokyo questioned whether the MTCR's Code of Conduct adequately represented the Asian view). Iran called for a study group on missile nonproliferation.

Russia's and China's initial opposition to the MTCR and their mixed perceptions of the regime were discussed in Chapter 3. It also should be noted that Moscow and Beijing both criticized North Korea's August 1998 missile test, reflecting their concerns over missile proliferation, especially because it provokes U.S. missile defenses. This concern implies that both Russia and China have a stake in checking missile proliferation through the MTCR. Both Russia and China also took stronger steps to curb their missile technology exports in the middle and late 1990s, though these efforts had mixed results. Further, if economic crises in these states deepen, their firms would face pressures to export technology, and their governments may be unwilling, or unable, to halt such exports. Thus, in the middle-term, Russia's and China's strict compliance with the MTCR remains uncertain, and would depend on prevailing political and economic circumstances.

Regime Continuation—Power, Interests, and Knowledge

The sources of cooperation in regimes—state power, national interests, and knowledge (about the perils of missile proliferation)—can generally be expected to perpetuate the MTCR in the middle term. State power has been a prominent feature in the MTCR. Washington consistently used its power to draw supplier states into the regime, and also used its leverage over regional powers to curb their missile programs. Thus, if U.S. power in the international system endures, this structural feature will help further the MTCR's continuation. Washington's ability to impose sanctions that deter violations, and to provide benefits (such as access to space launches and to U.S. markets and aid) in exchange for regime compliance, can make key suppliers more willing to maintain technology embargoes. The EU and Japan could also offer incentives to states complying with nonproliferation norms.

Besides hegemonic power, the functional demand for and interest in regimes also maintains them. Certain interest-based factors can perpetuate the MTCR. First, the security interest in a missile control regime remains high. Because proliferation ranks among the foremost international security concerns, a number of states that initially opposed the MTCR (for example, Russia and China), or that were targets of the regime (Argentina, Brazil, and South Africa), subsequently joined the regime or accepted its principles against missile technology exports.

The economic interests for violating the regime are not substantial. The MTCR's members—especially its core comprising the Western group—have no strong commercial motivations to undertake missile sales in the near term (but missile sales could revive in the middle term, as discussed below). Moreover, the small financial gains from exporting missile-relevant dual-use technologies are outweighed by the security costs of increased missile proliferation, and by the economic costs of U.S. sanctions for violating the regime. However, economic and industrial lobbies in supplier states remain under commercial pressure to export dual-use technologies such as electronics, chemicals, and manufacturing equipment. If national governments are influenced by or cannot check these domestic lobbies, the MTCR would be weakened.

Social cost considerations also perpetuate the MTCR. States such as Brazil and South Africa joined the regime to prove their international standing, and are reluctant to tarnish their international image by transferring missile technology. In addition, patterns of institutionalized cooperation generally endure and this will also perpetuate the MTCR. The regime is a useful multilateral forum for exchanging information on missile proliferation, and it reduces the transaction costs of multiple bilateral deliberations on the issue. For these reasons, the MTCR is likely to persist and its members can be expected to control missile technology exports, though these controls may be somewhat relaxed in the middle term under economic and political pressures.

MISSILE TRENDS AND NORMS —
IS A BROADER MISSILE REGIME NECESSARY?

The preceding discussion suggests that the MTCR will persist for at least the short term, and its supply embargo remains necessary to delay and constrain target missile programs. If its supply embargo can be maintained, is a broader missile control regime necessary? This question may be examined in light of developments in missile defense and the trends in missile proliferation.

Missile Defense

Regional missile powers may eventually acquire missiles such as Taepodong-1s that can strike Europe, and (albeit initially a very small number of) upgraded Taepodong-2s that can strike the United States. This increased missile capability will create interest in an expanded missile nonproliferation regime to contain the threat. However, if the missile threat can be countered through missile defense, then the interest in more missile controls would be reduced. Thus "knowledge" or information about the technology and politics of missile defense will play an important role in this issue. If missile defense technologies work, and their political consequences (on strategic arms control and Russia's and China's willingness to undertake nuclear force reductions) are manageable, then state interests will shift from missile control to missile defense. But missile defenses may have technological problems and political costs. Any unilateral and unchecked U.S. national missile defense initiatives may prompt Russia and China not only to maintain large offensive forces but also to reduce their commitment to the nonproliferation regime and transfer technology to regional powers, which would worsen the missile threat. In this situation, the interest in an expanded missile control regime will persist, especially because arms control initiatives that limit missile proliferation would also permit defenses to be limited and thereby make them less destabilizing.

Limited Missile Elimination Initiatives

The MTCR's scope does not include missile elimination, but two initiatives outside the MTCR have reduced the global inventory of missiles. First, the START treaties eliminated hundreds of U.S. and Russian long-range missiles (2,810 ICBMS and SLBMs had been eliminated by January 2001). In addition, the 1987 Intermediate Nuclear Force (INF) treaty eliminated about 2,700 missiles; Moscow scrapped some 1,800 IRBMs, and the United States destroyed 108 Pershing-2 IRBMs and over 600 cruise missiles. Second, Washington commercially purchased a few Scuds from East European states. In 1996, the U.S. Army Space and Strategic Defense Command bought four Scud launchers and 31 Scud-B missiles that were used as targets in missile-defense tests.[25]

A further missile elimination initiative, within the MTCR framework, is a policy that required nonnuclear states entering the regime to eliminate their offensive missiles and related technology. Argentina transferred over a dozen missile engines and bodies to Spain for destruction in 1993, and also dismantled missile production facilities. South Africa scrapped missile components and equipment before joining the MTCR in 1995. Other candidates for missile destruction include former Warsaw Pact states seeking to enter NATO, the EU, and the MTCR. Hungary destroyed an estimated twenty Scud-Bs in May 1995, Poland received $1.5 million for Scud destruction in 1996, the Czech Republic eliminated its Scud-Bs between 1988 and 1991, and also eliminated its sixteen SS-23 missiles in 1995 and their two missile launchers in 1996. After protracted negotiations with Washington since 1997, Bulgaria and Slovakia agreed to destroy their few SS-23s. However, Slovakia may retain Scud-Bs, and Kazakhstan, Belarus, and Turkmenistan also retain Scuds, as well as Frogs or SS-21 systems.

The last point brings out this policy's limitations: it does not apply to states that are not (and are not interested in becoming) MTCR members. Moreover, the policy has encountered some prominent obstacles. In 1994–98, Ukraine refused to destroy its Scuds, which delayed its MTCR membership. During Secretary of State Madeleine Albright's March 1998 visit to Kiev, Washington allowed Ukraine to retain its Scuds and still enter the MTCR; Ukraine had adopted strict missile export controls and also scrapped a nuclear deal with Iran.

The destruction of a few hundred missiles (mainly Scuds and SS-23s) by East bloc states and new MTCR entrants was significant because it set a precedent for such initiatives, and the destroyed missiles also became unavailable for export to regional powers. Yet the number of missiles destroyed was still *less than* the number of new missiles (of comparable or longer range) built by regional powers, China, and Russia in the 1990s.

Mixed Trends in Missile and WMD Control

Limited missile-elimination measures have reduced but are not sufficient to halt and reverse missile proliferation. Two contradictory trends emerge from recent developments in missile proliferation. On the positive side, several states curbed their missile aspirations in the 1990s, largely because they had no pressing security need for missiles. Further, some states have no security requirements to replace missiles nearing retirement. This is especially true of former East bloc states. Moreover, if international diplomacy persuades a key proliferator, North Korea, to freeze its missile program and curb its missile exports, the missile nonproliferation regime will be greatly strengthened. Without technical assistance from foreign suppliers such as North Korea, Russia, and China, the missile programs of Pakistan, Iran, Iraq, Syria, Libya, and other regional powers would be restricted to short or intermediate range missiles for several years. During this time, international diplomacy and political-economic pressure and incentives may persuade these states to at least restrain if not totally curb their missile programs.

Regional powers would have to weigh any strategic and security benefits from longer range missiles against the resulting diplomatic and economic costs. The costs of long-range missile programs are that they raise international proliferation concerns, and therefore hinder a regional power's attempts to integrate politically with the international community and gain economic aid and technology transfers. The benefits of a long-range missile are that it may dissuade foreign military strikes against regional powers. Illustrating this, Muammar Qadaffi noted in a 1990 speech: "If we had possessed a deterrent—missiles that could reach New York—we would have hit it at the same moment [as the 1986 U.S. air strike on Libya]. Consequently, we should build this force so that they and others will no longer think about an attack."[26]

Thus, as explored in Chapter 6 and 7, if regional powers such as North Korea, Iran, India, and Pakistan prefer deeper integration with the global community and their regional security environment stabilizes, they may restrain their missile activity to SRBMs or low-capability IRBMs. In such a situation, missile proliferation could be contained, and there would be a less pressing need for a broader missile nonproliferation regime. But if these political developments do not materialize in the middle term, regional powers may continue missile activity and build long-range missiles. Their SRBM and IRBM programs would provide them with the infrastructure for quicker further expansion to long-range missiles— missiles that have benefits even in purely regional conflicts because they can be a means of keeping foreign powers out of regional conflicts.

The negative trends in missile proliferation, and a situation where missile proliferation increases, should be critically considered. The demand for missiles can increase because Scud missiles purchased by several Middle Eastern states in the 1970s and 1980s (and CSS-2 missiles in Saudi Arabia) are nearing retirement. These states would seek to replace those missiles, especially if their neighbors maintain or build new missile arsenals. Several Middle Eastern states are building or acquiring missiles (Syria has aquired Scuds, Egypt is upgrading its Scuds, and Iran is developing Shehab missiles). Initially, missile replacements for states such as Syria, Iraq, and Libya may involve short-range missiles such as 300–600 km range Scud derivatives and M-9s. In time, 1,000 km range Nodongs and longer range Taepodong type missiles could also be built (by Iran, Pakistan, and North Korea) and exported to new clients. If even a few states acquire new generations of missiles, others would also seek missiles (and seek to replace retiring missiles) to counter a neighbor's missile force, and missile proliferation will expand.

In addition, a few states may acquire "strategic" chemical and biological weapons capabilities. Such acquisitions would greatly heighten security concerns among neighboring states and revive their demand (and development efforts) not only for ballistic missiles but also for a WMD-based deterrent. States that have renounced their missile aspirations could, in the absence of international commitments binding them and their neighbors to refrain from missile development, be more inclined to seek missile programs. Such renewed missile programs are unlikely to be halted by technology controls since missile technology would be more easily available in the future. In such a situation, the limited success achieved by the MTCR in the 1990s would disappear, and the missile nonproliferation regime (and possibly even other WMD regimes) could collapse.

International Norms, UN Initiatives, the GCS, and the Code of Conduct

Norms against missile possession and development were not firmly established during the MTCR's first decade. This made it diplomatically easier for states to engage in and avoid serious international repercussions for missile activity. The contrast between norms against nuclear, biological, and chemical (NBC) activities and those against missile activities is worth noting. Any test or use of NBCs would be strongly deplored with trade and aid sanctions. Such sanctions on France, China, India, and Pakistan for their nuclear tests in 1995–96 and 1998 demonstrated the strength of global norms (leading to substantive international responses) against NBC activity. Yet missile tests by India, Pakistan, and Iran were less intensely condemned (though North Korea's missile tests were strongly condemned); no formal UN General Assembly or Security Council resolutions were passed against these missile tests, in contrast to formal resolutions against nuclear tests.

In the UN and other international venues, a growing sentiment for firmer responses to missile proliferation has emerged since the late 1990s, but missile ownership had still not been legally banned. In April 1999 after New Delhi's and Islamabad's missile tests, the UN Secretary General underscored the need for multilaterally negotiated norms against missiles. That year, the UN General Assembly resolutions on arms control and disarmament had a section devoted to missiles, and the UN First Committee also discussed the issue. On October 4, 2000, Iran introduced a resolution on missiles at the UN First Committee. It requested the Secretary General to convene an expert panel and prepare a comprehensive report on all aspects of missile proliferation.[27] The 23-state expert group (comprising Algeria, Argentina, Australia, Brazil, Canada, Chile, China, Egypt, France, Germany, India, Indonesia, Iran, Israel, Japan, Pakistan, Russia, Slovakia, South Africa, South Korea, Ukraine, the United Kingdom, and the United States) met in August 2001, April 2002, and July 2002.

Nongovernmental experts also discussed missile nonproliferation proposals.[28] In parallel, the International Code of Conduct drafted by MTCR members and Moscow's proposed Global Control System (that intended to include non-MTCR members in negotiations) both sought to establish CBMs.

The MTCR's October 2000 draft Code of Conduct referred to Principles, Commitments, Incentives, CBMs, and Organizational Aspects of a code-based (but not legally based) missile regime. Under its CBMs, countries would give annual declarations explaining their ballistic missile and space policy, and also give notice of missile and space rocket launches. Moreover, the Code included a "Commitment by subscribing states to exercise maximum possible restraint in the development, testing and deployment of ballistic missiles capable of delivering weapons of mass destruction, including, where possible, to reduce national holdings of such missiles."[29] The draft Code was refined at the MTCR's September 2001 plenary. It was further discussed at a February 2002 meeting in Paris attended by eighty-six states and at a June 2002 meeting in Madrid attended by nearly a hundred states. The Code's initial signatories included the U.S., Russia, and Libya, but excluded China, Egypt, India, Iran, Israel, North Korea, Pakistan, and Syria. The Code contained important transparency measures, but it did not legally ban missiles; it did not offer incentives for states to renounce missiles (the draft Code's section on incentives was excluded from the final Code); and some states noted that the Code's transparency measures could legitimize rather than proscribe missile programs. The Code also lacked verification mechanisms. Thus, the Code was less comprehensive than, but by 2002 had attained diplomatic priority over, the GCS.

The GCS concept was proposed by Boris Yeltsin at the June 1999 G-8 summit; it was further discussed in March 2000 and February 2001 meetings in Moscow. Its core concepts included a six-part nonproliferation block (the MTCR, Code of Conduct, incentive mechanisms, security assurances, nonproliferation measures, diplomatic and economic enforcement measures), and a six-part transparency block (the two missile and space transparency CBMs of the Code of Conduct, plus launch notifications, technical monitoring of launches, an international data center, and additional CBMs).[30]

The Revival of Missile Sales and Space Exports

Some of the MTCR's gains in curbing missile sales are being reversed. In the 1990s, France approved a cruise missile sale to Bahrain, and the United States exported 100–200 km range ATACM systems to South Korea, Greece, and Turkey. If a few suppliers enter the missile market, others will face fewer constraints to also exporting missiles. Thus, in a situation where the MTCR begins breaking down or being circumvented, the Russian Iskander ss-x-26 missile (a solid-fuel 280 km range Scud successor with satellite and inertial guidance), Chinese M-11s and M-9s, Ukrainian Scuds, and North Korean Nodongs could all be offered for export. Further potential missile suppliers include Iran, which has reportedly given missile assistance to Libya, and possibly supplied Scuds to Congo in 1999;[31] Pakistan, which could sell Shaheen or Ghauri missiles to clients such as Saudi Arabia to bolster political ties and gain economic revenues; and India, which could transfer the India-Russia Brahmos cruise missile and the Prithvi ballistic missile.

Moreover, especially with the growth of the communications industry, states may develop and export space launch technology, causing the further proliferation of dual-use rocket technology.

In a future scenario where any, or all, of the above situations materialize, a broader missile regime going beyond the MTCR's technology embargoes would become necessary, since the MTCR would not be sufficient to tackle missile proliferation. On policy grounds, a broader missile nonproliferation regime containing space service regimes (and other incentives against rocket acquisition), regional missile-free zones and global medium-range missile bans (that provide legal barriers to proliferation), flight-test bans, and verification mechanisms offers a more robust institutional basis through which to contain missile proliferation.

SPACE SERVICE REGIMES

Rockets have both military and civilian applications. Rockets can launch satellites used for communications, weather forecasting, and remote sensing.[32] Yet rockets can also be used (with reentry vehicles) as ballistic missiles. Therefore, states may acquire missile capability through space launch programs. In 2002, nine states or agencies had satellite launch programs (the United States, Russia, Ukraine, the European Space Agency, Japan, China, India, Israel, and Brazil), as shown in Table 8.1; but additional states (South Korea, North Korea, Argentina, Spain, Italy, and Iran) were seeking to build launchers.

Should new space launch programs be permitted? (The 1967 Outer Space Treaty legally establishes space to be free for use by all states and not subject to national appropriation or exclusive control by any regime.) Should they be

Table 8.1. A Comparative Study of Eight Space Programs

Country/ Agency	No. of Launches		First Launch		First use of Cryogenic Technology	Annual Space Expenditure 1990s ($ mil.)	(% GDP)
	1957–1988	1989–2001	LEO	GEO			
U.S.	890	358	1958	1967	1966	25,000	0.5
Russia & CIS	2,107	571	1957	1967	1985	1,000–6,000*	1.0
Europe/ESA	23	113	1979	1980	1979	3,200	0.10
China	23	47	1970	1984	1984	1,000+	0.25
Japan	36	20	1970	1975	1986	2,100	0.05
India	5	10	1980	2001	2001	200–300	0.08
Israel	1	3	1988	-	-	20+	0.03
Brazil	-	2	1997	-	-	70–200	0.02

* Russia's space expenditures have declined from Cold War levels of $6 billion to post–Cold War levels of $1 billion.

NOTE: In recent years, there were 59 space launches in 2001 (including 22 U.S and 26 CIS launches, and 1 failure); 85 launches in 2000 (including 28 U.S. and 39 CIS launches, and 3 failures); 78 launches in 1999 (including 31 U.S. and 30 CIS launches, and 5 failures); and 81 launches in 1998 (including 36 U.S. and 25 CIS launches, and 5 failures, plus a North Korean launch attempt). U.S. totals include military, civilian (NASA), and space shuttle launches; Commonwealth of Independent States (CIS) totals are mostly Russian but include 3 to 5 Ukrainian launches (including Zenit/Sealaunch) each year.

LEO: low earth orbit; GEO: geostationary earth orbit (36,000 km altitude) encouraged with technological assistance? Should they be placed under international trusteeship or UN controls? Or should they be discouraged by the MTCR in the interests of international security? The draft Code of Conduct grappled with these questions. Its principles noted that on the one hand, "all countries alike must be able to continue to reap the benefits of the utilization of space for peaceful purposes," but on the other, "space launch vehicle programs should not be used to conceal ballistic missile programs, considering that there are similarities between both types of programs in terms of technology, facilities and expertise."[33]

Echoing similar themes, in the late 1980s, Moscow supported a broader technology-transfer regime such as a world space organization that would link "states with the advanced technological base of missile production and countries interested in obtaining access to space."[34] France's May 1991 "Arms Control and Disarmament Plan" declared that the MTCR ought to serve as a staging post to a more general (geographically more extensive, better controlled, and universally applicable) agreement. Such an agreement would lay down rules to promote civilian cooperation in space, while averting technology diversion to military missiles. France further recommended confidence-building measures in space and a code of conduct for civilian and military satellites.[35]

Each of the above proposals remained unfulfilled. The only MTCR-related initiative on space programs was through a September 1993 U.S. policy. This policy allowed states entering the MTCR to retain their space programs, but a state's offensive ballistic missiles and related technology would have to be destroyed. In addition, "For MTCR member countries, we [the United States] will not encourage new space launch vehicle programs, which raise questions on both nonproliferation and economic viability grounds. The United States will, however, consider exports of MTCR-controlled items to MTCR member countries for peaceful space launch programs on a case-by-case basis."[36]

This policy facilitated Brazil's entry into the MTCR while allowing Brazil to continue its VLS satellite launcher, which was in an intermediate stage of development. Ukraine kept its space program and South Korea was allowed to build liquid-fuel space launchers when entering the MTCR. However, Washington did not permit Argentina and South Africa to retain their dual-use rocket infrastructure when they entered the MTCR. These space programs were eliminated because they were in their initial stages (and therefore not economically viable, a criterion in the 1993 U.S. policy), and based on existing missile programs (which were of proliferation concern, another criterion in the 1993 U.S. policy).

From a purely economic perspective, space programs do not generate immediate profits. Developing even a rudimentary space launch capacity takes at least five to ten years and costs $1-2 billion (at the rate of $200 million annually).

Yet such a capacity would not bring economic gains, because the primary space suppliers largely fulfill the demand for satellite launch services. Thus the small savings that may eventually result from marginally cheaper indigenous satellite launches are generally less than, and insufficient to recover, the substantial costs to initiate and operate a space launch program.

Despite the adverse short-term economic calculations, Argentina, Spain, Italy, and South Korea revived their space aspirations in the late 1990s, partly to acquire launch autonomy and with a view to long-term gains in the space industry. The long-term demand for satellite launches depends on the competitiveness of existing launchers, and on the demand for communications services. If the aggregate demand for communications satellites increases, the demand for space launchers could also increase.[37]

Moreover, if new types of low earth orbit (LEO) satellite constellations enter the market, regional powers could find a niche in the space industry for 10 to 50 ton LEO-capable rockets. Previously, communication satellites were typically launched into high altitude geostationary orbits by heavy launchers (the equivalent of ICBMs) that were beyond the technical capability of regional powers. Yet new concepts such as Loral-Qualcomm's Globalstar and Motorola's Iridium involve placing lightweight communication satellites into LEO. Such LEO launch vehicles (the equivalent of IRBMs) are within the technical and economic capability of many states. LEO systems entered the market in the late 1990s but were not commercially viable and Iridium declared bankruptcy in 1999–2000. If the industry revives, an increased demand for technically attainable LEO rockets could prompt additional states to enter the satellite launch industry and acquire IRBM capability. Thus the increased demand for (and consequent greater willingness to supply) space launch technology could result in the further proliferation of dual-use rocket and missile technology.

The space launch programs of states that have signed WMD-control agreements may not raise immediate proliferation concerns. Yet other states that have not joined or are suspected of violating WMD-control treaties, but still declare that they have peaceful space aspirations, present greater challenges. A pragmatic approach to this challenge would withhold rocket technology transfer to any state and discourage launch programs for new space-aspiring states. In return, existing space agencies could either launch satellites at concessional prices for new space-aspiring states, or could offer them satellite-based data (relevant to weather forecasting, natural resource management, and communications), especially if they join missile nonproliferation treaties. These incentives could restrain additional states from building their own dual-use rockets.[38] Such a mechanism would have three advantages. First, it would not be discriminatory because it would apply the same criteria to all new space aspirants. Second, it would be relatively cheap, because an LEO launch costs only $1–10 million. Third, the small economic costs of this program would be outweighed by the security benefits of curtailing proliferation. Washington and Moscow explored such a proposal with North Korea in 2000.

LEGAL BARRIERS: REGIONAL AND GLOBAL MISSILE NONPROLIFERATION TREATIES

Missile restraints and elimination can be pursued through regional and international treaties and political initiatives. These include a comprehensive global missile ban, regional missile bans, a partial INF type missile ban, and no-new-missile initiatives. The UN, GCS, and Code of Conduct sought missile CBMs since the late 1990s but did not specifically seek legal missile bans; however, several proposals have explored global and regional bans.

A Global Missile Nonproliferation Treaty

Policy makers and analysts have occasionally called for the worldwide elimination of all missiles through international treaties similar to the NPT. In 1986 arms control talks with Moscow, the Reagan administration proposed a zero ballistic missile (ZBM) initiative to eliminate all U.S. and Soviet ICBMs and SLBMs within a ten-year period.[39] Similar missile disarmament schemes were discussed by Alton Frye in 1992 and 1996, the FAS in 1993, and Jonathan Dean in 1998.[40] At the 1993 MTCR plenary meeting, Canada suggested an internationally negotiated agreement to prohibit ballistic missiles. This would reduce the demand for ballistic missiles, which was an issue that the MTCR did not address. The suggestion received a cool response from the majority of MTCR partners, and the nuclear weapon states were hesitant about such a treaty being called "discriminatory" in light of the forthcoming NPT review conference; Canada revised this plan in later years.[41]

A universal global missile ban is politically difficult because the P-5 states base their deterrents on intercontinental ballistic missiles. While the United States has good alternate delivery systems (long-range bombers and air-launched cruise missiles), the other four P-5 states lack effective air delivery systems and rely heavily on long-range ballistic missiles. However, two of the P-5 (the U.S. and Russia) have given up their intermediate-range missiles under the INF treaty, and two other P-5 states (Britain and France) may be amenable to an INF or modified INF treaty since they have no intermediate-range missiles.

A Global IRBM Ban and Regional Missile Free Zones

In an April 1991 op-ed piece, former ACDA director Kenneth Adelman proposed a global INF type treaty banning Scuds and intermediate-range missiles.[42] ACDA considered initiatives to extend the INF ban worldwide, and in June 1994 ACDA director John Holum suggested inviting all nations to join the obligations of the INF treaty.[43]

Bans on intermediate-range missiles, multiple-stage systems, and new missiles appear feasible not only for the P-5, but also for regional missile powers. Such bans could be introduced to regions where missile proliferation has already occurred, such as the Middle East, South Asia, and the Korean peninsula. Under these bans, regional powers may temporarily retain existing short-range missiles such as Scuds (having a range of 300–600 km). Yet most regional powers may have no vital security interests for longer range missiles, though China, India, and Israel warrant further examination.

Beijing may consider restricting its SRBM deployments if Taiwan minimizes its offensive arms buildup and U.S. arms transfers to Taipei are restrained. Beijing may consider restricting its IRBM programs if all Asian powers (specifically India) do so. India has 1,000–2,000 km range Agni-1 and Agni-2 missiles and is building a new 3,000–4,000 km range Agni-3 to strengthen its deterrent against China. It may be covered by a South Asian strategic restraint regime under which it can keep one type of Agni IRBM, and undertake not to build any new missiles, not to modify existing missiles into ICBMs, and to restrict the quantity of such missiles. Israel, which has 1,400 km range Jericho-2s, may sign a similar MOU with the United States and adopt flight-test and missile CBMs through an arms control and regional security (ACRS) arrangement. Moreover, faced with the prospect of two thousand missiles among neighboring states in a decade, Israel may find it prudent to avert this development by offering to freeze its own missile production if other states do so. Indeed, restraints on Israel would provide greater legitimacy to any broader Middle East nonproliferation initiative. Arab states with modern air forces—such as Saudi Arabia and Jordan—could feasibly renounce missiles under regional initiatives. If its regional rivals accept missile restraints, Tehran may consider restrictions on the production and testing of its Shehab-3s and not develop new missiles.

Beyond global IRBM bans, all the P-5 states and regional powers may be amenable to a political undertaking to build no new ballistic missiles. Going further, in the middle term, deeper ZBM-type bans on all missiles over a 100 km range could be pursued; William Durch notes that under such a ban, "Giving up the ATACMs would be the U.S. price for a regime designed to rid other regions of Scuds, SS-21s, Al Husayns, Jerichos, Prithvis, Hatfs, Ghauris, Taepodongs, Shehabs, and other similar missiles."[44] Regional ZBM treaties could immediately be introduced to create missile-free zones in Latin America, Europe, Middle East Gulf Cooperation Council (GCC) states, and the Asia-Pacific and Southeast Asia. Indeed, Japan's March 2001 security and missile nonproliferation talks for

Asian states received a positive response; the *Bangkok Post* enthusiastically noted: "Reasoned talks among reasonable nations can help stop such [missile] threats. . . . Such talks can build trust and confidence. They can help to establish a mood where countries can agree to stop building missiles, and start destroying them instead."[45] Table 8.2 shows the architecture for an expanded missile nonproliferation regime with treaty bans.

The establishment and long-term viability of missile restraints will hinge upon continued progress in global arms control and favorable regional security conditions. Until regional tensions ease, Iran, Arab states, and Israel are unlikely to undertake even limited missile transparency measures.[46] However, regional security improvements, deeper political liberalization in Tehran, and a regime change in Baghdad could increase middle-term prospects for their adopting WMD and missile restraints. A dynamic of security improvements resulting in missile restraints is apparent in the Korean peninsula. Seoul and Pyongyang were both willing to negotiate missile constraints in the late 1990s, during a thaw in bilateral relations and improvements in North Korea's relations with the West.

In South Asia, both regional security and global arms control dynamics come into play. In general, if Delhi and Islamabad cap their nuclear programs under a fissile material cutoff treaty (FMCT), their need for additional missiles (to deliver nuclear weapons) would also be limited and they could accept missile restraints. Yet Islamabad may not accept an FMCT and missile restraints if Delhi acquires theater missile defense (TMD) systems that neutralize Islamabad's missile forces, or if Delhi expands its missile force. In turn, Delhi is unlikely to accept missile limitations and the FMCT in the face of a Chinese strategic arms buildup. Beijing could oppose the FMCT and build up its nuclear forces under pressure from a large U.S. national missile defense (NMD), or, conversely, may accept the FMCT and restrain its nuclear expansion if NMD is limited.

The Feasibility of Legal Barriers

How feasible and desirable is a global IRBM ban? If such a treaty had come into force in 1987 (the year that the MTCR and the INF treaty were established), and North Korea, Iran, Pakistan, India, and Israel had signed such a treaty, they would then have been legally constrained from building IRBMs that are of particular concern since the late 1990s. Indeed, 500–1,000 km range missile limits could have been acceptable to Pakistan, North Korea, and Iran because these missiles could still target neighboring states. Intermediate-range missile bans and regional missile-free zones are feasible for three reasons.

First, ballistic missiles have limited military utility. They are not very accurate and cannot hit a military or industrial asset when fired hundreds of kilometers from a target (though China has improved the accuracy of its SRBMs by

Table 8.2. The Architecture for a Missile Nonproliferation Regime

	Code of Conduct	Regional Missile Free Zone	Global IRBM Ban	Flight Test Ban	Space Service Regime	Verification
MTCR				Universal (test exceptions with verification)		
Key Suppliers	Universal	Europe, Subsaharan Africa, Latin America, Southeast Asia and Pacific	Koreas, Middle East, U.S., Russia, France, U.K. Stretched IRBM Ban: Israel, India, Pakistan		Suppliers: Spacefaring states. Recipients: Missile treaty members.	Members of missile treaties and space regime

IRBM Ban permits missile up to 300–500 km Scud-B/C; Stretched IRBM Ban permits only one missile of 1,000–4,000 km, but no ICBM.
Other: A "No New Ballistic Missile" undertaking could cover all states including China, which would be outside any IRBM ban.
Flight Test Bans would permit very few reliability tests and missile defense tests, which would be verified.

using global positioning systems); aircraft are more accurate than missiles. Ballistic missiles mainly have political utility by functioning as national morale boosters and terror weapons. Therefore, although new military doctrines in several states seek long-range strike capabilities, governments may not be averse to eliminating missiles having limited military utility, especially if their neighbors do not acquire them and if international norms proscribe them.

Second, missiles have been purchased in many cases for prestige reasons (missiles are equated with technological advancement and modernization) and to reach parity with a neighbor's missile force. For example, prestige influenced Saudi Arabia's missile purchases. The modern Saudi air force, equipped with advanced strike aircraft such as F-15s and Tornadoes, could undertake almost any military mission with greater precision than ballistic missiles. But the fact that Saudi Arabia did not have any missiles while its neighbors Iran and Iraq, and even a small neighboring state such as Yemen, had missiles was one factor influencing the Saudi leadership to seek missiles. This logic behind missile acquisition implies that states would be willing to eliminate missiles if neighboring states undertake similar actions.

Third, a missile-limited zone is verifiable to a substantial degree, as discussed below.

Despite the above logic favoring a regional or global missile nonproliferation treaty, such a treaty may initially not be signed by key states. The NPT was not signed by key states for more than a decade after its initiation; only in the 1990s did a few important states finally enter the NPT. Three middle-term benefits of a missile nonproliferation treaty should be noted. First, treaties can constrain states from acquiring new missiles. Treaties can check domestic lobbies that seek to act against the treaty's norms. Antiproliferation forces in a country may point to treaty obligations to counter hawkish proliferation-oriented domestic lobbies. Second, states that have missile forces will be more likely to eliminate them if their neighbors do not have missile forces or missile aspirations (which would be indicated if they sign a missile nonproliferation treaty). Third, a broad missile nonproliferation regime would provide greater legitimacy to, and consequently increase chances for the success of, missile elimination endeavors with regional powers. Otherwise, international pressure on regional powers may encounter heavy domestic resistance—as it did in Ukraine, which refused U.S. requests to give up its Scuds, and as it did in Bulgaria, where newspapers noted that "SS-23s Are Our Country's Shield," and questioned, "Why the United States Wants Our Missiles?"[47]

FLIGHT-TEST BANS

Regional missile-free zones and intermediate-range missile bans would be enhanced with two types of flight-test limitations—test notifications and moratoriums that can be *politically* reassuring, and test bans that are *technologically* significant barriers to proliferation.[48]

Test notifications, guidelines (such as agreements to not test in the direction of a neighboring state), and moratoriums are useful confidence-building measures. These measures have important political-security benefits because they contribute to the stability of regional security environments. Unannounced missile tests can shock neighboring states (as was the case with North Korea's 1998 Taepo-dong test) and increase their security concerns (and their demand for missiles). Test notifications remove the shock factor in any missile test. Further, test mora-toriums allow the continuation of a broader regional security dialogue. For exam-ple, any North Korean missile test in 1999 would have increased tensions and led to militarization and potential conflict. Instead, in September 1999, North Korea announced a freeze on tests as long as a dialogue continued, and Washington announced the lifting of trade sanctions and continued the dialogue with Pyongyang.

Some caveats are in order. Test restraints do not automatically generate coop-eration. Even if missile test CBMs are adhered to (for example during the April 1999 round of missile tests by India and Pakistan), they can still be followed by conflict (that occurred between New Delhi and Islamabad that summer). Moreover, in historical perspective, the majority of missile tests, announced or unannounced, have not been destabilizing; but tests in regions and times of conflict, or tests by new missile powers, are likely to be more destabilizing.

More comprehensive flight-test bans (that were excluded from the MTCR's Code of Conduct) would make the development of new missiles *technologi-cally* harder and thus be a significant barrier to proliferation. A test ban makes states less confident about improvements in the range, power, guidance, and other aspects of existing missiles. It also hinders their development of any new mis-sile (unless they are building missiles that have previously been tested in another country).

The number of tests required to build a missile should be further analyzed. A healthy rocket project goes through many flight tests. Early U.S. missiles required thirty to fifty tests before being declared operational, but emerging mis-sile powers may be satisfied with less thorough testing.[49] India's Prithvi mis-sile was deployed after twelve tests, Israel's Jericho-2 after five to seven tests, France's 2,750 km range S-2 after twelve tests, but North Korea's Nodong was deployed after a single test. Regional powers may henceforth not require any tests for Scud and Nodong type missiles. However, the development of more powerful and multistage missiles is more complicated. For example, initial flight tests of India's and Brazil's space launchers failed because of problems in stage separation. Moreover, of the eight new strategic missiles tested in the 1980s (the

MX, Trident-2, Pershing-2, SS-24, SS-25, SS-N-20, SS-N-23, and SS-18 follow-on), all but two failed their first test. This suggests that, despite computer simulations and better-trained manpower that reduce the need for a large test series, some testing is ultimately necessary to have confidence in advanced missiles.[50] Therefore, a test ban can be useful in curbing the development of long-range, multiple-stage, and accurate missiles.

One additional issue in a flight-test ban is that the P-5 states and regional missile powers periodically test their missiles. In this case, the number of such tests can be predetermined, advance notification may be provided, and the tests may be nonintrusively observed to ensure that new missiles are not being tested.

VERIFYING MISSILE CONTROLS

Verifying a state's compliance with missile nonproliferation agreements is hard because a determined violator can secretly build missiles in underground factories and hide them. Many Iraqi Scud launchers were not detected despite a massive allied air campaign against them in the Gulf War. However, five general points should be noted. First, an arms control agreement assumes that parties will cooperate with it by declaring production facilities and baseline inventories and allowing monitoring. Second, cooperation can be furthered by offering incentives to complying states and imposing costs on violators. Third, minor verification drawbacks may not damage an arms control regime. Fourth, verification at the level of "police patrols" (where every single missile component must be monitored) has high transaction costs and may be close to impossible; yet verification relying on "fire alarms" (where the detection of some missile-relevant activity brings greater international scrutiny and pressure on target states) may be adequate, because the transfer or development of only a few components will not give states a complete missile program.[51] Fifth, some degree of missile detection is technologically possible through satellites and other means.[52] For example, during the Cold War, U.S. satellites extensively monitored Russian missile plants, test centers, missile fields, and the number and size of missiles and their silos and transport vehicles. Such monitoring enabled them to determine that Russia's SS-25 was not an upgrade of the SS-13 (as was declared by Moscow) but an entirely new missile that was 10 percent longer and wider and having 90 percent more throw-weight than the SS-13.[53] In the 1980s, U.S. satellites detected a ballistic missile at a test range in South Africa, a Condor missile on its launch pad in Argentina, and the trucks carrying Chinese-supplied CSS-2 missiles in Saudi Arabia. Moreover, the experience of the START and INF treaties, and of UNSCOM in Iraq, has provided several techniques for verification. Fixed missiles can be detected by observing missile silos and facilities, and mobile missiles can be monitored by specifying the missile bases and through factory monitoring.[54] An extensive technical analysis of missile verification is beyond the scope of this study, but several technical monitoring issues are worth noting.

Declared missile bases and factories can be monitored.[55] Portal or perimeter inspections can observe weapons when they leave the plant or base, and X-ray equipment that is not highly intrusive can determine (from some distance) the length of the transporting vehicle and the missiles to verify that new missiles are not being developed. For example, under the INF treaty, U.S. and Russian inspectors conducted 850 inspections in thirteen years and monitored missile plants in Magna, Utah, and Votkinsk (Russia). In general, large systems (rocket boosters) are more amenable to such verification, while smaller systems such as missile parts may be undetected, although the final assembly of such systems would require a large workshop that is harder to hide. Moreover, cameras and sensors at missile test stands can measure the size and burn time of motors to verify their compliance with an agreement; this technique was used by UNSCOM in Iraq. Another means of production monitoring is through satellites. U.S. satellites have detected ground tests of rocket motors in Iran's missile plants. In addition, internal stockpiling could be inspected periodically, and a fixed number of challenge inspections (with varying degrees of intrusiveness comparable to the standards of perimeter monitoring) would make clandestine production difficult. Even if intrusive monitoring of missile factories is not permitted, the limited floor space of a factory would enable only a few missile components (such as engines) or complete missiles to be internally stockpiled.

Mobile missile launchers would have to be maintained in declared bases and not be permitted beyond certain operating areas. Missiles outside these areas would be in violation of an arms control arrangement. Missiles can then be monitored from perimeters or satellites without impeding their survivability, because during a tactical alert or strategic warning, mobile launchers can be moved outside the base (but still remain in a general operating area of several hundred square kilometers). Launchers may also be moved with prior notification for exercises.

Missile programs can be partly distinguished from space programs in a few ways. First, missile programs have larger plant capacities and higher production rates than space programs; typically only a few rockets are built per year in space programs, while several may be built for military programs.[56] Thus the difference between the number of units (such as airframes and engines) constructed, and the number of actual launches, can be estimated. A high difference would be a cause for concern and grounds for challenge inspections, but the accumulation and overproduction of a few units would be acceptable. Further, production capacity can be estimated by measuring the floor space available for constructing large rockets. Second, in terms of propellants, cryogenic liquids are less likely to be used in missiles. Solids or storable liquids such as nitrogen tetroxide and UDMH are better for missiles. In practice, however, many regional power ballistic missiles (Scuds and Nodongs) use liquid fuels, and several space launchers use solid fuel, and the difference is also not applicable for sounding rockets. Another point of difference is that missiles are generally light and mobile and capable of short-notice launches. Space launchers (especially those that use volatile liquid fuel) take hours or days to prepare for launching, and may be heavy and not rapidly transported.

Missile test bans can be monitored. Especially in their early development stage, missiles are launched from fixed complexes that include launch pads, tracking stations, and down-range instrumented areas; activity at these sites can be observed. Further, a rocket's exhaust can be detected. Every Scud launch during the Gulf war was observed. Indeed, information from the exhaust's spectrum can identify the propellants, while a more detailed spectrum analysis can determine reaction products and proportions, and the absolute brightness of the exhaust provides information about the rate at which fuel is burned, which determines the thrust and hence the range of the missile. Tests may also be monitored nonintrusively by observing the length of the transporting vehicle or missile and verifying that new missiles are not being developed and tested.

Missile tests can be distinguished from a space launch.[57] First, a missile reenters the atmosphere while a space launcher does not. Thus a ban on reentry other than by parachute would be part of a missile test ban. The areas of reentry can also be defined, so that reentry angles used by missiles (typically 22 to 45 degrees) are barred, but other reentry angles are permissible for spacecraft. Second, a ban on multiple independently targetable reentry vehicles (MIRVs), and a ban on depressed trajectory flights (typical for SLBMs), are both feasible, since these activities have no overlap with space flights. Third, the nonintrusive inspection of space payloads would verify that multiple satellites released from a single launcher are not MIRVs. Such inspections would also preclude heat shields from being tested in the guise of a failed satellite launch (moreover, bans could be imposed on tests of sounding rockets boosted downward, since this technique could test heat shields). Fourth, the nonencryption of telemetry would be part of a flight-test ban; the interception of proscribed telemetry signals could expose military-related upgrades on any space launch.

Verifying controls on cruise missiles is far more challenging, but single-purpose cruise missile platforms can be detected.[58] Short-range missiles are hard to distinguish from artillery rockets, and artillery rockets or short-range missiles can also be reconfigured to increase their range.[59] However, mutually agreed inspections and declarations of short-range missiles and artillery rockets can overcome verification difficulties on this issue.

The broad principles discussed above suggest that verification is feasible, though it may have drawbacks. For example, one drawback is that a missile ban would not preclude many missile components from being tested in a space program. This allows key components and major boosters to be tested up to the threshold of a breakout. However, states would still require additional testing to have confidence in missile reentry and targeting systems that are not part of space launchers. Another drawback is that a very determined violator has a fair probability of evading international monitoring. Yet, while some missile development activities can be hidden and covert, others such as testing can be detected, and states cannot confidently develop accurate and long-range missiles without testing. Further, low levels of verification uncertainty may be tolerable, because a violator may clandestinely build only a small number of missiles; any large-scale program is more likely to be detected. In summary, verification may be imperfect but can still be adequate; verification mechanisms are substantially useful in monitoring and enhancing confidence in missile nonproliferation agreements.

ASSESSMENT

The MTCR's technology barriers and political CBMs of the Code of Conduct are useful and practical short-term policy options, but may not be entirely sufficient to contain missile proliferation in the long term. A broader missile nonproliferation regime containing incentives, legal barriers, and verification mechanisms can better address all issues relevant to missile proliferation. Offering security-related assurances to states encountering a missile ban violator, and political and economic penalties for violators as well as incentives for complying states, would enhance the viability of missile limitation initiatives. States could be given security incentives (such as no-first-use guarantees and positive and negative security assurances) and technical and economic incentives (such as space services) for strictly complying with missile nonproliferation agreements. While a broader missile nonproliferation regime will have drawbacks (it would not immediately or completely eliminate regional missile forces, and may not be fully verifiable), it could still considerably contain proliferation and be effective over the long term. On policy grounds, therefore, the establishment of verification initiatives, missile-free zones, intermediate-range missile bans, flight-test bans, and space service incentives are five feasible steps to strengthen the missile nonproliferation regime.

9

Conclusions

M ultilateral regimes can contain the spread of deadly technologies in two general ways. First, they can pursue a technological containment approach—an approach of containing strategic weapons proliferation through technological means, by denying regional powers the technological assistance required for weapons development. Second, regimes may adopt a political-legal approach, whereby all concerned states verifiably renounce certain weapons or the military use of a technology. Such agreements may allow technology transfer between states (or not actively oppose such transfer) on the condition that the transferred technology would be used only for peaceful nonmilitary applications. The Missile Technology Control Regime (MTCR) pursued the former approach. How effective is the MTCR? How effective is the technological containment approach? What broader foreign policy lessons does the MTCR experience offer?

The first question was addressed in Chapters 3–8. The MTCR was evaluated as being partly effective, and generally necessary but rarely sufficient, as a nonproliferation tool. The regime's technology barriers mainly delayed and raised the costs of target missile programs, which caused missile decisions to shift from technological to political considerations. These political considerations—related to security pressures from the regional environment, political-economic pressures from the global system, and foreign policies of engagement with regional powers in such a system—determined national missile outcomes. On policy grounds, this analysis suggested that the easing of regional tensions and international engagement with regional powers could at least temporarily curb missile proliferation. It also suggested that in the long term, a better constructed treaty regime that can withstand political fluctuations would provide valuable additional barriers against proliferation. Steps toward such a regime were outlined in Chapter 8.

A critical examination of how technological, security, and political-economic pressures influenced national missile decisions provides answers to our second and third questions. How well can multilateral regimes and unilateral approaches, engagement and containment policies toward target states, and the use of technological, economic, and political instruments, contain strategic weapons proliferation? Under what conditions are these policies successful, and when do they fall short? These questions are examined in this chapter.

THE POLITICS OF REGIMES

How was cooperation secured in the MTCR? How can it more generally be attained in supplier cartels and multilateral security regimes? The literature on cooperation is extensive and notes that the interaction between power, interests, and knowledge, along with the use of incentives, affect cooperation. These factors have sustained multilateral cooperation in the MTCR. The experience of the missile regime was that, in the 1980s, increasing *knowledge* about the perils of missile proliferation and the links between nuclear and missile proliferation created an *interest* in a regime to contain the missile threat. Over time, this knowledge and interest spread beyond the G-7 to other suppliers, who also joined the MTCR. But when states were reluctant to comply fully with the MTCR, in part because of conflicting economic interests to export missile technologies, *power* politics came into play. U.S. power (through sanctions and incentives) brought reluctant supplier states more firmly into the MTCR. The effect of sanctions, however, should not be exaggerated. As noted in Chapter 3, some MTCR-related sanctions (such as those against North Korea) had no effect, while other sanctions (such as those against Russian and Chinese firms) only partially and indirectly restrained technology transfers. In some of these cases, the *incentive* to lift or not impose sanctions induced compliance.

The role of incentives in international cooperation is worth further examination. Because of their high transaction costs, incentives may be difficult to offer, but when they are viable, they can consolidate cooperation.[1] Incentives made key suppliers such as Russia and China cooperate better with the MTCR. Political and security considerations (such as the benefits of improved ties with the United States), as well as increasing acceptance of nonproliferation norms, influenced Moscow and Beijing to more strongly curb their firms' technology transfers. But economic incentives consolidated their restraint from these transfers. In the 1990s, Moscow and Beijing benefited economically from lucrative U.S. space contracts (worth a billion dollars over a decade) in exchange for curbing relatively low-income rocket and space exports to regional powers (the Russia-India cryogenic deal was valued at $200 to 300 million, and Scud type exports were worth similar small amounts).

Moreover, these incentive structures were largely market-conforming, because they were perpetuated by economic forces such as the steady global demand for satellite launches but reduced space activity among regional powers. If incentive structures are not market-conforming (if firms do not need the original incentive because they find alternative markets for their products), they may not be able to withstand commercial pressures (from the alternative market) that undermine a regime's area of cooperation. The persistent regional power demand for dual-use technology—and the absence of further U.S. incentives for suppliers to withhold this technology (not all Russian and Chinese firms received U.S. satellite contract incentives, nor did all such firms incur large marginal costs from sanctions)—is one reason for continuing technology outflows from some Russian and Chinese firms in the late 1990s.

While the MTCR modestly curbed technology transfers to regional powers, it only partially curbed their missile programs. This issue—the impact of the MTCR's technology barriers on proliferation—warrants closer examination.

TECHNOLOGICAL CONTAINMENT

How effective are strategies of technological containment, or the use of technology embargoes as nonproliferation and arms control tools? The MTCR experience provides five insights into this question.

Mid to Low Success Rates, Decreasing with Time

First, technology embargoes can have a low to modest "success rate," and these success rates decrease over time. In general, nine out of fourteen target missile programs were constrained (to less than medium range missiles, though this excludes Brazil's space launcher) during the MTCR's first fifteen years; the regime also constrained the range of many continuing medium range missile programs. From these observations, and separating the effects of technology embargoes from those of political pressures on target missile decisions, a rough impact assessment, or success score, for the MTCR may be computed.[2]

Table 9.1 shows that the MTCR had a great impact on Libya (which could not build even short range missiles), but a negligible impact on India and Israel (who considerably advanced their missile activities despite the regime); its impact on other states fell somewhere in between these two extremes. In quantitative terms, the MTCR's success score is similar to success scores for economic sanctions, which have been computed to be 34 percent for all sanctions and 13 to 37 percent for Cocom's military impairment sanctions.[3]

A quantitative evaluation that the MTCR has a 30 to 40 percent success rate suggests that technology controls can be effective in about one-third of the cases where they are applied. This assessment helps but does not offer firm guidelines for policy making because it does not indicate which these cases may be, and does not provide information on how export controls function.

Table 9.1. Calculating MTCR Effectiveness

Target State	(a) Constraint in Target Missile Program	(b) Contribution of MTCR Embargo to Missile Constraint	(a × b) Net MTCR Impact	
	(1997 -> 2002)		1997	2002
Israel	Very Low	Low	Very Low	Very Low
India	Very Low	Low	Very Low	Very Low
Brazil	Low -> Very Low	Mid	Low/Very Low	Very Low
North Korea	Low -> Very Low	High	Low	Very Low
South Korea	High -> Mid	Low	Low	Low/Very Low
Taiwan	High	Mid	Mid	Mid
Argentina	High	Mid	Mid	Mid
South Africa	High	Mid	Mid	Mid
Iraq	High	Mid	Mid	Mid
Iran	Mid -> Low	High	Mid	Mid/Low
Pakistan	Mid -> Low	High	Mid	Mid/Low
Egypt	High -> Mid	Mid/High	Mid/High	Mid/Low
Syria	High -> Mid	High	High	Mid
Libya	High	High	High	High
Sum			**Mid**	**Mid-Low**

The constraint in a target missile program is calculated as follows:
Very Low or Negligible: Missile range over 1,500 km, multiple-stage missile or SLV
Low: Missile range constrained to 1,000–1,500 km, single-stage missile
Mid: Missile range constrained to 300 km Scud type system
High: Missile program absent or constrained under 200 km

Target Technological Capability, Nonproliferation Outcome, and Missile Quality

Second, the cases where technology embargoes are effective are (but only partly) a function of the technological capability of the target state. Three propositions clarify the issue. A first proposition, that technologically strong states are not affected by technology controls and therefore continue missile activity, is only weakly supported. Contrary to this proposition, five of the seven economically and technically capable missile aspirants—South Korea, Brazil, Taiwan, Argentina, and South Africa—curbed their missile programs in the 1990s (though Brazil advanced its space program). A second and converse proposition, that technologically weak states cease missile activity, is marginally supported. Four out of seven cases confirm this outcome: Egypt, Syria, Iraq, and Libya halted or considerably curbed their missile aspirations, but Pakistan, Iran, and North Korea advanced their missile activity. However, if this proposition is applied to a subset of cases—the very weak states—it is more strongly supported. The MTCR's technology barriers were sufficient for curbing the missile programs of very weak states such as Libya (at least for the regime's first fifteen years) and Syria during the regime's first decade.

Thus technology barriers alone can halt proliferation among technologically very weak states; but for all other states, their technical capability alone does not singularly determine whether they will attain a strategic weapons program when subject to a technology embargo. A third proposition—that technologically stronger states build more advanced missiles—is better supported. Of the five states that made political decisions to continue their missile quest and tested medium-range systems in the 1990s, those with an advanced industrial capability—India and Israel—built more powerful solid-fuel multiple-stage missiles or space launchers. Conversely, the technologically weaker states—North Korea, Iran, Pakistan—had less powerful liquid-fuel missiles (restricted to single-stage Nodong type systems for Iran and Pakistan). These observations should not suggest that technologically strong states always have better rocket programs. Rocket programs are influenced by many other factors such as technical strategies, and technologically strong states may fail where weaker states succeed (Japan's space program has had lower launch rates and commercial success than China's). Instead, the above observations mainly indicate a rough positive correlation between national technological capability and missile outcomes for states that make political decisions to continue their missile quest.

The Process of Technology Controls, and the Type of Technology Controlled

Third, analyzing the process through which technology embargoes operate, and the type of technology they seek to control, offers valuable information about their effectiveness. Technology barriers are useful because they form a (sometimes necessary) first step in a process that may lead to nonproliferation successes. Technology barriers *raise the costs* of production and shift national arms production decisions beyond technical considerations to include political and economic factors. Technology barriers *delay* target missile programs (the length of the delay varies from case to case, and is typically just a few years for a short-range missile program and five to ten years for a longer range missile program), and thereby offer additional time for dialogue with proliferators. During this time, security and political-economic factors influence national missile decisions. In cases where the regional security environment improves or external pressures influence target states, missile proliferation is restrained. In cases where a state's demand is high (due to high security threat perceptions or the importance of missile exports for a national economy) and international diplomatic or economic pressures are not very influential, missile proliferation continues.

The above point about the MTCR's differing effects on short-range and longer range missile programs raises another issue—the type of technology to be controlled. Technology embargoes may be less effective in controlling the spread of "low-tech" systems—systems such as short-range missiles, rudimentary chemical and biological weapons, and less sophisticated conventional weapons such as naval patrol boats and infantry fighting vehicles. Technology embargoes may be more effective in halting the proliferation of "high-tech" systems— systems such as long range missiles, nuclear weapons and miniaturized nuclear warheads, and better conventional arms such as advanced combat aircraft and sophisticated naval vessels.

The Number of Targets

Fourth, the number of target states can affect the outcome of technology control regimes. The MTCR was aimed at relatively few target states, and most of these states were already susceptible to U.S. leverage. Attempts to influence (through pressures or incentives) a larger number of states may have been beyond the capabilities of any single external power. Thus, when the number of target states is small, a regime focused solely on technology barriers may (when the targets are also susceptible to political influences) be effective, if only in the short term. When the number of target states is large (as in the nuclear arena, where over fifty states have nuclear technology), a broader regime may be necessary to tackle the issue.

The Completeness of a Supply Embargo

Fifth, in order to be effective, a technology control regime must secure the compliance of all major suppliers. Violations by even a single supplier can considerably undermine the regime. In the MTCR's case, technology transfers by one external supplier (North Korea, which was not an MTCR member) facilitated the quicker emergence of two additional medium-range missile powers, Pakistan and Iran, whose medium-range missiles are based on the North Korean Nodong missile. Given their modest technical capabilities, Pakistan and Iran may eventually have built medium-range missiles on their own, but foreign assistance considerably speeded up their missile programs.

Summing Up

Technology control regimes are not the only way to contain strategic weapons proliferation, but in some cases they may be the most feasible, or even the only available, option. This is because other approaches may not be politically feasible: creating international legal bans can be difficult, and even if such bans are created, states may not adhere to them or may violate them. The strategic weapons programs of these states can then only be contained through technological means. The MTCR experience suggests five lessons about the expected effectiveness of such technology control approaches. These lessons and findings have practical policy applications.

For example, they suggest that "smart sanctions" (a policy including stronger technology embargoes that the United States sought for Iraq in 2001) would have a limited middle-term effectiveness on Baghdad. Iraq is a technologically weak state, and therefore smart sanctions will delay its development of missiles (especially long-range missiles) but will become progressively ineffective with time and if foreign suppliers violate the sanctions regime. Suppliers may violate the regime if they are not offered incentives to comply or sanctioned if they do not comply with the arms embargo. In addition, Middle East geopolitics will crucially determine Iraq's long-term demand for weapons of mass destruction and missiles: if relations with Iran and the regional security environment stabilize, Baghdad would have fewer reasons to seek missiles and WMDs. Our findings also suggest that supplier controls would thwart terrorist groups (who have weak technological capabilities) from building advanced WMDs.

This study's findings also provide broader lessons for supply-side nonproliferation strategies. These apply not only to WMD proliferation but also to conventional arms control, particularly the control of offensive systems such as submarines and aircraft. Supply-side barriers can be effective if the number of targets is small, if the targets are susceptible to external political pressure, and if all suppliers conform to the regime. Even then, supply-side technology barriers would mainly slow but not halt weapons development in target states, and will ultimately be effective only when accompanied by security-enhancing and political-economic approaches.

REGIONAL SECURITY AND PROLIFERATION

How do regional security considerations influence a state's compliance with global nonproliferation regimes? This study suggests that they are crucial in determining a state's nonproliferation behavior. Three propositions clarify this issue. First, when regional tensions and security concerns are high and no external security assurance is offered to regional powers, missile programs continue. In this situation, diplomatic and political-economic pressure does not persuade proliferators to halt their missile programs. This is the case with India, Pakistan, Iran, and North Korea.

Second, when regional security concerns are high but external powers have strong security ties with regional powers, proliferation is restrained. This proposition holds for two of three cases—Taiwan and South Korea but not Israel. Moreover, at times when the United States reduced its security ties, Taiwan and South Korea more actively sought nuclear and missile programs. Conversely, the maintenance of U.S. security commitments through its troop deployments, naval presence, and arms transfers provided the necessary security assurances to restrain Taiwan and South Korea's nuclear and missile activity.

Third, when security threats recede, as they did for Argentina, Brazil, and South Africa, nonproliferation successes follow. It should be clarified that even after security threats decreased, Argentina and South Africa continued rocket activity for space-related commercial or prestige reasons, but they were then influenced by external political-economic pressure to rein in this activity.

The sources of security threats were outlined in previous chapters—security pressures arise from an adversary's WMD program, an adversary's conventional force and economic superiority, a state's inability to maintain a conventional military deterrent, and a state's international political isolation and the loss of allies. Addressing these sources of insecurity can critically alleviate a state's demand for WMDs and missiles.

In addition, pressures from an adversary's missile programs are not solely of a military-security nature, but also stem from competitive rivalry and prestige reasons to maintain parity with a neighbor. In the Korean peninsula, both rivals have sought to outdo each other with better missiles since the 1970s. The acquisition and development of North Korea's Frog-7 (obtained in 1975), South Korea's NHK-1 (tested in 1978), North Korea's Scud-B (acquired in 1979–80 and tested in 1984), South Korea's NHK-2 (tested and deployed in 1986–87), and North Korea's Scud-C (tested in 1990) illustrate this rivalry. Further, Pyongyang's Scud activity and 1993 Nodong test influenced Seoul's 1995 request to Washington to scrap their bilateral missile restraint agreement. The earlier 1993 launch of a South Korean satellite and Seoul's 1996 space plans may have influenced Pyongyang to upgrade its Taepodong into an SLV; this system's launch in 1998 influenced Seoul to seek 500 km range missiles in 1999.

Missile rivalry is also evident in other regions. In the Middle East, Egypt and Israel engaged in a missile race in the late 1950s and early 1960s. In Latin America, Argentina and Brazil both renounced their missile options by the mid-1990s; but the loss of prestige in falling behind Brazil's space program influenced Argentina to continue a space launcher quest throughout the late 1990s. In South Asia, Delhi's 1988 Prithvi test caused Islamabad to announce Hatf tests in 1989; news reports of Prithvi deployments in June 1997 made Islamabad announce a Hatf test in July 1997.

Finally, national missile decisions are linked with both regional security pressures and the global arms control regime. They are more strongly tied to the global arms control regime in the South Asian case, and less tightly linked with the global arms control regime in the Middle East and Korean cases. In South Asia, Pakistan may be amenable to restraining its nuclear and missile programs if the Kashmir dispute with India is resolved, and if Islamabad can maintain a conventional deterrent and does not face international political isolation and sanctions. Yet Delhi keeps its nuclear and missile programs to counter a long-term Chinese threat. Thus India may undertake deep restraints such as signing a fissile material cutoff treaty (FMCT) and accepting a missile freeze only if Beijing does so; but Beijing has opposed the FMCT because of Washington's missile defense initiatives. Thus, until the global arms control regime stabilizes and the NMD-FMCT-nuclear disarmament standoff is resolved, Delhi may not undertake deep nuclear and missile restraints, and Islamabad may also then back away from such restraints. In contrast to the South Asian countries, states in the Middle East and the Korean peninsula have not strongly linked their missile restraints with progress on global arms control issues (though their WMD and missile programs are a serious concern for the global regime). These states could accept missile restraints if their neighbors do so and if their regional security environment stabilizes; they would then be more influenced by external incentives or political-economic pressures to rein in their missile activity.

POLITICAL ENGAGEMENT AND POLITICAL-ECONOMIC PRESSURES

When and how do political engagement and external pressure influence target states? Analysts have extensively debated strategies of engagement and containment;[4] this book does not suggest a new theory of engagement, but rather highlights the structural conditions behind the issue. It explores whether higher levels of interdependence allow for successful external leverage on regional powers, and explains how systemic factors such as globalization and unipolarity affect levels of interdependence and nonproliferation outcomes.

Globalization has increased levels of interdependence between regional powers and the United States (which was the major external power driving nonproliferation endeavors and also dominating the world economy). Economic interdependence translates into bargaining power which allows for political influence on target states; and the level of interdependence is increased through strategies of engagement with regional powers. Interdependence does not directly lead to nonproliferation outcomes, but is the structural condition that affects interstate bargaining and influences nonproliferation outcomes. Two points on the level and symmetry of interdependence are worth noting.

First, high to moderate levels of interdependence between a regional power

and major external powers correlate positively and strongly with nonproliferation successes. Three of four regional powers that were highly interdependent
with the United States—South Korea, Taiwan, and Egypt (but not Israel)—were
influenced to halt their medium-range missile activity. Three of five states with
moderate levels of interdependence—Argentina, Brazil, and South Africa
(though not India and Pakistan)—were also influenced by U.S. pressure. As their
trade, aid, and investment ties with the United States or U.S.-influenced international financial institutions increased in the 1990s, they became more susceptible to U.S. pressure to curb their missile programs.

Thus, while interdependence is not a necessary or sufficient condition for
nonproliferation (it was only in the context of security improvements that inter-
dependence-induced pressure led to positive nonproliferation outcomes), high
degrees of interdependence enhance prospects for nonproliferation.

Conversely, low degrees of interdependence made North Korea and Iran less
susceptible to U.S. pressure; these states continued their missile activity in the
1990s. In such cases, engagement strategies and incentives may have to be pursued to influence target states. Engagement, however, is not risk-free. It can boost
a target state's economy and give it greater resources for strategic weapons development. The conditions under which engagement may influence proliferation
are related to symmetries in dependence and bargaining politics.

Second, the symmetry of interdependence affects proliferation outcomes.
Taiwan, South Korea, Israel, and Egypt are all highly interdependent with the
United States in both the economic and security areas. However, the first two
states were influenced to curb their missile programs substantially in the 1990s,
but Israel advanced its medium-range missile activity, and Egypt pursued a short-
range missile project. Asymmetry in security interdependence partly explains
this outcome. Taiwan and South Korea are far more dependent on Washington
for their security than vice versa and therefore have less reverse leverage to
counter U.S. pressure. On the other hand, although Israel and Egypt are both
highly dependent on U.S. aid, they are also strategically important regional allies
for Washington. Consequently, they have reverse leverage on Washington. Their
dependence enabled Washington to secure some nonproliferation goals such as
curbing Israel's missile-related exports, and halting Egypt's intermediate-range
missile activity. Yet because of their reverse leverage, Washington did not seek
to curb all aspects of their missile activity.

This framework roughly explains the links between interdependence and
leverage, but also has limitations. For example, despite its susceptibility to U.S.
influence and its lesser reverse leverage, South Korea eventually bargained with
Washington for the right to build a space launcher and a 300 km range missile

by 2001. This was mostly because Washington dropped its resistance to such programs and accepted them to be of lesser proliferation concern, and not because of any greater leverage acquired by Seoul.

To summarize, this study suggests that engagement can influence target states under four conditions: (1) if an external power attains a high degree of interdependence with the target state and can credibly threaten it with sanctions, or if, at low to moderate degrees of interdependence, it offers incentives (including the incentive to lift sanctions); (2) if such dependence is asymmetric in favor of the external power; (3) if domestic politics or strategic considerations do not hinder the external power from pressuring the target; and (4) if the preference orderings of the target state make it less resistant to pressure (if target states give greater priority to security, sovereignty, or regime survival over economic issues, they would more strongly resist external pressure). This framework may be tested on additional cases to more comprehensively explore the conditions under which interdependence between states enhances their leverage on each other.

On policy grounds, this analysis suggests that calls for the United States to distinguish between friends (or nonhostile nations) and foes (hostile states that gravely threaten U.S. national interests) in its nonproliferation policy, and to not seek nuclear and missile restraints from nonhostile states, may be conceding excessive ground on the issue. This is because, as the United States builds stronger ties and better relations with regional powers, it has more means to influence their missile activity. Thus, rather than simply concede ground on the nuclear and missile programs of friendly regional powers, Washington could in fact use its influence to rein in their nuclear and missile programs and strengthen the nonproliferation regime.

DEMOCRATIZATION AND ECONOMIC LIBERALIZATION

While external factors such as security threats and political-economic pressure are highly influential, domestic politics also affect proliferation outcomes. Economic liberalization increases a regional power's degree of interdependence with external powers, and makes it more susceptible to external pressure. The impact of democratization on proliferation is mixed, and security considerations are an intervening variable between democratization and nonproliferation outcomes. Two points are relevant to this analysis.

The first is that despite a high correlation between democratization and missile nonproliferation, democratization does not necessarily favor nonproliferation. Five states that have democratized since the mid-1980s—Argentina, Brazil, South Africa, South Korea, Taiwan—curbed their missile programs in the 1990s. Yet a deeper analysis comparing the timing of democratization with the timing of nonproliferation reveals that the impact of democratization is not as direct as assumed. Many of these states actually *increased* missile activity immediately following the transition to democratic regimes, and reined in their missile programs only a few years later.

A democratic *transition* alone has no immediate or direct influence on proliferation. A democratic *consolidation* that reduces the military's role in policy making increases prospects for nonproliferation, but even this issue requires further analysis. On the one hand, Argentina and Brazil curbed their missile programs upon democratic consolidation. But in South Korea and Taiwan, the consolidation of democracy correlated with calls for an expanded missile program; and democratic politics in established democracies such as India also made reversing proliferation harder. Thus democratization and democratic consolidation do not singularly bring about proliferation outcomes; they are most relevant when taking into account the democratization of a dyad, and the regional security environment.

Second, when examining dyads as the unit of analysis, the record is mixed. One democratized dyad—the Argentina-Brazil case—resulted in nonproliferation success, while in the India-Pakistan democratized dyad (from 1988 to 1999) proliferation continued. This is because security considerations are an important intervening variable. When democratization in a dyad leads to security improvements (such as between Argentina and Brazil), nonproliferation successes have followed. When democratization in the dyad has not resulted in security improvements (such as between India and Pakistan), nonproliferation remains elusive.

In summary, democratization and economic liberalization may enhance prospects for nonproliferation (as the Argentina-Brazil case illustrates), but democratization and economic reforms are not entirely sufficient for nonproliferation (as demonstrated in the India-Pakistan case).

INSTITUTIONAL DESIGN AND INTERNATIONAL COOPERATION

How does institutional design influence international cooperation and regime effectiveness? First, are international security regimes with a limited *domain* more effective than those that are more inclusive and include key regional powers? Second, are regimes with a small *scope* more effective than those with a larger scope? Moreover, are regimes that focus exclusively on the *technology* of an issue effective, or should they also include *political, security, and legal components?* Regimes may succeed or fail regardless of their particular scope and domain. But their institutional design still matters. The MTCR experience demonstrates that limiting the number of states and issues has the temporary advantage of making cooperation more likely, but can falter over the long term.

If a regime's scope and domain are not expanded to tackle new issues, or if a regime cannot stabilize technological advances through political-legal frameworks, then regime effectiveness will decline over time. Although they were formed under very different political circumstances, the examples of the MTCR and NPT are worth comparing.

The NPT, though negotiated among only a few states (the two superpowers largely formulated a draft treaty text, and a few treaty articles were amended or added at the Disarmament Conference to accommodate nonnuclear states), was wide in its scope and domain. It catered to a large number of states—nuclear and nonnuclear, allied and nonaligned—and encompassed multiple issues such as the economic issues of technology transfer and security issues of verification and nuclear elimination under a single treaty. The NPT regime took several years to attain completion; but in the long run it has been modestly successful, attaining near-universal membership and indefinite extension in 1995. Its institutional design and operating logic are robust and have withstood technological advances and changing structural conditions such as the transition from bipolarity to unipolarity in the world system; the NPT is also predicted to remain successful under a multipolar system.

In contrast to the NPT, the MTCR included few states and covered few issues during its formation. This was not necessarily inappropriate. In the 1980s, alternative strategies for a broad missile nonproliferation treaty may not have worked, simply because a large number of states did not then desire the elimination of their missile programs or missile exports. In such situations, it may be better to work from the bottom up, by initially including only a few states and a few issues, and then expanding the regime to cover additional states. This strategy has drawbacks because it may leave out states with important and legitimate requirements for a given resource or technology. It may also exclude key states that could undermine the regime. Yet it is pragmatic as it recognizes that most international behavior is driven by short-term calculations of interest, and that state power can be brought to bear to achieve key objectives in the middle term.[5]

The MTCR was initially successful in curbing missile technology exports and halting some target programs. However, additional gains eluded the regime after the mid-1990s. Political and bureaucratic inertia hindered proposals to expand the missile nonproliferation regime. This left missile nonproliferation efforts frozen at a narrow scope and without the institutional mechanisms to address key emerging issues such as banning new missiles, prohibiting missile tests, and dealing with space programs. If continuing political commitments to expanding the regime are not forthcoming, the regime may not only be unable to tackle these emerging issues, but its past gains could also be reversed under changing technical and political circumstances.

The difference between the formation of the MTCR and the NPT is reflected in a similar contrast between the Antarctic regime and the Oceans regime. The Antarctic regime evolved through the piecemeal approach, dealing with only a few issues at a time. The 1959 Antarctic Treaty deferred questions of sovereignty, economics (such as catch limits), and environment (wildlife preservation) to future treaties, but successfully addressed more pressing demilitarization issues.[6] In contrast, the Law of the Seas adopted a broad-based track similar to the NPT; all major security, sovereignty, and economic issues such as rights of passage, territorial waters, seabed resources, and economic zones were simultaneously negotiated under a single treaty.[7] In the long term, both the Oceans and Antarctic regimes, although formed through different approaches, successfully tackled the major relevant issues in their respective areas. The NPT has the framework to address all issues in the nuclear area, but the MTCR is institutionally ill-equipped to tackle emerging issues on the missile nonproliferation agenda.

Thus the MTCR experience suggests that small-domain and small-scope regimes and the piecemeal approach to regime formation may be initially appropriate. But in the absence of continuing and possibly politically and economically autonomous and institutionalized support mechanisms for regime expansion, regimes may freeze and their gains may be reversed over time. Security regimes, and international cooperation in general, are enhanced through more broad-based inclusiveness in a regime.

The need to balance technology, politics, security, and law is also worth noting. Regimes like the MTCR, which have only technological components, are undermined by technology diffusion and technological advances. Regimes such as the NPT that have legal barriers and political and security components can restrain destabilizing advances in technology. Nuclear technology has spread to over fifty countries, but the NPT provides the framework to ensure that less than ten are nuclear weapons powers. Rocket technology may eventually be acquired by many states, and a robust political-legal framework going beyond the MTCR will be necessary to prevent this technology from being used in ballistic missiles.

MULTILATERAL INSTITUTIONS,
INTERNATIONAL SECURITY, AND MISSILE PROLIFERATION

Scholarly debates about institutional effectiveness have shifted from asking whether institutions matter to inquiring how they matter. This study adds to such debates. The experience of a single regime (the MTCR) is not a firm basis for generalizing about all regimes, but it provides some crucial insights into the political, technological, institutional, and structural factors that influence security and arms control regimes.

First, *institutional design can have a significant impact on international cooperation and regime effectiveness.* Regimes that are exclusively technology-focused and lack a wider scope and more robust political-legal foundations are undermined by technological advances (in target states), commercial and economic pressures (from domestic lobbies in supplier states), and political changes (in the domestic politics of targets and suppliers, and in relations among suppliers or between suppliers and targets). This finding has important policy implications. It suggests that arms control regimes and possibly even defense regimes (as well as deterrence regimes that do not lock in strategic stability and instead allow new technologies to undercut deterrence) that rely exclusively on technological instruments can be undermined in time—perhaps within a decade—by technological advances and political changes.

Second, *two political factors affect the operation of regimes and can to some extent compensate for their institutional deficiencies.* The first factor is that regional security considerations influence state participation in global security regimes. In areas with regional tensions, an external security guarantee or improvements in regional security (that may result from democratization in both states of a dyad) increase the effectiveness of nonproliferation and security regimes. The second factor is that structural and domestic political-economic influences affect national decisions to comply with regimes. Increased interdependence in a globalized system makes regional powers vulnerable to external pressure to join regimes, especially when they pursue economic reforms that require integration with global markets. These findings can form the basis for further research on security regimes to generate wider policy applications; they also usefully predict the MTCR's future prospects.

Fifteen years after its creation, the missile regime stands at a critical juncture. The MTCR has substantially curbed missile proliferation and reduced it to a few hard cases. It may yet be successful if, during the additional time provided by technology barriers, international engagement and improvements in regional security persuade the few remaining proliferators of most serious concern, such as Iran and North Korea, to constrain their missile programs.

Yet an alternative scenario based on two destabilizing developments must also be considered. First, if key regional powers do not halt their missile activities, and they also export missiles to even a few other states, additional states will seek missile forces, and will be unconstrained from doing so by any international obligation or treaty. The demand for missiles will then increase, and former suppliers such as China and Russia could reenter the missile market. As a result, missile proliferation will revive, and may not be constrained to simply Scud or Nodong class missiles (that threaten only a neighboring state), but could include longer range multistage Taepodong class missiles that can strike distant states and seriously undermine regional and international security. Second, commercial developments such as the growth of the communications industry could make the development of rockets (to launch communications satellites) potentially lucrative. In this context, regional powers will have more legitimate grounds to pursue rocket programs, and foreign suppliers may be more inclined to transfer technology, resulting in the further proliferation of dual-use rocket and missile technology. To forestall these developments, an expanded regime with political and legal restraints on missile and rocket activities, and which addresses the dual-use dilemma, will be necessary to complement the MTCR. This regime could comprise regional missile-free zones, global intermediate-range missile bans, flight-test bans, verification provisions, and space service mechanisms. Such an expanded regime would provide a more robust institutional basis through which to contain missile proliferation and strengthen international security in the long term.

APPENDIX: TECHNICAL NOTES ON MISSILES

This book does not undertake a detailed technical examination of missiles, but a few basic features of missiles, their propulsion systems, and their WMD payloads are worth noting.

Ballistic Missiles, Cruise Missiles, and Other Missiles

The term "missile" refers to several types of systems—ballistic missiles, cruise missiles, artillery rockets, surface-to-air missiles (SAMs), and other low capability systems. The MTCR has been mainly concerned with ballistic missiles, which are the most threatening, though it can technically also cover cruise missiles and artillery rockets.

Cruise missiles are the technical equivalent of unmanned aircraft; they are generally slower and technically easier to intercept (British aircraft and anti-aircraft fire shot down many German V-1s in World War II, while air-to-air missiles have downed cruise missiles in recent tests), though they may still evade detection. The cruise missile threat should therefore not be underestimated, but should also not be overplayed. While over 70,000 cruise missiles have been manufactured by nineteen countries and exported to over seventy countries, two-thirds of these are antiship systems without much land attack capability, and most of the remaining systems have limited range and payload capacities.

SAMs and artillery rockets have very short ranges, but have some WMD delivery capability. Low-capability 1 to 10 km range SAMs are not significant threats, but bigger SAMs such as the 2.4 ton SA-2 and 4.7 ton Nike-Hercules have been converted into 40–180 km range surface-to-surface missiles. Artillery rockets with ranges of up to 150 km may also carry WMD payloads.

Solid and Liquid Fuel

Rockets use solid or liquid fuel propulsion systems. Most early U.S., Russian, and Chinese rockets used liquid fuel, while their later rockets used solid fuel; most regional powers have liquid-fuel Scud and Nodong missiles, but India's SLV-3 and SLV-derived Agni missile, Israel's Jericho, and Brazil's VLS use solid fuel. Liquid fuels have a greater specific impulse than solid fuels, which means they are more powerful and have greater range and payload capacities. Yet liquid-

Table A1. Technical Data for Selected Ballistic Missiles

Missile	Weight (tons)	Range (km)	Time of Flight (min)	Velocity (km/sec)	Altitude of Flight (km)	Distance From:	To:
Scud-B	6	300	4	1.8	75	Iraq	Western Iran
Scud-C	9	600	6	2.2	150	Iraq	Tehran, Israel
Nodong	16	1,000	8	3	240	N. Korea	W. and N. Japan
Taepodong-1	20	1,500+	10	3.5	350	N. Korea	S. and E. Japan
Agni-2	20	2,000	11.5	4	465	India	China
Css-2	64	2,500–3,500	13–16	4.5–5	570–760	S. Arabia	Israel
ss-20	40	5,000	20	6	1,000	Russia	France
ICBM	50–200	10,000	32	7	1,350	Russia	U.S.

fuel systems have many pipes, valves, and moving parts and are hard to handle. They may also be volatile and stored separately from a missile, and take time (a few minutes for Scuds, and hours or even days for other systems) to load onto a missile, and are therefore less optimal for quick launch military purposes. Thus, in theory, liquid fuels (and cryogenic fuels, which are liquefied gases) are better for satellite launchers which do not require rapid launches, while solid fuels are better for fast-launch rugged military missiles. In practice, both solid and liquid fuels are used in missiles and satellite launchers.

WMD Payloads and MTCR Thresholds

Ballistic missiles can carry conventional and WMD payloads. In terms of payload weights, early-generation nuclear weapons typically weigh over one ton, though they may eventually be miniaturized to under 500 kg. Chemical and biological payloads can be much lighter. The MTCR originally covered missiles that could deliver a 500 kg payload (the estimated smallest weight of a regional power nuclear warhead) to a 300 km range. It subsequently covered missiles capable of and intended for any WMD payload, such as chemical and biological payloads that are lighter than 500 kg. A missile's range increases if its payload weight is decreased; thus a missile having a 200 km range with a 500 kg warhead may have a 300 km range with a 200 kg warhead.

In general, ballistic missiles are optimal for nuclear delivery but less optimal for chemical and biological weapons delivery, which may be better undertaken by aircraft and cruise missiles.[1] Chemical agents deteriorate at high temperatures and can become ineffective under the heat of ballistic missile reentry or impact. Biological agents are most effective when distributed over a wide area, a task better carried out by aircraft and cruise missiles. Despite these limitations, chemical and biological agents can still be delivered on ballistic missiles, especially when they are placed in several small bomblets sheltered inside a larger heat-shielded warhead. For nuclear delivery, ballistic missiles that cannot be easily intercepted are preferable to aircraft, though regional powers may find it hard to build a compact lightweight nuclear warhead for missiles. The problem is especially relevant for SRBMs and IRBMs that have small diameters, but is somewhat reduced for ICBMs which have a larger diameter and can accommodate larger warheads.

Finally, in terms of ease of manufacture, regional powers can more easily build SRBMs but find it difficult to build IRBMs and ICBMs. For example, low-power SRBM engines are much easier to build than high-power IRBM and ICBM engines; and SRBMs with slow reentry velocities require only rudimentary heat shielding (that can be more easily developed by regional powers) while high-velocity ICBMs require sophisticated heat shielding.

NOTES

1. INTRODUCTION

1. *A Blueprint for New Beginnings: A Responsible Budget for America's Priorities* (Washington, D.C.: Government Printing Office, February 28, 2001).

2. President William Jefferson Clinton, Georgetown University, September 1, 2000. Clinton noted that "the rapid spread of technology across increasingly porous borders raises the specter that more and more states, terrorists and criminal syndicates could gain access to chemical, biological or even nuclear weapons and to . . . ballistic missiles capable of hurling those weapons halfway around the world."

3. William Schneider, "Europe Comes into Range," *Financial Times,* August 25, 1998.

4. "Missile Threat to U.S. 'Serious,' Report Warns," *Los Angeles Times,* September 10, 1999; National Intelligence Council, *Foreign Missile Developments and the Ballistic Missile Threat to the United States Through 2015* (Washington, D.C.: September 1999).

5. Peter Lavoy, "Nuclear Myths and the Causes of Nuclear Proliferation," *Security Studies* 2, no. 3/4 (Spring/Summer 1993): 192–212; Scott Sagan, "Why Do States Build Nuclear Weapons? Three Models in Search of a Bomb," *International Security* 21, no. 3 (Winter 1996/97): 54–86.

6. Robert Keohane and Lisa Martin, "The Promise of Institutionalist Theory," *International Security* 20, no. 1 (Summer 1995): 40.

7. A missile's weight may roughly, but does not necessarily, reflect its range. For example, China's first-generation 1,000 km range DF-2 weighed 32 tons and the 2,800 km range DF-3 (with a 2 ton payload) weighed 64 tons.

8. *Foreign Media Reaction Report,* "North Korea's Missile Test Over Japan: A Provocative Shot Across the Bow," September 3, 1998.

9. For a review of geography, proximity, psychological aspects, and conflict, see Paul Diehl, "Geography and War: A Review and Assessment of the Empirical Literature," *International Interactions* 17, no. 1 (1991): 11–27.

10. In July 1998, the Rumsfeld Commission suggested that the United States could face missile threats from North Korea, Iran, and Iraq significantly sooner and with far less warning than prior U.S. estimates, implying the need for accelerated missile defense. Missile defense budgets in subsequent years were $5–8 billion annually.

11. Beyond defense, control, and deterrence, missile threats can be countered via

counterproliferation strategies and the use of military force. These approaches are seldom used, the prominent exceptions being a 1981 Israeli strike on Iraq's Osirak nuclear reactor, a 1998 U.S. cruise missile strike on suspected chemical sites in Sudan, and the December 1998 U.S.-U.K. bombing of Iraqi WMD targets. Military assets and naval vessels have also blocked potential WMD cargoes from reaching target states in a few instances.

12. Most missile defense tests in the early and mid-1990s failed. Later tests had more success. Israel's Arrow-2 had several test successes between 1998 and 2000; the THAAD hit targets in its tenth and eleventh tests in 1999 (its first three tests, in 1995, were not intended to hit targets, and the fourth through ninth tests missed their targets); the Patriot PAC-3 had seven of eight successes against ballistic missile targets and four of four successes against air-breathing targets in 1999–2001, but failed its first operational test in 2002; and the Navy Area Theater system exceeded its budgets and was canceled. The NMD system failed two of its first three tests but succeeded in its next three tests from 1999 to early 2002, though critics argued that it could be evaded by decoys.

13. Joseph Biden, "Missile Defense Delusion," *Washington Post,* December 19, 2001. See also Dean Wilkening, *Ballistic Missile Defence and Strategic Stability,* Adelphi Paper 334, 2000; Ivo Daalder, James Goldgeier, and James Lindsay, "Deploying NMD: Not Whether, But How," *Survival* (Spring 2000).

14. *Foreign Media Reaction Report,* "Asian Security Issues: Countering Pyongyang's Brinkmanship; Debating U.S.-Japan Ties; Taiwan; Spratlys," January 26, 1999; "China Aims More Missiles at Taiwan," *Washington Post,* February 11, 1999.

2. REGIMES, TECHNOLOGY, POLITICS, AND PROLIFERATION

1. Stephen Krasner, "Structural Causes and Regime Consequences: Regimes as Intervening Variables," *International Organization* 36, no. 2 (Spring 1982): 186.

2. These principles are similar to those of the broader nonproliferation regime, which are that "a proliferated world is likely to be a nasty and dangerous place, entailing threats to the security and domestic well-being of virtually all nations." Lewis Dunn, "Nuclear Proliferation and World Politics," *Annals of the American Academy of Political and Social Science* 430 (March 1977): 97. In contrast, the logic of deterrence argues that nuclear deterrence prevents wars. For a discussion of this debate, see Scott Sagan and Kenneth Waltz, *The Spread of Nuclear Weapons: A Debate* (New York: W. W. Norton, 1995).

3. Charles Lipson, "Why Are Some International Agreements Informal?" *International Organization* 45, no. 2 (Autumn 1991): 504–38.

4. For verifying biological weapons nonproliferation, see the discussion in John Steinbruner, *Principles of Global Security* (Washington, D.C.: Brookings Institution, 2000).

5. For the application of this logic to multiple players and iterations over extended periods to perpetuate cooperation and preclude defection, see Robert Axelrod, *The Evolution of Cooperation* (New York: Basic Books, 1984).

6. "U.S. Seeks Changes in Germ War Pact," *New York Times,* November 1, 2001.

7. "Statement by the Assistant to the President for Press Relations," and "Missile Technology Regime: Fact Sheet to Accompany Public Announcement," The White House, Office of the Press Secretary, April 16, 1987.

8. Regimes generally originate through four channels or tracks—the evolutionary, spontaneous, contractual, and piecemeal tracks. The evolutionary track is one where institutions arise from widespread practice over time. The spontaneous process involves regime formation as a consequence of a dramatic, often unilateral action, that is subsequently accepted by others on a de facto basis. The evolutionary and spontaneous paths do not generally involve a negotiations process. In the contractual track, states negotiate a formal contract laying down rules for (typically many aspects of) an issue area. In the piecemeal track, parties negotiate on a few issues, with the anticipation that this will spill over into a broader regime covering additional issues over time. Oran Young, "International Regimes, Problems of Concept Formation," *World Politics* 32, no. 3 (April 1980): 331–56.

9. Mancur Olson, *The Logic of Collective Action: Public Goods and the Theory of Groups* (New York: Schocken Books, 1965), p. 2.

10. George Downs, David Rocke, and Peter Barsoom, "Managing the Evolution of Multilateralism," *International Organization* 52, no. 2 (Spring 1998): 397–419.

11. Duncan Snidal, "Coordination Versus Prisoner's Dilemma: Implications for International Cooperation and Regimes," *American Political Science Review* 79, no. 4 (December 1985): 929, 936.

12. Miles Kahler, "Multilateralism with Small and Large Numbers," *International Organization* 46, no. 3 (Summer 1992): 707.

13. Kenneth Oye, ed., *Cooperation Under Anarchy* (Princeton: Princeton University Press, 1986), pp. 20–21.

14. James Caporaso, "International Relations Theory and Multilateralism: The Search for Foundations," *International Organization* 46, no. 3 (Summer 1992): 610.

15. The degree of international legalization can be measured along three dimensions— obligation (the degree to which states are legally obliged to an agreement), precision (the extent to which rules are precisely identified), and delegation (the extent to which third parties are delegated to implement and enforce an agreement). Kenneth Abbott, Robert Keohane, Andrew Moravcsik, Anne-Marie Slaughter, and Duncan Snidal, "The Concept of Legalization," *International Organization* 54, no. 3 (Summer 2000): 401–19. On a scale of 1 to 8, the European Union and WTO-TRIPs ranked at 1, WTO-national treatment ranked at 2 (it was low on precision), U.S.-Russian arms control treaties ranked at 3 (they

were low on delegation), the Helsinki Final Act and technical standards ranked at 7, and the G-7 ranked at 8.

16. Andreas Hasenclever, Peter Mayer, and Volker Rittberger, *Theories of International Regimes* (Cambridge: Cambridge University Press, 1997).

17. Robert Gilpin, *The Political Economy of International Relations* (Princeton: Princeton University Press, 1987).

18. Charles Kindleberger, "International Public Goods Without International Government," *American Economic Review* 76, no. 1 (March 1986): 10; Charles Kindleberger, "Dominance and Leadership in the International Economy," *International Studies Quarterly* 25, no. 2 (June 1981): 242–54. Leadership does not have a totally benign nature; Kindleberger adds that leaders may become corrupted into taking dominant advantage, and leadership often has strong elements of arm twisting and bribery.

19. Arthur Stein, "Coordination and Collaboration: Regimes in an Anarchic World," *International Organization* 36, no. 2 (Spring 1982): 299–324.

20. Linkage strategies are common in other regimes. For example, in the Oceans regime, developing countries sought and gained access to a large 200 mile economic zone but the superpowers obtained rights of passage for their naval vessels. Edward Wenk, *The Politics of the Ocean* (Seattle: University of Washington Press, 1972).

21. Stephen Krasner, "State Power and the Structure of International Trade," *World Politics* 28, no. 3 (April 1976): 317–43.

22. Robert Keohane, *After Hegemony: Cooperation and Discord in the World Political Economy* (Princeton: Princeton University Press, 1984), pp. 101, 106.

23. Ernst Haas, "Why Collaborate? Issue-Linkage and International Regimes," *World Politics* 32, no. 3 (April 1980): 357–402.

24. Judith Goldstein and Robert Keohane, eds., *Ideas and Foreign Policy: Beliefs, Institutions and Political Change* (Ithaca: Cornell University Press, 1993), p. 20.

25. Katja Weber, "Hierarchy Amidst Anarchy: A Transaction Cost Approach to International Security Cooperation," *International Studies Quarterly* 41, no. 2 (June 1997): 321–40. Where threats are low and transaction costs are either low or high, neither cooperation nor informal alliances arise; when threats are high, low transaction costs result in binding alliances while high transaction costs give rise to confederations.

26. Robert Jervis, "Security Regimes," in Stephen Krasner, ed., *International Regimes* (Ithaca: Cornell University Press, 1982), pp. 173–94; Helga Haftendorn, Robert Keohane, and Celeste Wallander, *Imperfect Unions: Security Institutions Over Time and Space* (Oxford: Oxford University Press, 1999).

27. Charles Lipson, "International Cooperation in Economic and Security Affairs," *World Politics* 37, no. 1 (October 1984): 1–23.

28. John Mearsheimer, "Back to the Future: Instability in Europe After the Cold War," *International Security* 15, no. 6 (Summer 1990): 5–56; Joseph Grieco, "Anarchy and

the Limits of Cooperation: A Realist Critique of the Newest Liberal Institutionalism," *International Organization* 42, no. 3 (Summer 1988): 485–507.

29. Zachary Davis, "The Realist Nuclear Regime," *Security Studies* 2, no. 3/4 (Spring/Summer 1993): 79–99.

30. James Fearon, "Bargaining, Enforcement and International Cooperation," *International Organization* 52, no. 2 (Spring 1998): 269–305.

31. See, for example, David Baldwin, *Economic Statecraft* (Princeton: Princeton University Press, 1985); Michael Mastanduno, *Economic Containment: CoCom and the Politics of East-West Trade* (Ithaca: Cornell University Press, 1992).

32. Technological advances—the development of new and better technologies, advances in a state's technological capabilities (which enable it to develop and absorb new technologies), and the diffusion and transfer of technology between states (which enhance a state's technological capabilities)—are ubiquitous in world affairs. They critically sustain commercial competitiveness and economic development, and also have military spinoffs. Technological superiority allows states to balance rivals having larger economic and military capacities. As Betts notes, "Technological innovation traditionally plays a crucial role in American defense policy. In its military competition with the Soviet Union after World War II the United States used qualitative advantages in weaponry to compensate for Soviet quantitative advantages." Richard Betts, ed., *Cruise Missiles: Technology, Strategy, Politics* (Washington, D.C.: Brookings Institution, 1981), p. 1. Betts also cautions, "Military, budgetary, diplomatic, and political implications of technological advances, however, are seldom understood and often are not clear until long after new weapons have been deployed. Ensuring that . . . inadvertant negative consequences [of new military systems] do not outweigh their benefits has become progressively more important."

33. Sverre Lodgaard and Robert Pfaltzgraff, eds., *Arms and Technology Transfers: Security and Economic Considerations Among Importing and Exporting States* (Geneva: United Nations Institute for Disarmament Research, 1995), p. xi.

34. Gary Hufbauer, Jeffrey Schott, and Kimberly Ann Elliott, *Economic Sanctions Reconsidered: History and Current Policy* (Washington, D.C.: Institute for International Economics, 1990), p. 93; David Cortright and George A. Lopez, eds., *Economic Sanctions: Panacea or Peacebuilding in a Post–Cold War World?* (Boulder: Westview, 1995).

35. Gary Bertsch, Richard T. Cupitt, and Steven Elliott-Gower, *International Cooperation on Nonproliferation Export Controls: Prospects for the 1990s and Beyond* (Ann Arbor: University of Michigan Press, 1994); Richard Cupitt, Suzette Grillot, and Yuzo Murayama, "The Determinants of Nonproliferation Export Controls: A Membership-Fee Explanation," *Nonproliferation Review* 8, no. 2 (Summer 2001). See also Richard Cupitt, *Reluctant Champions* (New York: Routledge, 2000).

36. Peter Zimmerman, "Technical Barriers to Nuclear Proliferation," *Security Studies* 2, no. 3/4 (Spring/Summer 1993): 354.

37. Radio South Africa (Johannesburg) External Service, "Africa Today," July 17, 1986.

38. Stephanie Neuman, "Third World Arms Production and the Global Arms Transfer System," in James E. Katz, ed., *Arms Production in Developing Countries: An Analysis of Decision Making* (Lexington, Mass.: D.C. Heath, 1984), pp. 18–19.

39. Robert Harkavy, *The Arms Trade and International Systems* (Cambridge, Mass.: Ballinger, 1975), pp. 183–200; Steven Miller, *Arms and the Third World: Indigenous Weapons Production,* Program for Strategic and International Security Studies, Graduate Institute of International Studies, Geneva, PSIS Occasional Paper 3, December 1980; David Louscher and Michael Salomone, *Marketing Security Assistance: New Perspectives on Arms Sales* (Lexington, Mass.: D. C. Heath, 1987), pp. 167–68; Herbert Wulf, "Arms Production in the Third World," in *World Armaments and Disarmament: SIPRI Yearbook 1985* (London: Taylor and Francis, 1985), pp. 32–40; Edward Laurance, *The International Arms Trade* (New York: Lexington, 1992), p. 105.

40. U.S. Department of Defense, *The Military Critical Technologies List* (Washington, D.C.: GPO, October 1992).

41. James Sperling, David Louscher, and Michael Salomone, "Taking a Walk on the Supply Side: The Prospects for Weapons and Weapons Technology Diffusion and Control," Paper Presented at the Midwest Political Science Conference, Chicago, April 1997. The authors suggest that states with scores above 0.5 can develop most military technologies; states with scores between 0.5 and 0.125 are not highly competent across all fifteen categories, but they are still fairly competent in many categories.

42. Stephen Meyer, *The Dynamics of Nuclear Proliferation* (Chicago: University of Chicago Press, 1984).

43. Albert Hirschman, *National Power and the Structure of Foreign Trade* (Berkeley: University of California Press, 1945; reprint 1980), p. 3; David Baldwin, *Paradoxes of Power* (New York: Basil Blackwell, 1989), chap. 8, "Interdependence and Power: A Conceptual Analysis."

44. Robert Keohane and Joseph Nye, *Power and Interdependence* (Boston: Little, Brown, 1977).

45. The symmetry of dependence should also be considered. For states in a more balanced trading or security relationship, the stronger state does not have absolute leverage on the other, because mutual dependence between states (such as interdependence that is not highly asymmetrical) leads to bargaining that is not a zero-sum game. Thomas Schelling, *The Strategy of Conflict* (Cambridge: Harvard University Press, 1960), chap. 4, "Toward a Theory of Interdependent Decision." Asymmetric interdependence also does not automatically allow the less dependent actor to exercise political influence over the other. The exchange of economic resources for political concessions works if it makes both parties better off than they would be if they bargained over distributional gains from the economic relationship alone. This tradeoff is entirely independent of the degree of

asymmetry in the economic relationship, or its direction. R. Harrison Wagner, "Economic Interdependence, Bargaining Power, and Political Influence," *International Organization* 42, no. 3 (Summer 1988): 481–83.

46. When domestic pressures prevent a government from pursuing policies against other states, its credibility declines. Its ability to influence other states then falls as its reputation as a bluffer grows. Bruce Russett and Harvey Starr, *World Politics: The Menu for Choice* (San Francisco: Freeman, 1981), pp. 237–38.

47. Japan halted its economic aid to protest nuclear testing by India, Pakistan, and China in the late 1990s, and to protest missile testing by North Korea in 1998, but Japan has not pursued a sustained missile nonproliferation dialogue with regional powers. Similarly, West European states cut economic aid to India and Pakistan following their 1998 nuclear tests, but this was an ad hoc measure and not part of a broader nonproliferation initiative.

48. Regional powers received (1) economic development aid from international development banks such as the World Bank, (2) financial loans from the International Monetary Fund, and (3) foreign direct investment. Figures for these three sources of foreign assistance, indicated as seven-year totals for 1990–96 in billion dollars, and as a percentage of GNP, are as follows: South Korea (1.6, -, 8.1; 0.25%); Taiwan (-, -, 8.3; 0.5%); Egypt (3.6, 0.1, 4.9; 3%); South Africa (0.1, 0.6, 1.0; 0.3%); Brazil (14.7, 0.1, 23.2; 0.6%); Argentina (12.9, 5.1, 15.6; 1.7%); Israel (-, 0.2, 5.6; 0.6%); India (20.7, 3.6, 7.0; 1.4%); Pakistan (9.1, 1.0, 2.8; 3.5%); Iran (0.8, -, -; 0.1%).

49. The United States is dependent on foreign sources for over half of the major non-fuel minerals needed by an industrial nation. However, it could stockpile reserves and had or could develop substitutes for these minerals. The United States is partly dependent on Brazil and South Africa, and to a lesser extent on Argentina, India, and Israel, for about ten of thirty-eight major minerals. U.S. Geological Survey, *Mineral Commodity Summaries,* 1997.

50. Robert Gilpin, "Three Models of the Future," in C. Fred Bergsten and Lawrence B. Krause, eds., *World Politics and International Economics* (Washington, D.C.: Brookings, 1975), p. 40.

51. In 1992–96, the United States supplied over 90 percent of Israel's, Taiwan's, and Egypt's arms imports, and approximately 60 percent of South Korea's, 75 percent of Argentina's, and 60 percent of Brazil's, but a low 10 percent of India's, Pakistan's, and South Africa's. U.S. Arms Control and Disarmament Agency, *World Military Expenditures and Arms Transfers* (1995 and 1997 editions).

52. Data from Stockholm Institute of Peace Research databank.

53. Gabriel Almond, "Capitalism and Democracy," *PS: Political Science and Politics,* September 1991, pp. 467–74; Symposium of the *Journal of Democracy* 5, no. 4 (October 1994); Stephen Haggard and Robert Kaufman, *The Political Economy of Democratic Transitions* (Princeton: Princeton University Press, 1995).

54. Etel Solingen, "The Political Economy of Nuclear Restraint," *International Security* 19, no. 2 (Fall 1994): 126–69; Etel Solingen, *Regional Orders at Century's Dawn: Global and Domestic Influences on Grand Strategy* (Princeton: Princeton University Press, 1998).

55. Bryan Johnson, Kim Holmes, and Melanie Kirkpatrick, *1999 Index of Economic Freedom* (Washington, D.C.: The Heritage Foundation, 1999).

56. Democratic norms and cultural explanations suggest that a democratic political culture favors the peaceful resolution of internal disputes. The culture, perceptions, and practices that permit compromise within democracies spill over to relations with other democracies. Decision makers also expect their counterparts in other democratic states to follow peaceful norms of conflict resolution; they therefore do not fear war and are less likely to initiate a preemptive war.

The structural and institutional model for the democratic peace focuses on restraints imposed by a population unwilling to pay the price of war. Checks and balances on the executive and the need for public debate to enlist support for war considerably slow decisions for war, and reduce the likelihood that such decisions will be taken. Leaders in opposing states, perceiving leaders of democracies as so constrained, therefore do not fear surprise attack, and in turn do not initiate a preemptive war to forestall being subject to a surprise attack.

For a literature review, see Michael Brown, Sean Lynn Jones, and Steven Miller, eds., *Debating the Democratic Peace* (Cambridge: MIT Press, 1996); Zeev Maoz, "The Controversy Over the Democratic Peace: Rearguard Action or Cracks in the Wall," *International Security* 22, no. 1 (Summer 1997): 162–98.

57. Mitchell Reiss, *Without the Bomb: The Politics of Nuclear Proliferation* (New York: Columbia University Press, 1988).

58. George Perkovich, *India's Nuclear Bomb: The Impact on Global Proliferation* (Berkeley: University of California Press, 2000).

59. An illustrative example is Pakistan, where Prime Minister Benazir Bhutto noted, "My father [Prime Minister Zulfiqar Ali Bhutto] gave this country a nuclear program, I gave this country the delivery system to carry nuclear payloads." See Reuters, "Bhutto Claims Credit for Pakistan's Long-range-Missile," April 10, 1998.

60. In the case of Pakistan, two prime ministers—Zulfiqar Ali Bhutto and Nawaz Sharif—sought to strengthen their hands versus Pakistan's military by attempting to control the national nuclear program. See Stephen Cohen, "Pakistan: Once Again a Pivotal State (But for How Long?)," Brookings Institution, July 1999.

61. Keith Jaggers and Ted Robert Gurr, "Transitions to Democracy: Tracking Democracy's Third Wave with the Polity III Data," *Journal Of Peace Research* 32 (November 1995): 469–82. Freedom House ranks for Political Rights, Civil Liberties, and Freedom (with 1 representing most free and 7 representing least free) in 1998 were as follows: Argentina (3, 3, Free), Brazil (3, 4, Partly Free), India (2, 3, Free), South Africa

(1, 2, Free), South Korea (2, 2, Free), Israel (1, 3, Free), Taiwan (2, 2, Free), Pakistan (4, 5, Partly Free), Iran (6, 6, Not Free), Egypt (6, 6, Not Free), North Korea (7, 7, Not Free). Freedom House, *The Comparative Survey of Freedom* (Washington, D.C.: Freedom House, 1999).

62. Gary King, Robert Keohane, and Sidney Verba, *Designing Social Inquiry: Scientific Inference in Qualitative Research* (Princeton: Princeton University Press, 1994), p. 211; Harry Eckstein, "Case Study and Theory in Political Science," in Fred Greenstein and Nelson Polsby, eds., *Handbook of Political Science* (Reading, Mass.: Addison-Wesley, 1975), 7:108–15.

63. Stanley Lieberson, "Small N's and Big Conclusions," in Charles Ragin and Howard Becker, *What Is a Case? Exploring the Foundations of Social Inquiry* (Cambridge: Cambridge University Press, 1992), pp. 105–18.

3. BUILDING A SUPPLY-SIDE REGIME

1. *The Globalist,* February 21, 2001.

2. United States Central Intelligence Agency, *Unclassified Report to Congress on the Acquisition of Technology Relating to Weapons of Mass Destruction and Advanced Conventional Munitions, 1 January Through 30 June 2000* (Washington, D.C.: February 2001).

3. Ibid.

4. Aaron Karp, *The United States and the Soviet Union and the Control of Ballistic Missile Proliferation in the Middle East* (New York: Institute for East-West Security Studies, 1990); Jurgen Scheffran and Aaron Karp, "National Implementation of the MTCR: The U.S. and German Experiences," in Hans Gunter Brauch, Henry van der Graaf, John Grin, and Wim Smit, eds., *Controlling the Development and Spread of Military Technology* (Amsterdam: Vu University Press, 1992), pp. 238–40; W. Seth Carus, *Ballistic Missiles in the Third World* (Westport, Conn.: Praeger, 1990).

5. The transaction was advanced by the State Department despite objections from the Defense Department and NASA. Moreover, labor and eventually even corporate groups opposed U.S. rocket technology transfers. The AFL-CIO protested against corporate-driven exports of U.S. satellite technology because they feared this would stimulate foreign competition and hurt American workers. In 1977, U.S. satellite manufacturers also voiced concerns about foreign competition resulting from U.S. technology transfer. U.S. Senate, *U.S. Export Control Policy and Extension of the Export Administration Act,* Hearing Before the Subcommittee on International Finance of the Committee on Banking, Housing and Urban Affairs, March 12, 1979, p. 39.

6. Henry Sokolski, *Best of Intentions: America's Campaign Against Strategic Weapons Proliferation* (Westport: Praeger, 2001), p. 66.

7. "Statement by ACDA Director Ikle to the Conference of the Committee on

NOTES TO CHAPTER 3

Disarmament: Arms Transfers, Nuclear Cooperation, and Non-Proliferation, 19 July, 1976," *Documents on Disarmament 1976* (Washington, D.C.: U.S. Arms Control and Disarmament Agency, 1978), p. 500.

8. Janne Nolan, "The U.S.-Soviet Conventional Arms Transfer Negotiations," in Alexander George, Philip Farley, and Alexander Dallin, eds., *U.S.-Soviet Security Cooperation* (Oxford: Oxford University Press, 1988), p. 515.

9. U.S. Arms Control and Disarmament Agency, *World Military Expenditures and Arms Transfers, 1969–78* (Washington, D.C.: GPO, December 1980), p. 21.

10. "Statement by the Director of the Department of State Bureau of Politico-Military Affairs (Gelb) Before a Special Panel of the House Armed Services Committee: Conventional Arms Transfers, October 3, 1978," *Documents on Disarmament 1978,* October 1980, p. 596.

11. Maurice Eisenstein, "Third World Missiles and Nuclear Proliferation," *The Washington Quarterly,* Summer 1982, p. 115.

12. Unless otherwise cited, much of the discussion in this and the following section is drawn from Richard Speier, *The Missile Technology Control Regime: Case Study of a Multilateral Negotiation,* Manuscript Submitted to the United States Institute of Peace, Washington, D.C., November 1995.

13. National Security Decision Directive 50, August 6, 1982, Implementing Guidelines to the Space Assistance and Cooperation Policy, Section C.

14. Ibid., Section B.

15. 500 kg was the estimated weight of a light nuclear payload and was determined by analysts at a research lab. The 300 km range figure was derived by inspection of the Korean peninsula. The 10 km CEP figure was the estimated CEP that would result in significant damage from a 20 kiloton nuclear weapon targeted against a dispersed urban area.

16. Martin Navias, *Going Ballistic: The Build-up of Missiles in the Middle East* (London: Brassey's, 1993), p. 198.

17. "Statement by the Assistant to the President for Press Relations," and "Missile Technology Regime: Fact Sheet to Accompany Public Announcement," The White House, Office of the Press Secretary (Santa Barbara, California), April 16, 1987.

18. Testimony of Dr. Janne E. Nolan, in U.S. Senate, *Ballistic and Cruise Missile Proliferation in the Third World,* Hearing Before the Subcommittee on Defense Industry and Technology, Committee on Armed Services, May 2, 1989, p. 55.

19. Statement of Vincent DeCain, in U.S. House, *Missile Proliferation: The Need for Controls (Missile Technology Control Regime),* Hearing Before the Subcommittees on Arms Control, International Security and Science and on International Economic Policy and Trade, Committee on Foreign Affairs, July 12 and October 30, 1989, p. 10.

20. *Arms Control Reporter* 1990, p. 706.B.32 (6–90).

21. *Washington Post,* April 6, 1990.

22. Moscow exported rockets and missiles to Algeria (Frog-7, 1975), Cuba (Frog-4, 1961), Egypt (Frog-7, 1971; Scud-B, 12 launchers and over 100 missiles, 1973), Kuwait (Frog-7, 1978), Iraq (Frog-7, 1969; Scud-B, 800 missiles, 1976–85), Libya (Frog-7, 1978; Scud-B, 72 missiles, 1976), North Korea (Frog-7, 1969), North Yemen (SS-21, 1988), South Yemen (Frog-7 and Scud-B, 6 launchers, 1979; SS-21, 4 launchers, 1988), and Syria (Frog-7, 1973; Scud-B, 18 launchers, 1974; SS-21, 1983). These exports were part of larger arms transfer packages. William Potter and Adam Stulberg, "The Soviet Union and the Spread of Ballistic Missiles," *Survival* 32, no. 6 (November/December 1990): 544–50; Wyn Bowen, *The Politics of Ballistic Missile Nonproliferation* (New York: St. Martin's, 2000), p. 15.

23. Following 1955 nuclear cooperation agreements, Moscow transferred two SS-2 missiles and their blueprints in 1958, from which China built an experimental 600 km range "Type-1059" (later designated DF-1) ballistic missile. Both a Soviet-acquired version and a Chinese version were flight-tested in 1960. The 1,000 km range DF-2 (CSS-1) was developed from notes and drawings of the Soviet R-5/SS-3; a flight test failed in 1962 but was successful in 1964, and an extended 1,250 km range version (DF-2A) was tested in 1965. The 2,500 km range DF-3 (CSS-2), similar to the Soviet R-12/SS-4, was successfully tested in 1966. Robert Norris, Andrew Burrows, and Richard Fieldhouse, *Nuclear Weapons Databook Volume V: British, French, and Chinese Nuclear Weapons* (Boulder: Westview, 1994), pp. 358–65.

24. William Potter and Adam Stulberg, "The Soviet Union and the Spread of Ballistic Missiles," *Survival* 32, no. 6 (November/December 1990): 546.

25. Alexander Pikayev, Leonard Spector, Elina Kirichenko, and Ryan Gibson, *Russia, the U.S. and the Missile Technology Control Regime,* Adelphi Paper 317, 1998, p. 40. Some reformers also noted that Washington was ignoring the difficult situation it faced in dealing with weakened state institutions and enforcement mechanisms—a weakness that did not allow easy cancellation of the deal. Washington's 1992 missile sanctions affected the pro-U.S. foreign policy pursued by Moscow after the failed August 1991 coup, and Prime Minister Chernomyrdin canceled a trip to the United States. However, after the 1993 missile compromise, pro-Western groups reestablished bureaucratic support for accommodation with the West.

26. Michael Beck, Maria Katsva, and Igor Khripunov, "Assessing Proliferation Controls in Russia," *Nonproliferation Export Controls: A Global Evaluation* (Athens: University of Georgia Center for International Trade and Security, 2001).

27. Alexander Pikayev, "Russia and the Missile Technology Control Regime," in Gary Bertsch and William Potter, eds., *Dangerous Weapons, Desperate States* (New York: Routledge, 1999), p. 208.

28. U.S. Department of State, "Missile Technology Control Regime," archived at http://www.state.gov/www/global/arms/treaties/mtcr_anx.html.

29. "Reckless Russian Rocket Exports," A Nonproliferation Education Center Policy

Brief, May 30, 1997 (Washington, D.C.: Nonproliferation Policy Education Center); Stephen Blank, "Russia as Rogue Proliferator," *Orbis* 44, no. 1 (Winter 2000): 96–97; "Russia, China Aid Iran's Missile Program," *Washington Times*, September 10, 1997, p. 1.

30. The nine firms investigated by Moscow were Glavkosmos, Baltic State Technical University, Grafit Research Institute, Polyus Scientific Research Institute, Tikhomorov Instrument Building State Research Institute, Komintern Plant in Novosibirsk, Russian Scientific and Production Center (INOR), MOSO, and Europalas 2000.

31. The firms sanctioned by Washington in January 1999 were the Mendeleyev Chemical Technical University in Moscow, the Scientific Research and Design Institute of Power and Technology, and the Moscow Aviation Institute. "U.S. Punishes 3 Russian Institutions," *Washington Post,* January 12, 1999.

32. Washington's ban on all contact or educational exchanges with the BSTU (Baltic State Technical University) rector Mr. Savalyev remained in force. This was because of the university's program to teach Iranian students courses in advanced physics, metallurgy, and gas and fluids dynamics. The courses offered by Savalyev and BSTU had previously been investigated by the Russian government, which then banned some of these and also reprimanded Savalyev. See Patrick Tyler, "A Case Shows Russia's Quandary in Preventing Leaks of Arms Lore," *New York Times,* May 10, 2000. Moscow noted that the lifting of sanctions was the result of joint U.S.-Russian efforts and Washington's appraisal of a Russian commitment to export controls, but was surprised that sanctions against other firms and against Mr. Savalyev remained. Russian Foreign Ministry Press Release 354-26-4-2000, April 26, 2000.

33. Bill Gertz, "Russia Sells Missile Technology to North Korea," *Washington Times,* June 30, 2000.

34. Fred Wehling, "Russian Nuclear and Missile Exports to Iran," *Nonproliferation Review* 6, no. 2 (Winter 1999): 134–44.

35. The Nuclear Non-Proliferation Project, Carnegie Endowment for International Peace, *Proceedings of the June 1997 Conference.*

36. Beck, Katsva, and Khripunov, "Assessing Proliferation Controls in Russia" (see note 26 above).

37. Alexander Pikayev, "The Business of Russian Cooperation with Iran," *Proliferation Brief* 4, no. 6 (April 6, 2001).

38. *Arms Control Reporter* 1993, p. 706.B130 (7–93).

39. "International Control of Missile Technology Queried," *FBIS-SOV,* June 8, 1994, citing *Nezavisimaya Gazeta* (Moscow), June 7, 1994, p. 1.

40. The Nuclear Non-Proliferation Project, Carnegie Endowment for International Peace, *Proceedings of the June 1997 Conference.*

41. "Syria's Acquisition of North Korean Scuds," *Jane's Intelligence Review,* June 1991, pp. 249–51.

42. Testimony of Dr. Gordon Oehler, "Hearing on the Proliferation of Chinese Missiles," U.S. Senate, June 11, 1998.

43. Robert Ross, "China," in Richard Haass, ed., *Economic Sanctions and American Diplomacy* (Washington, D.C.: Council on Foreign Relations, 1998), pp. 22–25.

44. Jim Mann, "China Said to Sell Pakistan Dangerous New Missiles," *Los Angeles Times,* December 4, 1992, pp. A1, 18.

45. Robert Shuey and Shirley A. Kan, *Chinese Missile and Nuclear Proliferation: Issues for Congress* (Washington, D.C.: Foreign Affairs and National Defense Division, Congressional Research Service, November 16, 1995).

46. John Wilson Lewis and Hua Di, "China's Ballistic Missile Programs," *International Security* 17, no. 2 (Fall 1992): 5–40; John Lewis, Hua Di, and Xue Litai, "Beijing's Defense Establishment: Solving the Arms-Export Enigma," *International Security* 15, no. 4 (Spring 1991): 87–108.

47. Hao Jia, "China's Nuclear Nonproliferation Policy and International Regimes" (Ph.D. dissertation, George Washington University, 1999), p. 286.

48. Mingquan Zhu, "The Evolution of China's Nuclear Nonproliferation Policy," *Nonproliferation Review* 4, no. 2 (Winter 1997): 40–48; Zachary Davis, "China's Nonproliferation and Export Control Policies," *Asian Survey* 35, no. 6 (June 1995): 587–603; Banning N. Garrett and Bonnie S. Glaser, "Chinese Perspectives on Nuclear Arms Control," *International Security* 20, no. 3 (Winter 1995–96): 43–78; Wendy Frieman, "New Members of the Club—Chinese Participation in Arms Control Regimes 1980–1995," *Nonproliferation Review* 3, no. 3 (Spring/Summer 1996): 26.

49. East Asia Nonproliferation Project, Center for Nonproliferation Studies, Monterey, California; Jing dong Yuan, "China's Nonproliferation Policies 1989–1999," Paper Presented at the International Studies Association Annual Meeting, 1999; Richard Cupitt, "Export Controls in the People's Republic of China," *Bulletin of Asia Pacific Studies,* March 1999, pp. 29–72.

50. Evan Medeiros and Bates Gill, *Chinese Arms Exports: Policy, Players, and Process* (Carlisle, Penn.: Strategic Studies Institute, August 2000), pp. 36–38.

51. R. Jeffrey Smith, "China Linked to Pakistani Missile Plant," *Washington Post,* August 25, 1996, p. A01; "The Secret Missile Deal," *Time,* June 30, 1997.

52. Shirley Kan, *China's Proliferation of Weapons of Mass Destruction and Missiles,* CRS Report to Congress, March 12, 2001.

53. "Russia, China Aid Iran's Missile Program," *Washington Times,* September 10, 1997, p. 1; Aaron Karp, "Lessons of Iranian Missile Programs for U.S. Nonproliferation Policy," *Nonproliferation Review* 5, no. 3 (Spring/Summer 1998): 22.

54. Kan, *China's Proliferation of Weapons of Mass Destruction.*

55. Bill Gertz, "Beijing Delivered Missile Technology to Libya," *Washington Times,* April 13, 2000.

56. "Selling Missiles to China," *Washington Times,* March 23, 1998, p. A19. This

report appeared ahead of Robert Einhorn's expert-level talks in China on March 23 and John Holum's Global Security discussions on March 25.

57. Beijing's November 21, 2000, statement allowed Washington to waive sanctions that were simultaneously imposed on Iran and Pakistan for Beijing's past transfers to these states. A series of high-level meetings, including an unannounced trip to Beijing that month by Robert Einhorn, assistant secretary of state for nonproliferation affairs, and Gary Samore of the National Security Council, concluded an agreement; President Clinton and Jiang Zemin approved the agreement at a mid-November economic summit in Brunei. John Lancaster, "U.S. Waives Proliferation Penalties on China," *Washington Post,* November 22, 2000, p. A20.

58. "U.S. Pressures China Over Arms Exports," *Washington Times,* August 7, 2001.

59. "Reaction to Missile Technology Sales, Sanctions" *FBIS-CHI,* August 27, 1993, p. 1; "Official Protests to U.S. Envoy," ibid.

60. Evan Medeiros, Monterey Institute, author interview, July 2001.

61. Bates Gill and Evan Medeiros, "Foreign and Domestic Influences on China's Arms Control and Nonproliferation Policies," *China Quarterly* no. 161 (March 2000).

62. A press report stated that in December 1994, Zaire had a $100 million deal for 18 Scud-C missiles. *Le Point* (Paris), January 28, 1995, p. 19, in *FBIS-EAS-95-025,* January 28, 1995. Another report stated that between April and October 1995, Peru held meetings with North Korea to discuss a $52.5 million purchase of Scud-C missiles, although Peru's President Alberto Fujimori denied the report. *EFE* (Madrid), December 20, 1995, in *FBIS-LAT-95-244,* December 20, 1995, cited in Center for Nonproliferation Studies, *Chronology of North Korea's Missile Trade and Developments: 1994–1995.* For the Vietnamese transaction, see "Vietnam Stocking Up Scuds," *Jane's Defence Weekly,* April 14, 1999.

63. "N. Korea Sells Iran Missile Engines," *Washington Times,* February 9, 2000. The engines were transported from North Korea in an Iran Air Boeing 747.

64. "North Korea Sends Missile Parts, Technology to Iran," *Washington Times,* April 18, 2001.

65. "North Korea Admits Selling Missiles," *Washington Post,* June 16, 1998.

66. The following discussion on MTCR meetings is drawn from *Arms Control Reporter,* various years.

67. "Missile Technology Control Regime: Joint Appeal," Tokyo, November 6, 1997. MTCR documents are archived with the Stockholm International Peace Research Institute, http://projects.sipri.se/expcon/mtcr_documents.htm, and at www.mtcr.info.

68. "Plenary Meeting of the Missile Technology Control Regime, Ottawa, Canada, 25–28 September 2001," Press Release, September 28, 2001.

69. "Bonn Stops Ghost Ship," in "Shipment of Scud Missile Parts to Syria Halted," Foreign Broadcast Information Service, *FBIS-WEU,* January 15, 1993, p. 21.

70. U.S. Senate, *Ballistic and Cruise Missile Proliferation in the Third World,* Hearing

Before the Subcommittee on Defense Industry and Technology, Committee on Armed Services, May 2, 1989, p. 54.

71. For example, the 1993 U.S. sanctions blocked $1 billion worth of U.S. high technology exports, particularly satellite systems, to the Chinese Ministry of Defense and Ministry for Aerospace Industry. The restrictions could have expanded to $3–4 billion if Washington determined that complete missiles, and not just missile components, had been shipped to Pakistan (*Arms Control Reporter* 1993, p. 706.B143 (9–93)). U.S. space technology companies including Martin Marietta and Hughes Aircraft lobbied the Clinton administration to lift the sanctions which would otherwise cause large layoffs (*Arms Control Reporter* 1993, p. 706.B152 (11–93)).

By November 1993, Washington offered to reinterpret U.S. export laws to permit the export of two of the seven satellites banned by sanctions. In return Beijing was asked to open formal talks on its missile sale policy. In January 1994, despite lack of progress at the January 24–27 talks in Paris, the U.S. Commerce Department approved the sale of three satellites to China. The Commerce Department sidestepped MTCR restrictions by considering the export license requests as applications for the whole satellite system (whose exports would be permitted under U.S. MTCR-related laws) rather than for the embedded technology which was barred from export. *Arms Control Reporter* 1993, p. 706.B157 (1–94); *Arms Control Reporter* 1994, p. 706.B165 (3–94).

72. The White House, "Fact Sheet—Statement on National Space Transportation Policy," August 5, 1994.

73. Beck, Katsva, and Khripunov, "Assessing Proliferation Controls in Russia" (see note 26 above). This study measured national export control systems along several indicators: licenses, lists, international regime membership, catch-all provisions, training, agency process, customs, verification, and penalty for violations.

4. ARGENTINA, BRAZIL, SOUTH AFRICA

1. *Orlando Sentinel,* July 2, 2000, p. H1.

2. Decree 604 of April 9, 1985, citing Legislation 951 (December 13, 1984), noted that the Condor-1 was in its final stages, and that it could produce a satellite launch vehicle, could generate space exports, and represented a technological advance. To establish an adequate link between Condor-1 and Condor-2, the firms IFAT, Desintec, and Consen would provide technical assistance, materials, and teams for the Condor-2, and would buy some production for export. The decree mandated that the air force staff in the Cordoba area would oversee the project and handle contracts, and the ministries of defense, economy, and foreign relations, and the central banks, would allow completion of the project. It was signed by President Alfonsin and the ministers of defense, foreign relations, and the economy.

Decree 1315 of August 13, 1987, gave further approval to the Condor-2; it looked forward to external technology flows and to commercial links with foreign firms. The decree approved a contract between the air force and the firms Consultec and Desintec to constitute the Integrada Aerospace Corporation to complete the Condor-1 and Condor-2, whose activities were in the national interest. It authorized the defense ministry and air force to fund the project. It was signed by President Alfonsin. Daniel Santero, *Operacion Condor II: La Historia Secreta del Misil Que Desactivo Menem* (Buenos Aires: Ediciones Letra Buena, 1992).

3. Robert Shuey, *Missile Proliferation: A Discussion of U.S. Policy Objectives and Policy Options* (Washington, D.C.: Congressional Research Service, February 21, 1990), p. 32; Robert Shuey, *Missile Proliferation: Survey of Emerging Missile Forces* (Washington, D.C.: Congressional Research Service, October 3, 1988; updated February 9, 1989); Scott Tollefson, "El Condor Pasa: The Demise of Argentina's Ballistic Missile Program," in William Potter and Harlan Jencks, eds., *The International Missile Bazaar: The New Suppliers' Network* (Boulder: Westview, 1994), pp. 255–78; Janne Nolan, *Trappings of Power* (Washington, D.C.: Brookings, 1991), p. 53. The Consen Group included Consen SA, IFAT Corporation Ltd (Institute for Advanced Technology), and Desintec AG (a subsidiary of IFAT). Some of the Condor technology made its way to Iraq and Egypt; Egypt's Abu Zaabal Chemical Company helped the Taj al-Maarik solid-fuel plant in Latifiyah (al Hillah), while Western firms supplied equipment to the Saad 16 Al Kindi Research Complex.

4. Aaron Karp, *Ballistic Missile Proliferation* (Oxford: Oxford University Press, 1996).

5. R. Graham, "Argentina to Seek Venture for Condor Missile Team," *Financial Times,* April 10, 1990, p. 9.

6. "Argentina, Acceding to U.S., Ends Missile Program," *New York Times,* May 30, 1991.

7. *Arms Control Reporter* 1991, p. 706.B.60–61 (6–91).

8. U.S. Deputy Assistant Secretary of State for Political-Military Affairs Robert Walpole visited Falda del Carmen with Argentine Defense Secretary Juan Ferreira Pino to confirm the deactivation of the Condor. In April and May 1992, another U.S. delegation headed by Undersecretary of State for International Security Reginald Bartholomew was in Argentina. In September 1992, a technical mission led by the State Department's Head of Security and Licenses Granting Office, William Skok, visited Argentina to discuss its export controls and adoption of COCOM and MTCR guidelines. *Proliferation Issues,* March 13, 1992, pp. 13–14, citing *Clarin* (Buenos Aires), March 1, 1992, p. 10; Nuclear Non-Proliferation Network News, March 26, 1993.

9. The Capricornio had three problems: it could not acquire a U.S. gyroscopic platform for its guidance system; it was unable to develop solid-fuel systems; and it could not attain mechanical reliability. In September 1992, Spanish technicians toured Argentine workshops for fuel, ballistic trials, metallurgy, electronics and control, com-

posite materials, and navigational and guidance systems. "Condor II Revival in Support of Spanish Space Program," *International Defense Review,* November 1992, p. 1062.

10. Argentina's nuclear and missile projects were pursued by separate bureaucracies: Argentina's navy sought to collaborate with the atomic energy agency and develop nuclear reactors for submarines (though these plans were not seriously pursued), while the air force dominated the Condor rocket project.

11. Stanley Hilton, "The Argentine Factor in Twentieth Century Brazilian Foreign Policy Strategy," *Political Science Quarterly* 100, no. 1 (Spring 1985): 27.

12. Mitchell Reiss, *Bridled Ambition: Why Countries Constrain Their Nuclear Capabilities* (Washington, D.C.: Woodrow Wilson Center, and Baltimore: Johns Hopkins Press, 1995).

13. *Arms Control Reporter* 1991, p. 706.B.73 (1–92), citing *FBIS-LAT,* October 28, 1991.

14. "Argentina Lagging on Missile Pledge," *New York Times,* August 19, 1992.

15. In February 1990, President Carlos Menem denied that the Condor-2 was delayed by U.S. pressure, and instead noted that delays were for economic reasons. Yet an air force officer stated that the Condor project was suspended so that Argentina could export five hundred IA-63 Pampa aircraft to the U.S. air force. On April 24, 1990, Menem noted that the Condor project was curbed to avoid a confrontation with the United States and other countries. *Arms Control Reporter* 1990, p.706.B.33 (6–90); "Menem Says Missile Scrapped over U.S. Concerns," in *FBIS-LAT,* April 26, 1990, p. 20.

16. "Cheney's Remarks on Military Cooperation Reported," *Noticias* (Buenos Aires), February 20, 1992, in *FBIS-LAT,* February 24, 1992, p. 22. Carlos Menem showed the Argentine military that his government could reestablish military contacts with the United States and secure A-4 aircraft and spare parts, but the Condor would have to be curbed. The Bush administration supplied Menem with detailed intelligence on the Condor program that the military had kept from him. Henry Sokolski, "Nonproliferation: Strategies for Winning, Losing and Coping," Paper Presented at the American Political Science Association Annual Convention, Boston, Massachusetts, September 2, 1998.

17. *Arms Control Reporter* 1993, p. 706.B.107 (3–93).

18. In June 1993, Washington pressed Buenos Aires to account for missing Condor components, particularly three "Sageme wings" which housed missile guidance and control systems. Washington also requested Argentina to destroy the Falda del Carmen facilities at Cordoba, but the Argentine air force protested, arguing that the destruction was expensive and not required under the prior U.S.-Argentina agreement. In August 1993, Defense Minister Camilion stated that the Cordoba facilities would be recycled to preserve their valuable components, and that Argentina would deliver more Condor components to Spain in September, including two of the three Sageme guidance boxes—the third was not functional. Thrust vector control parts and two launching trucks were also

sent to Spain. *Arms Control Reporter* 1993, p. 706.B.122 (6-93); *Arms Control Reporter* 1993, p. 706.B.136 (9–93).

19. "Editorial Criticizes Handling of Condor Missile Issue," *FBIS-LAT,* June 23, 1993, p. 029, citing "The United States, Chile and Argentina," *La Prensa* (Buenos Aires), June 20, 1993, p. 10. Opposition members of Parliament also questioned Menem's actions. Radical Civic Union (UCR) deputies asked the executive branch not to accept a U.S. petition to destroy the Falda del Carmen plant in Cordoba and its solid-fuel blending equipment and other components. They noted that Argentina had sovereign rights to a solid-fuel manufacturing plant under international controls. "UCR Deputies Reject U.S. Petition to Destroy Missile Plant," *FBIS-LAT,* March 11, 1993, p. 015.

20. "Space Offers Fast Track to Technology Mainstream," *Aviation Week & Space Technology,* March 4, 1996, p. 49.

21. Scott Tollefson, "Brazilian Arms Transfers, Ballistic Missiles, and Foreign Policy: The Search for Autonomy" (Ph.D. dissertation, Johns Hopkins University, 1991); Pericles Gasparini Alves, "Brazilian Missile and Rocket Production and Export," in William Potter and Harlan W. Jencks, eds., *The International Missile Bazaar: The New Suppliers' Network* (Boulder: Westview, 1994), pp. 99–127; Steven Flank, "Reconstructing Rockets: The Politics of Developing Military Technology in Brazil, India, and Israel" (Ph.D. dissertation, Massachusetts Institute of Technology, 1993).

22. "First Tests Ever on Brazil's ss-300," *Jane's Defence Weekly,* December 20, 1986, p. 1428.

23. The Brazilian Commission for Space Activities (COBAE) was responsible for the MECB. The civilian Space Research Institute (INPE) built Brazil's satellites. The air force's Aerospace Technology Center (CTA) and its Space Activities Institute developed the 49 ton VLS.

24. *Jane's Space Directory,* 1994–95, p. 196.

25. "Officer Reveals Smuggling of Technology for SLV," *Agencia Estado* (São Paulo), December 4, 1995, in *FBIS-LAT-95-233,* December 4, 1995.

26. *Arms Control Reporter* 1995, p. 706.B.188 (8–95).

27. The greater amount of steel requires more fuel, and also increases engineering problems. The VLS team engineer noted that the four-engine option was chosen because of Brazil's inability to produce larger turbines—anything over 1 meter in diameter. Another criticism was the use of solid instead of liquid fuel. Solid fuel was less powerful but easier for the national industrial base. Liquid-fuel engines would have to be imported, but this was difficult because of the MTCR's restrictions. "Obstacles to VLS Development Reviewed," *FBIS-LAT,* August 15, 1989, pp. 28–30, citing *Folha de São Paulo,* July 14, 1989, p. G-3.

28. Robert Shuey, "Assessment of the Missile Technology Control Regime," in Hans Gunter Brauch et al., *Controlling the Development and Spread of Military Technology* (Amsterdam: Vu University Press, 1992), pp. 182–83.

29. Inadequate domestic infrastructure such as wind tunnels and heat treatment ovens caused Brazil to send these rocket casings to Lindberg. Eventually, the MTCR embargo spurred indigenous efforts to build heat treatment ovens. Pericles Gasparini Alves, "Brazilian Missile and Rocket Production and Export," in Potter and Jencks, *The International Missile Bazaar*, p. 115.

30. Emanuel Adler, *The Power of Ideology: The Quest for Technological Autonomy in Argentina and Brazil* (Berkeley: University of California Press, 1987), chap. 11 (pp. 280–326).

31. Jorge Domínguez, ed., *International Security and Democracy: Latin America and the Caribbean in the Post–Cold War Era* (Pittsburgh: University of Pittsburgh Press, 1998).

32. Ken Conca, "Technology, the Military and Democracy in Brazil," *Journal of InterAmerican Studies and World Affairs* 34, no.1 (Spring 1992): 153.

33. Brazil sought to back away from (but not go against) the United States and adopt a more autonomous policy since the 1970s. In 1977, it abrogated a 1952 military assistance agreement with the United States. Brazil also diversified its sources of technology: it signed a nuclear agreement with Germany in 1975 (after Washington suspended nuclear cooperation with Brazil in 1974), and negotiated the China-Brazil Earth Resource Satellite (CBERS) project in 1985.

34. "Libya Offers to Finance Brazilian Missile Project," *Jane's Defence Weekly*, February 6, 1988, p. 201.

35. John Barham, "Brazil Ignores U.S. Protest Over Arms for Libya," *Sunday Times*, January 31, 1988. At this time, Brazil's economy was stagnant (its growth rate was −0.3 percent in 1988) and its arms industry suffered from declining exports after the Iran-Iraq war ended.

36. Ibid.

37. On this issue, the Brazilian firm Embraer, which depends on U.S. markets for its civilian planes, and other Brazilian civilian firms were competing against Engesa, from which Libya sought 250 Osorio battle tanks. The Embraer president stated that he would have to lay off 3,000 workers if the United States imposed sanctions. Tollefson, "Brazilian Arms Transfers," pp. 309–11.

38. Jose Monserrat Filho, "The New Brazilian Space Agency: A Political and Legal Analysis," *Space Policy* 11, no. 2 (May 1995): 121–30.

39. Wyn Q. Bowen, "Brazil's Accession to the MTCR," *Nonproliferation Review* 3, no. 3 (Spring-Summer 1996): 88.

40. Bill Keller, "South Africa Says It Built 6 Atom Bombs," *New York Times*, March 25, 1993, p. 1; Peter Liberman, "The Rise and Fall of South Africa's Bomb," *International Security* 26, no. 2 (Fall 2001): 54.

41. *Cape Business News* noted that Denel built four rockets and launched three from the Overberg range as part of its Greensat orbital management system. *Cape Business News*, "South Africa—New Life for Local Space Programme," September 1997.

42. United Nations Department for Disarmament Affairs, *South Africa's Nuclear-tipped Ballistic Missile Capability* (New York: United Nations, 1991).

43. R. Jeffrey Smith, "President Waives Sanctions for Israel: S. African Firm Cited in Missile Parts Deal," *Washington Post,* October 27, 1991. In 1989, the *Washington Times* reported, "The South African government will soon test launch a new intermediate range missile with the help of Israel." The Israeli Embassy noted that in March 1987 their government decided not to initiate any new defense contracts with South Africa, and another Israeli source said that the United States was pressing Israel to halt ties with South Africa, which (the *Times* believed) were still strong despite Israeli promises to end all military cooperation by 1991. U.S. intelligence also believed that the South African IRBM would launch satellites. Bill Gertz, "S. Africa on the Brink of Ballistic Missile Test," *Washington Times,* June 24, 1989.

44. The 600 hectare Overberg launch site included an airstrip for 747-size jets, a rocket launch pad, and all the infrastructure necessary to test and assemble launch vehicles, such as tracking stations, thermal vacuum chambers to simulate space conditions for testing equipment, insulated hangars for dry testing rockets at noise levels beyond human tolerance, and computers. In the 1980s some 5 billion Rand was spent on the Overberg facility. In 1992, military funding was withdrawn, and the following year funding for Greensat's commercial applications also stopped. By the mid-1990s, Houwteq's operations slowed while Denel sought an international partner, and the staff was reduced from 500 to 28 (mostly security staff for the deserted range and state-of-the-art launch infrastructure). *Cape Business News,* "South Africa—New Life."

45. Fred Bridgland, "S. Africa Scraps Missile Plan after U.S. Pressure," *Daily Telegraph,* July 1, 1993, p. 12; Fred Bridgland, "Space Program Grounded in S. African Scorched Earth, Missiles to Go Same Way as A-bombs to Keep Them from ANC," *Sunday Telegraph,* April 4, 1993, p. 19.

46. R. Jeffrey Smith, "President Waives Sanctions for Israel: S. African Firm Cited in Missile Parts Deal," *Washington Post,* October 27, 1991.

47. Brian Chow, *Emerging Space Launch Programs: Economics and Safeguards* (Santa Monica, Calif.: Rand Corporation, April 1992).

48. Henry Sokolski, "Faking It and Making It," *National Interest* 51 (Spring 1998): 71. Sokolski noted that Washington's new position on missile sanctions was: "The sanctions would remain in place until South Africa agreed to stop importing missile technology for its rocket and further agreed to control its export of missile technology in accordance with the guidelines of the MTCR. The U.S., finally, would only back South Africa for membership in the MTCR if it agreed to abandon its space launch vehicle program."

49. "Missile Talks Stumble in South Africa," *Washington Post,* February 16, 1992.

50. This decision was not publicly announced when President de Klerk announced South Africa's past nuclear program. Keller, "South Africa Says It Built 6 Atom Bombs," p. 1.

51. *Arms Control Reporter* 1993, p. 706.B.114 (4-93).

52. *Arms Control Reporter* 1993, p. 706.B.121 (6-93). Houwteq manager Ian Farr noted that the Overberg facility could support up to ten launches a year, and even one or two launches might bring in 500 million Rand and create 100 to 200 hi-tech jobs plus other off-site jobs. Farr also anticipated that new LEO projects like Globalstar and Iridium could use the Overberg facility. *Cape Business News,* "South Africa—New Life."

53. "Space Industry in South Africa," The Permanent Mission of South Africa to the United Nations, Press Release No. 1993, June 30, 1993, by South African President R. F. Botha.

54. *Arms Control Reporter* 1994, p. 706.B. 177 (11-94).

55. "Missile Technology Regime Approves Membership," *FBIS-AFR,* September 15, 1995, p. 11.

5. SOUTH KOREA, TAIWAN, ARAB STATES

1. "Nationally Produced Ground-to-Ground Missiles Tested," *Seoul Haptong,* September 27, 1978, in *FBIS Asia and Pacific,* September 27, 1978, p. E1.

2. "Development of Missiles," *Korea Herald,* September 28, 1978, p. 4, in *FBIS Asia and Pacific,* September 28, 1978. The article added that the development of missiles and the defense industry "was made possible by the support of the entire population rendered in the form of the defense tax and voluntary contributions."

3. David A. Fulghum, "Advanced Threats Drive Arrow's Future," *Aviation Week & Space Technology,* October 12, 1998, pp. 56–57.

4. Janne Nolan, *Military Industry in Taiwan and South Korea* (London: Macmillan, 1986), p. 74.

5. Lee Jung-hoon, "The Missile Development Race Between South and North Korea, and the U.S. Policy of Checking," *East Asian Review* 9, no. 3 (Autumn 1997): 86–88.

6. "Extending Missiles' Range," *Chosun Ilbo,* April 21, 1999.

7. The Korea Aerospace Research Institute (KARI), the Korea Advanced Institute for Science and Technology (KAIST), Seoul University, and Hanyang University developed the KSR-1. Doo-won Heavy Industrial, Hanhwa, Korean Fiber, Danam Industries, and Ace Antenna produced the KSR-2. *Arms Control Reporter* 1993, p. 706.B.161 (3-94); "South Korea Internal Developments," *Nonproliferation Review,* Winter 1997, p. 161.

8. North Korea has about 1 million active duty personnel and 3,000 tanks, compared with 670,000 personnel and 2,100 tanks for South Korea. However, analysts have argued that South Korea still has an adequate defense capability against any North Korean invasion. Its military equipment is more modern, geography favors the defense, and South Korea's military budgets of $10–15 billion are far greater than North Korea's budgets of $2–3 billion. See Michael O'Hanlon, "Stopping a North Korean Invasion: Why Defending South Korea Is Easier Than the Pentagon Thinks," *International Security* 22,

no. 4 (Spring 1998): 135–70. For South Korea-China normalization, see Victor Cha, "Engaging China: Seoul-Beijing Détente and Korean Security," *Survival* 41, no. 1 (Spring 1999): 73–98.

9. Joseph Yager, *Nonproliferation and U.S. Foreign Policy* (Washington, D.C.: Brookings, 1980), p. 313. For U.S. leverage, see also Peter Clausen, *Nonproliferation and the National Interest: America's Response to the Spread of Nuclear Weapons* (New York: Harper Collins, 1993), pp. 129–30; Leonard Spector, *The Undeclared Bomb* (Washington, D.C.: Carnegie Endowment, 1988), p. 341; Mitch Reiss, *Without the Bomb: The Politics of Nuclear Nonproliferation* (New York: Columbia University Press, 1988), p. 93; William Gleysteen, *Massive Entanglement, Marginal Influence: Carter and Korea in Crisis* (Washington, D.C.: Brookings, 1999).

10. The military regime lacked domestic legitimacy and therefore sought acceptance from external powers, particularly the United States; the dismissal of scientists from ADD catered to Washington. Strong personal ties between Chun Du Hwan and President Reagan (and Prime Minister Nakasone in Japan) also brought Seoul closer to Washington. Seung-Young Kim, "Security, Nationalism, and the Pursuit of Nuclear Weapons and Missiles: The South Korean Case, 1970–82," *Diplomacy & Statecraft* 12, no. 4 (December 2001): 53–80.

11. Robert Shuey, *Missile Proliferation: A Discussion of U.S. Objectives and Policy Options* (Washington, D.C.: Congressional Research Service, February 21, 1990), p. 40.

12. Representative Ha Kyong-kun's policy report on "Sovereignty Over Missiles and Admission to the MTCR," December 1996, cited in Lee Jung-hoon, "The Missile Development Race Between South and North Korea, and the U.S. Policy of Checking," *East Asian Review* 9, no. 3 (Autumn 1997): 88. This note was written by Korea's foreign affairs ministry under pressure from the United States. Taewoo Kim, "South Korea's Missile Dilemmas," *Asian Survey* 34, no. 3 (May/June 1999): 494.

13. With the dissipating Cold War and democratic transition in 1987, the Korean public echoed dissension about the excesses of an arms race, and the Roh Tae Wuh regime took some conciliatory steps. The Kim Young Sam government (inaugurated in January 1993) continued the same policies—democratization makes arms control politically attractive, and stirs expectation of welfare spending that would theoretically lower defense budgets. On the other hand, the Roh regime was accused of being soft toward the North, and conservative forces opposed reconciliation with the North. Chung-in Moon, "South Korea," in Muthiah Alagappa, *Asian Security Practice* (Stanford: Stanford University Press, 1998).

14. *FBIS-EAS,* June 11, 1996, citing "ROK-U.S. Memorandum Must Be Revised," *Seoul Sinmun,* June 11, 1996, p. 3.

15. "ROK Wants Repeal of ROK-U.S. Missile Memorandum," *FBIS-EAS,* July 24, 1996, p. 53, citing *Yonhap,* July 24, 1996. In August 1996, South Korea was also planning a cruise missile test; Bill Gertz, "S. Korea Counters North's Missiles," *Washington Times,* December 2, 1996, pp. 1, 13.

16. Jongchul Park, "U.S.-DPRK Missile Talks and South Korean Response," *Korea and World Affairs* 20, no. 4 (Winter 1996): 612–13; Lee Jung-hoon, "The Missile Development Race Between South and North Korea and the U.S. Policy of Checking," *East Asian Review* 9, no. 3 (Autumn 1997): 92.

17. "U.S., North Korea Meet on Missiles; Japan, S. Korea Press on Defenses," *Arms Control Today* 28, no. 7 (October 1998): 28.

18. *Korea Herald,* April 20, 1999; "Seoul's Missile Development Gains Momentum," *Korea Herald,* July 13, 1999.

19. *Korea Herald,* April 28, 1999.

20. "South Korea Is Seen Trying to Extend Missile Capability," *Washington Post,* November 13, 1999.

21. "Future Challenges of Non-Proliferation in Northeast Asia," Seminar, Brookings Institution, January 27, 2000.

22. These details were announced by South Korea's vice defense minister Ahn Byung Kim before the national assembly's defense committee. "ROK to Develop Space Projectiles 'Without Limits'," *FBIS-EAS-1999-0427,* April 27, 1999, citing *Seoul Yonhap,* April 27, 1999.

23. South Korean officials would not accept inspections that they perceived would violate Korea's sovereign rights to a space project: "We have maintained a very strong position on the issue of commercial rocket development." "U.S., ROK to Meet on Extending ROK Missile Range," *FBIS-EAS-98-260,* September 17, 1998, citing *Seoul Yonhap,* September 17, 1998.

24. "Missile Talks Deadlocked Because of Difference in Negotiating Procedure," *Korea Herald,* November 20, 1999.

25. "Seoul, Washington Near Accord on South's Missile Development," *Korea Herald,* July 15, 2000.

26. Willis Witter, "South Korea Plans Enhanced Missiles," *Washington Times,* January 18, 2001.

27. "ROK Researcher on Launch Vehicle R&D," *FBIS Document KPP20000228000143,* January 1, 2000.

28. Nolan, *Military Industry in Taiwan and South Korea,* p. 57.

29. Statement by Professor James Hsiung, in U.S. Senate, Committee on Foreign Relations, *Taiwan: One Year After United States–China Normalization* (Washington, D.C.: Government Printing Office, 1980).

30. "Missile Project May Resume Despite U.S. Stance," *FBIS-CHI-95-046,* March 9, 1995; Aaron Karp, "The Frantic Third World Quest for Ballistic Missiles," *Bulletin of the Atomic Scientists,* June 1988, p. 19.

31. *Renmin Ribao Overseas Edition,* May 5, 1989, in *FBIS-CHI,* June 13, 1989; see also Robert Kairnol, "Taiwan's Space and Missile Programs," *International Defense Review,* August 1989, p. 1077.

32. Henry Sokoloski, "Fighting Proliferation with Intelligence," *Orbis* 38, no. 2 (Spring 1994): 245.

33. Bernice Lee, *The Security Implications of the New Taiwan*, Adelphi Paper 331, October 1999, p. 25. Bilateral trade increased from $50 million in 1978 to $1.1 billion in 1985 and $20-25 billion annually in the period 1995–98. China became Taiwan's second largest export market after the United States, accounting for 17 percent of Taiwan's exports in 1995; and Taiwanese investment in China was a cumulative $30 billion by 1995, or a third of Taiwan's total capital outflow.

34. In 2000, Taiwan had 376,000 active duty military personnel versus 2.5 million for China, but it could call upon 1.6 million reservists; Taiwan had 4,000 heavy armored units (tanks, armored personnel carriers, artillery) and 340 advanced combat jets, compared with 50–100 advanced jets for China. See David Shlapak, Davis Orletsky, and Barry Wilson, *Dire Strait? Military Aspects of the China-Taiwan Confrontation and Options for U.S. Policy* (Santa Monica: RAND, 2000); Michael O'Hanlon, "Why China Cannot Conquer Taiwan," *International Security* 25, no. 2 (Fall 2000): 51–86.

35. The Nixon administration blocked Taiwan's 1969 attempt to purchase a reprocessing plant, but by 1975 Taiwan was constructing its own laboratory-scale plutonium reprocessing unit. The Ford administration then asked Taiwan to dismantle the unit and halt future reprocessing. Clausen, *Nonproliferation and the National Interest*, p. 129; Spector, *The Undeclared Bomb*, pp. 346–47.

36. "Defense Minister Comments on Sky Bow Missile," *FBIS-CHI*, January 4, 1996, p. 62; however, the defense ministry had dropped hints of missile activity in March 1995 even before the Chinese missile tests. In March 1995, Defense Minister Chiang Chung-ling noted in the Legislative Yuan that "If we want the Chung-shan Institute of Science and Technology to resume the Sky Horse (Tien Ma) missile research project, it is easy. It will not take long." "Missile Project May Resume Despite U.S. Stance," *FBIS-CHI-95-046*, March 9, 1995.

37. "Taiwan: Legislators Urge Cruise Missile Development," *FBIS-CHI*, May 1, 1996, p. 87. See also John Garver, *Face Off: China, the United States, and Taiwan's Democratization* (Seattle: University of Washington Press, 1997), p. 157; Evan Feigenbaum, *Change in Taiwan and Potential Adversity in the Strait* (Santa Monica: Rand, 1995), xii.

38. "Missile Project May Resume Despite U.S. Stance," *FBIS-CHI-95-046*, March 9, 1995.

39. Bryan Bender and Robert Kairnol, "Taiwan Puts $600m into Missile Programmes," *Jane's Defence Weekly*, March 10, 1999, p. 4.

40. "Facing China Missiles, Taiwan VP Wants Deterrent," CNN, December 9, 1999. The minister of defense clarified that this was only a "viewpoint" and not official "policy." *United Daily News* (Taipei), December 10, 1999.

41. *United Daily News* (Taipei), December 10, 1999.

42. Lewis Frank, "Nasser's Missile Programs," *Orbis* 11, no. 3 (Fall 1967): 746–57.

43. "Increase in Egypt's Scuds Leads to BAE Pull-Out," *Jane's Defence Weekly*, September 5, 1992, p. 31.

44. Barbara Starr, "CIA Discloses Source of Egyptian Scud-B Parts," *Jane's Defence Weekly*, July 9, 1997, p. 5; *Washington Times*, June 21, 1996.

45. Center for Nonproliferation Studies, Monterey, California, Fact-sheet on Egypt's Weapons of Mass Destruction Program, 1998.

46. Andrew Rathmell and M. Ziarati, "Egypt's Military-Industrial Complex," *Jane's Intelligence Review*, October 1994, pp. 455–60. The AOI includes the Sakr missile facility which produces the Redeye SAM, antitank missiles, Matra Magic AAMs, and short-range ballistic missiles; the Arab-British Dynamics (ABD) company, which produces Swingfire antitank systems; the Arab-British Company (ABECO), which builds engines for the Alpha jet and Mirage 2000; and the Helwan aircraft factory and Helwan Engine Company, which assembles engines for the MiG-21 and Su-7 jets. The NODP supervises the Field Services Equipment Group, where engines are manufactured by Helwan, and the Chemical and Explosives Group, where rocket propellants and small arms ammunition are produced by the Abu Zaabel and Kata factories.

47. Avner Cohen, *Israel and the Bomb* (New York: Columbia University Press, 1998), p. 246. The Kennedy administration approved Hawk sales to Israel in 1962.

48. "Egypt's Musa Warns of Israeli Mideast Policies," *FBIS-NES*, July 13, 1998.

49. Steve Rodan, "Israel, USA Claim Egyptian Missile Links with North Korea," *Jane's Defence Weekly*, February 23, 2000, p. 18.

50. Egyptian-U.S. ties were strengthened in the 1970s after the Sadat government distanced itself from Moscow. Egypt received billions of dollars in U.S. aid after the Camp David accords. Washington's multibillion dollar aid to Egypt is motivated by Egypt's strategic importance for Middle East stability, and Washington's interest in the absence of a credible Arab military option against Israel. William Quandt, *The United States and Egypt* (Washington, D.C.: Brookings, 1990); A. F. K. Organski, *The $36 Billion Bargain: Strategy and Politics in U.S. Assistance to Israel* (New York: Columbia University Press, 1990).

51. Martin Navias, *Going Ballistic: The Build-up of Missiles in the Middle East* (New York: Brassey's, 1993), p. 120.

52. "Egypt, Iran Import Engines for Missiles," *Middle East Newsline*, March 28, 2000; "Israel, USA Claim Egyptian Missile Links with North Korea," *Jane's Defence Weekly*, February 23, 2000, p. 18.

53. Timothy McCarthy and Jonathan Tucker, "Saddam's Toxic Arsenal," in Peter Lavoy, Scott Sagan, and James Wirtz, eds., *Planning the Unthinkable: How New Powers Will Use Nuclear, Biological, and Chemical Weapons* (Ithaca: Cornell University Press, 2000), pp. 47–78.

54. "Flight Tests by Iraq Show Progress of Missile Program," *New York Times*, July 1, 2000.

55. Joseph S. Bermudez, "Syria's Acquisition of North Korean Scuds," *Jane's Intelligence Review*, June 1991, pp. 249–50.

56. *Missile News*, August 1996.

57. U.S. Director of Central Intelligence, Nonproliferation Center, *Unclassified Report to Congress on the Acquisition of Technology Relating to Weapons of Mass Destruction and Advanced Conventional Munitions, 1 January Through 30 June 1999* (Washington, D.C.: Central Intelligence Agency, 1999).

58. National Intelligence Council, *Foreign Missile Developments and the Ballistic Missile Threat through 2015: Unclassified Summary of a National Intelligence Estimate* (Washington, D.C.: National Intelligence Council, 2002).

59. "Ortrag Ends Libyan Launch Work," *Aviation Week and Space Technology*, December 14, 1989, p. 22; Leonard Spector, *Tracking Nuclear Proliferation* (Washington, D.C.: Carnegie Endowment for International Peace, 1995), p. 141; Joshua Sinai, "Ghadaffi's Libya: The Patient Proliferator," *Jane's Intelligence Review* (December 1998), pp. 27–28.

60. "UK Paper on FRG Assistance for Libyan Missile," *Sunday Correspondent* (London), October 15, 1989, p. 3; *Nuclear Developments*, November 6, 1989, pp. 19–20.

61. "Where Governments Fail: The Case of Leybold AG," *Mednews*, October 12, 1992, pp. 1–7.

62. "Libya-Egypt: Major Breach of Arms Embargo," *Intelligence Newsletter*, December 1, 1994, p. 7.

63. "Italy: Police Seize Missile-Production Machine Bound for Libya," *Il Giornale* (Milan), August 10, 1997, p. 10, in *FBIS-TAC-97-223*, August 11, 1997.

64. "Tehran Deal to Help with Libyan Missile," *The Times* (London), November 22, 1997, p. A4.

65. Bill Gertz, "Beijing Delivered Missile Technology to Libya," *Washington Times*, April 13, 2000.

66. Office of the Secretary of Defense, *Proliferation: Threat and Response* (Washington, D.C.: January 2001).

67. Press reports of Libya's missile purchases have not been confirmed. The *Wall Street Journal* noted that between 1986 and 1991, Libya purchased Scuds from North Korea and that both nations agreed to establish a missile production facility in Libya ("The Postwar Scud Boom," *Wall Street Journal*, July 10, 1991). *Ha'aretz* reported on May 29, 2000, that Syria and Libya acquired North Korean Scud-D missiles (*Middle East Newsline* 2, no. 218, June 8, 2000). *Jane's* noted that Libya "already has, or is just receiving, North Korean Nodong ballistic missiles" (*Jane's Intelligence Review*, April 2001, p. 24).

68. "Iraq Lacks the Means and Expertise to Manufacture Advanced Weaponry," *Al-Qabas* (Kuwait), February 1, 2000.

69. "German Assessment: Iraqi Missiles Will Reach Europe by 2005," *Deutsche Presse Agentur* (Berlin), February 23, 2000.

6. ISRAEL, INDIA, PAKISTAN

1. "Gandhi Makes Statement on 18 July Satellite Launch," *FBIS South Asia*, July 21, 1980, p. E1.

2. "An Indian Satellite," *Dawn*, July 20, 1980, in *FBIS South Asia*, July 22, 1980, pp. F1–F2.

3. "Media Hail Launch, Criticize U.S.," *JPRS-TAC-89-022* (Near East and South Asia), May 31, 1989, p. 31.

4. "Gandhi Hails Missile Test," *JPRS-TAC-89-022* (Near East and South Asia), May 31, 1989, p. 31.

5. "Army Chief: Surface-to-Surface Missiles Tested," *FBIS-NES*, February 6, 1989, p. 72.

6. "Further on Beg Comments," *FBIS-NES*, February 6, 1989, pp. 72–73.

7. "Pakistan Test-fires Ghauri Missile," *Dawn*, April 7, 1998.

8. "Ghauri Gives Pakistan Edge Over India: Gohar," *Dawn*, May 7, 1998.

9. "India Is Now a N-weapons State: PM," *Times of India*, May 16, 1998.

10. "India Joins Nuclear Club," *Times of India*, May 12, 1998.

11. "Pakistan, Answering India, Carries Out Nuclear Tests," *New York Times*, May 29, 1998.

12. *World Press Review,* August 1998, p. 12.

13. Ibid., p. 9.

14. Avner Cohen, *Israel and the Bomb* (New York: Columbia University Press, 1998), p. 116.

15. Pierre Langereux, "Dassault Lifts the Lid on the Jericho Missile Story," *Air & Cosmos/Aviation International* no. 1590, December 6, 1996, p. 36; Seymour Hersh, *The Samson Option* (New York: Random House, 1991), p. 173.

16. William Beecher, "Israel Believed Producing Missiles of Atom Capability," *New York Times*, October 5, 1971, pp. 1, 15.

17. W. Seth Carus, "Israeli Ballistic Missile Developments," in *Report of the Commission to Assess the Ballistic Missile Threat to the United States*, July 15, 1998, Appendix III, p. 89 [Rumsfeld Commission Report].

18. Steven Flank, "Reconstructing Rockets: The Politics of Developing Military Technology in Brazil, India, and Israel" (Ph.D. dissertation, Massachusetts Institute of Technology, 1993), p. 304.

19. Navias, *Going Ballistic: The Build-up of Missiles in the Middle East*, p. 112; Aaron Karp, *Ballistic Missile Proliferation: The Politics and Technics* (Oxford: Oxford University Press, 1996), p. 141.

20. Cohen, *Israel and the Bomb,* p. 65.

21. The distance between Israel and these states made any Israeli action to remove the threat complicated and expensive, and Israel therefore required a broader political-diplomatic strategy and assistance from the United States and the international community against this threat. Zeev Schiff, "IDF Review Ranks Iran, Iraq as Primary Threat," *Ha'aretz,* May 5, 1999, p. B1. Israeli analysts simultaneously expressed concern over Egypt's military and air force modernization. Amir Oren, "Egypt: A Peacetime Threat," *Ha'aretz,* July 7, 1998.

22. Washington's close ties with (and consequent leverage on) Israel commenced with its arms transfers in the mid-1960s; in the early 1970s, U.S. aid sharply increased. While geopolitical considerations maintained the U.S.-Israeli relationship, domestic politics— a strong domestic pro-Israel lobby—also sustain American executive and legislative support for Israel. Bernard Reich, *United States and Israel: Influence in the Special Relationship* (New York: Praeger, 1984).

23. Peter Clausen, *Nonproliferation and the National Interest: America's Response to the Spread of Nuclear Weapons* (New York: Harper Collins, 1993), p. 125.

24. Aaron Karp, "Ballistic Missile Proliferation," in *SIPRI Yearbook 1990,* p. 336, citing State Department daily press briefing, April 23, 1990, p. 14.

25. U.S. Arms Control and Disarmament Agency, *World Military Expenditures and Arms Transfers 1996;* Yitzhak Shichor, "Israel's Military Transfers to Taiwan and China," *Survival* 40, no. 1 (Spring 1998): 71, 76.

26. R. Jeffrey Smith and David Hoffman, "President Waives Sanctions for Israel," *Washington Post,* October 27, 1991; Stephen Labaton, "The Middle East Talks; Baker Defends Waiver of Sanctions Against Israel on Missiles," *New York Times,* October 28, 1991.

27. Vikram Sarabhai, *Science Policy and National Development* (ed. Kamla Chowdhry) (Delhi: Macmillan, 1974), p. 61.

28. In 1982, the scientific adviser to the defense minister formed a review team comprising DRDO chief Abdul Kalam and members from the three armed services and defense production centers. Within four months this team presented its report to the defense minister, the three chiefs of the defense forces, and the defense secretary. Consequently, the decision was taken to develop five types of missiles, and to run these programs simultaneously. "Importance of Missile Program Stressed," *JPRS-TND-94-014,* July 13, 1994, pp. 34–37.

29. *Times of India,* July 10, 1991, p. 12.

30. "Missile Development Likely To Be Expedited by BJP Govt," *Deccan Herald,* March 16, 1998. Another press report called attention to the high content of imports in the IGMDP, and the initially low priority to the Agni in the IGMDP. It noted that "of the Rs. 748.66 crores spent on the [IGMDP] program by September 1990 . . . 291.14 crores, or more than a third of the outlay, was in the form of import content. That only Rs. 55

crore has been spent so far on the Agni project, whereas the projected fund requirement for Prithvi and Trishul together is Rs. 250 crores a year, speaks of the level or priority accorded to Agni, if expenditure is any indicator." V. Sudarshan, "Smoke Without Fire: India's Agni Fantasy," *The Pioneer,* September 6, 1997, p. 8, cited in "Article Views Agni Missile Program," *FBIS-TAC-97-251,* September 8, 1997.

31. "Agni Test-Fired, Significance Viewed," *Deccan Chronicle,* February 20, 1994, p. 1.

32. Ashley Tellis, *India's Emerging Nuclear Posture: Between Recessed Deterrent and Ready Arsenal* (Santa Monica: RAND, 2001), p. 561.

33. *Jane's* noted that DRDO was considering two options for the Agni-3. One option would use a solid booster of 1.8 meter diameter with 36 tons of propellant fuel (the PSLV utilizes a 36 ton liquid-fuel booster), while the second option would add a third stage to the Agni-2, though stage separation is a complicated process. *Jane's Missiles & Rockets,* January 1, 2000. Indian scientists note that the Agni-3 "will be rail-mobile and have a range of 3,500–4,000 km. Its first test may occur in late 2003." K. Santhanam, "Agni-I: A Short Range Nuclear-Missile India Urgently Needs," *Times of India,* January 27, 2002.

34. Gary Milhollin, "India's Missiles—With a Little Help from Our Friends," *Bulletin of the Atomic Scientists,* November 1989, pp. 311–15.

35. A. Baskaran, "Different Stages of Technological Capabilities and the Effectiveness of Export Controls: The Case of India's Space and Missile Programs," Paper Presented at the 9th International Summer Symposium on Science and World Affairs, Ithaca, July 1997.

36. Waheguru Pal Singh Sidhu, *Enhancing Indo-U.S. Strategic Cooperation,* Adelphi Paper 313, September 1997, pp. 26–27.

37. Brahma Chellaney, "The Missile Technology Control Regime," in Francine R. Frankel, *Bridging the Nonproliferation Divide* (Lanham, Maryland: University Press of America, 1995), p. 205.

38. George Perkovich, *India's Nuclear Bomb: The Impact on Global Proliferation* (Berkeley: University of California Press, 1999); Sumit Ganguly, "India's Pathway to Pokhran II," *International Security* 23, no. 4 (Spring 1999): 148–77.

39. Prime Minister Vajpayee explained the nuclear decision as follows: "I have been deeply concerned at the deteriorating security environment, specially the nuclear environment, faced by India for some years past. We have an overt nuclear weapons state [China] on our borders, a state which committed armed aggression against India in 1962. Although our relations with that country have improved in the last decade or so, an atmosphere of distrust persists mainly due to the unresolved border problem. To add to the distrust that country has materially helped another neighbor of ours [Pakistan] to become a covert nuclear weapon state." "Prime Minister Atal Behari Vajpayee's Letter to President Clinton, May 12, 1998," *New York Times,* May 13, 1998.

40. A representative news article noted that "the short range Prithvi program has been

stalled for at least eight months since user trials were completed and American pressure has a great deal to do with it." "Prithvi in the Fridge?" *Indian Express,* March 31, 1995, p. 8.

41. "Deploy Agni, Says House Panel Report," *Times of India,* May 1, 1997; Pravin Sawhney, "India's Missile Policy: Focus Must Shift to Agni," *Times of India,* March 4, 1997.

42. Dieter Braun, "Wie friedlich ist Neu-Delhi's Atom-programm?" *Europa-Archive,* September 25, 1974, p. 626.

43. Pakistan also sought missiles in the 1980s after being subject to Scud attacks from Afghanistan, which suggests that its missile motivations were not aimed solely at countering India's missile program.

44. Nazir Kamal and Pravin Sawhney, "Missile Control in South Asia and the Role of Cooperative Monitoring Technology," Sandia National Laboratories, CMC Occasional Papers 4, October 1998, p. 37.

45. At a June 1991 press briefing, a Chinese foreign ministry spokesman stated, "China did supply some conventional weapons to Pakistan, including a very small number of short-range tactical missiles . . . . China's short-range missiles [are] those with a range of 200 kilometers. . . . On the range of missiles, there are different definitions in the international community." "China's Missile Exports and Assistance to Pakistan: Statements and Developments," Center for Nonproliferation Studies, Monterey Institute for International Studies.

On the 1992 transfers, see Jim Mann, "China Said to Sell Pakistan Dangerous New Missiles," *Los Angeles Times,* December 4, 1992, pp. A1, 18; Robert Ross, "China," in Richard Haass, *Economic Sanctions and American Diplomacy* (Washington, D.C.: Council on Foreign Relations, 1998), pp. 22–25.

The *Washington Post* noted that the Pakistan Embassy made no secret of the M-11 purchases, which the embassy said were in response to India's Prithvi missile development; the embassy had added that sanctions should not be levied because the range of the M-11 falls below the 300 km MTCR limit. R. Jeffrey Smith and Thomas Lippman, "Pakistan M-11 Funding Is Reported," *Washington Post,* September 8, 1994, p. A32.

46. Brian Cloughley, *A History of the Pakistan Army* (Karachi: Oxford University Press, 1999), p. 352.

47. Other sources note that Islamabad set up a missile development board in 1992 with assistance from SUPARCO, and that the Hatf-III was a SUPARCO rocket that was tested in July 1997. *The Nation,* July 4, 1997.

48. "Article Views Effect of Prithvi on Regional Security," *FBIS-TAC-97-161,* June 10, 1997, citing *The Nation,* June 10, 1997, pp. 1, 13.

49. David Wright notes that flying on the optimal minimum energy trajectory, a 1,100 km missile has an apogee of 300 km. Increasing the altitude to 350 km would limit the range to 700 km, which is consistent with the parameters for the April 6 flight. Wright

also notes that the actual flight time was ten rather than eight minutes. Citing the official version of the test, John Pike notes that the trajectory of the first Ghauri missile test was from Tilla Jogian, near Jehlum, to Taftan in Balochistan, traveling close to 1,100 km, and that the missile reached an altitude of 350 km during a flight of eight minutes. David Wright, "An Analysis of the Pakistani Ghauri Missile Test of April 6, 1998," *Science and Global Security* 7 (1998): 227–35; Federation of American Scientists, Washington, D.C. *Dawn* noted that on April 14, 1999, the second Ghauri was launched from Tilla, near Jhelum, and flew for twelve minutes toward Jiwani some 1,150 km away. "Ghauri-II Launched, More Tests Planned," *Dawn,* April 15, 1999.

50. "Sharif: No Foreign Consent for Ghauri Test," *FBIS-TAC-98-108,* April 18, 1998, citing *The Nation,* April 18, 1998.

51. Press reports noted Bhutto had stated that "my father late Zulfikar Ali Bhutto gave the country a peaceful nuclear program and it was [under] my guidance that the delivery system was made indigenously . . . I want recognition and if this does not happen, I will tell the masses about the entire story. . . . The Ghauri missile was earlier named after Zulfikar, the sword of 4th Muslim caliph Hazrat Ali (RA)." "Bhutto Views Ghauri Testing, Other Issues," *FBIS-NES,* April 11, 1998, citing *The Nation,* April 11, 1998. Dr. Abdul Qadeer Khan noted that the missile was eventually named Ghauri "after Sultan Shahab-ud-Din Ghauri." "Qadeer Khan on Ghauri Missile Test," *FBIS-TAC-98-097,* April 7, 1998, citing *The Nation,* April 7, 1998.

52. Bill Gertz, "Iran-Bound Mystery Freighter Carried Parts for Missiles," *Washington Times,* July 16, 1992, p. A3.

53. "A Silent Partner," *Jane's Defence Weekly,* May 20, 1998, pp. 16–17. This article notes that the November 1995 delegation was headed by Choe Kwang, vice chairman of the National Defense Commission, minister of the People's Armed Forces, and marshal of the Korean People's Army. He met with President Sardar Leghari, Defense Minister Aftab Shaban Miran, and Pakistan's armed service chiefs. North Korea is also believed to have provided Pakistan with the TEL launcher for the Ghauri test. North Korea may have benefited by obtaining Chinese guidance technologies from Pakistan, and also acquired data from the Ghauri test where the missile flew farther than during North Korea's 1993 Nodong test.

54. "Pakistani Daily Reports Ghauri Missile Development," *FBIS-TAC-98-005,* January 5, 1998, citing *Jang* (Rawalpindi), January 3, 1998, p. 4.

55. "U.S. Sanctions Against Kahuta Labs Viewed," *FBIS-TAC-98-125,* May 5, 1998, citing *The Nation,* May 5, 1998.

56. Javed Nasir, "The Post-Ghauri Scenario," *The Nation,* April 28, 1998.

57. David Wright, "An Analysis of the Pakistani Ghauri Missile Test of 6 April 1998," Union of Concerned Scientists and Security Studies Program, MIT, May 1998.

58. Giving more details of the Ghauri launch, Dr. A. Q. Khan stated that the Ghauri was originally to be launched from Kahuta but the location was changed to Tilla Jogian,

near Jehlum. He added that "the weather was stormy and some persons had apprehensions that the missile might get short-circuited"; he also noted that the whole project was completed in prefabricated sheds: "If we went for proper concrete sheds, it would have taken a longer time." "Scientist Gives Details of Ghauri Project," *FBIS-TAC-98-124,* May 4, 1998, citing *The Nation,* May 3, 1998, pp. 1, 13.

59. "COAS Terms Ghauri as Necessary Step," *FBIS-NES-98-106,* April 16, 1998, citing *The Nation,* April 16, 1998.

60. Hanif Khalid, "How Shaheen Was Developed," *Jang,* April 19, 1999. This report noted that the Shaheen-1 had an indigenously built terminal guidance system, whose "development was the biggest challenge for Pakistani scientists and engineers."

61. R. Jeffrey Smith, "China Linked to Pakistani Missile Plant," *Washington Post,* August 25, 1996, p. A01; "The Secret Missile Deal," *Time,* June 30, 1997.

62. Dr. S. M. Mand, "We Invited Dr. Khan to Come and See What an Atomic Test Looked Like," *The Herald,* June 1998, pp. 26–27. "Without Kahuta, Nothing Can Be Done," *The Herald,* June 1998, pp. 27–29. Subsequent press reports give similar dates, noting that the Shaheen-1 "was developed in 2 years and 3 months before it was ready for launch in early 1998, though the government allowed its flight test in April 1999." "Serial Production of Shaheen-1 Under Way," *The News,* September 21, 2000.

63. "Pakistan Unveils Shaheen-2," *Jane's Defence Weekly,* April 5, 2000; "India, Pakistan: Nuclear Arms Race Gets Off to a Slow Start," *Jane's Intelligence Review,* January 2001.

64. Ziba Moshaver, *Nuclear Weapons Proliferation in the Indian Subcontinent* (New York: St. Martin's, 1991), p. 65; see also Samina Ahmed, "Pakistan's Nuclear Weapons Program," *International Security* 23, no. 4 (Spring 1999): 178–204.

65. M. A. Niazi, "Ghauri Dilemmas," *The Nation,* April 17, 1998.

66. Javed Nasir, "The Post-Ghauri Scenario," *The Nation,* April 28, 1998.

67. Maleeha Lodhi, "Confronting the Missile Challenge," *The News,* April 12, 1998.

68. Ibid.

69. Stephen Cohen, "Pakistan: Once Again a Pivotal State (But for How Long?)," Brookings Institution, July 1999.

70. For example, commentators noted: "Since March 1993 [the] Pakistani media has been up in arms and scores of editorials and articles have been published about the Prithvi menace, but little is known as to what successive governments have done to counter the Prithvi threat. . . . What steps are being taken for matching response to the Indian missile and nuclear plans should be discussed in the Parliament by the Defense Committees and proper plans should be made for the immediate manufacture of reliable and accurate SSMs, SAMs and ATMs with better range and improved performance." Ayaz Ahmed Khan, "Countering the Prithvi Threat," *The Nation,* June 30, 1997, p. 7.

71. "COAS Terms Ghauri as Necessary Step," *FBIS-NES-98-106,* April 16, 1998, citing *The Nation,* April 16, 1998.

72. Hasan Askari Rizvi, "Civil-Military Relations in Contemporary Pakistan," *Survival* 40, no. 2 (Summer 1998): 96–113; Stephen Cohen, *The Pakistan Army* (Oxford: Oxford University Press, 1998), pp. 164–80; Hasan Askari Rizvi, *Military, State and Society in Pakistan* (New York: St. Martin's, 2000).

73. In the 1980s, Washington's substantial economic and military aid did not give it leverage over Pakistan's nuclear program because of the balance in security interdependence. Pakistan's frontline status against the Soviet Union in Afghanistan caused Washington to need Pakistan perhaps as much as vice versa. Therefore, Washington did not press the issue of Pakistan's nuclear activity. After the Soviet withdrawal from Afghanistan in 1990, Washington had much less strategic need for Islamabad's support in the region and it imposed Pressler Amendment sanctions in 1990. See, for example, Dennis Kux, *The United States and Pakistan, 1947–2000: Disenchanted Allies* (Washington, D.C.: Woodrow Wilson Center Press, 2001).

74. "U.S. To Be Realistic on Missiles," *The Hindu*, July 15, 1998. At Senate hearings, Assistant Secretary of State for South Asia Karl Inderfurth was asked why the issue of missile testing was not among U.S. nonproliferation objectives for the region. He responded: "I think they have been candid with us as to what they can and cannot do. . . . And I think certain forms of [missile] development programs will be going ahead. And I think we have to be realistic about that."

75. Strobe Talbott, Deputy Secretary of State, "Dialogue, Democracy and Nuclear Weapons in South Asia," January 16, 1999, Stanford University.

76. "Indian Missile Set for Production," *International Herald Tribune*, March 8, 2001.

77. "ICBMs Any Day, Says Kalam," *Hindustan Times* (New Delhi), September 18, 2000.

78. "India Denies Planning Long-range Missile Test," *Hindustan Times* (New Delhi), May 5, 2001.

7. NORTH KOREA AND IRAN

1. *Jerusalem Post*, July 24, 1998.

2. "Iran Claims Missile Self-Sufficiency," *Jane's Missiles & Rockets*, January 1999, p. 5.

3. "Iran Successfully Tests Medium-Range Missile," *Tehran Times*, July 26, 1998.

4. Unless otherwise cited, this section on the technical details of North Korea's missiles is largely drawn from Joseph Bermudez, *A History of Ballistic Missile Development in the DPRK*, Center for Nonproliferation Studies Occasional Paper 2, November 1999.

5. The General Bureau is responsible for planning, procurement, and distribution of materials for the Second Economic Committee (SEC) and its subsidiaries. The SEC oversees the planning, financing, production, and distribution of defense-related equipment. It has seven machine industries bureaus (MIBs) working on items ranging from

small arms to conventional weapons to missiles to nuclear, biological, and chemical systems. Joseph S. Bermudez, "North Korea's Deadly Industries Revealed," *Jane's Defence Weekly,* November 12, 1997, pp. 54–57.

6. *New York Times,* June 13, 1993, p. 7.

7. In January 1991, the freighter *Al-Yarmouk* departed from North Korea with twenty-four Scud-Cs and twenty launchers, and arrived in Latakia, Syria, on March 13. In late 1991 the North Korean vessel *Mupo* was turned back by Israeli gunboats and returned to North Korea without delivering Scuds to Syria. In early February 1992 the *Dae Hung Ho* departed from North Korea with Scud-Cs and assembly equipment such as machine tools; on March 9, 1992, the vessel docked at Bandar Abbas, Iran, and on March 11, 1992, sailed to Tartus, Syria. Missile manufacturing equipment was also transferred to Syria from Tehran. In August 1992 Syria conducted two Scud-C tests. In late October 1992, a vessel with up to one hundred missiles, fifty for Syria and fifty for Iran, departed from North Korea and arrived in Iran by early 1993. Greg Gerardi and James Plotts, "An Annotated Chronology of DPRK Missile Trade and Developments," *Nonproliferation Review* 2, no. 1 (Fall 1994): 65–93.

8. David Wright and Timur Kadyshev, "An Analysis of the North Korean Nodong Missile," *Science and Global Security* 4 (1994): 129–60.

9. Joseph Bermudez, "The Rise and Rise of North Korea's ICBMs," *Jane's International Defense Review,* July 1999, p. 57.

10. Center for Nonproliferation Studies, *Chronology of North Korea's Missile Trade and Developments: 1992–1993.*

11. Barbara Starr, *Jane's Defence Weekly,* June 25, 1994, p. 10.

12. "North Koreans Test Two-stage IRBM over Japan," *Jane's Defence Weekly,* September 9, 1998, p. 26; "North Korea Space Guide," Federation of American Scientists, 1998.

13. Federation of American Scientists homepage, http://www.fas.org/nuke/guide/dprk/missile/td-2.htm. This report notes that North Korea had built a new 33 m high launch tower in July 1999 when the Taepodong-2 rocket was stored near the launch pad. It would take two days to assemble the rocket on the pad and then check it electronically and load liquid propellants from tanker trucks. The FAS also cited press reports that North Korea conducted four static engine tests (some of which may have involved the Taepodong-2 first stage) at the Musudan site in December 1999 and January 2000, and conducted another static test at the launch pad in June 2001.

14. Don Oberdorfer, *The Two Koreas: A Contemporary History* (Reading: Addison-Wesley, 1997).

15. The table on page 236 shows the GNP, defense expenditure, and armed force size for South Korea and North Korea.

16. Kim Il Sung adopted a doctrine of four military lines in the 1960s, and 20–25 percent of GNP was allocated to the defense sector. In response, South Korea's military

	South Korea			North Korea		
	GNP	*DEFENSE SPENDING*	*MILITARY MANPOWER*	*GNP*	*DEFENSE SPENDING*	*MILITARY MANPOWER*
YEAR	*($ BIL.)*	*($ BIL.)*		*($ BIL.)*	*($ BIL.)*	
1968	5.2	0.29	620,000	2.8	0.70	384,000
1972–74	17.5	0.72	625,000	3.5	0.77	467,000
1979–80	60	4.4	601,000	14	1.47	782,000
1987–88	171	10	750,000	47	4.6	1,100,000
1997–98	430–440	12–15	672,000	14	2–2.2	1,050,000

SOURCE: International Institute of Strategic Studies (IISS), *The Military Balance,* various years.

manpower increased to 645,000 at the peak of inter-Korean military tension in 1970, and Seoul pursued an assertive force-modernization program after 1974 (in the wake of U.S. military withdrawal plans and Seoul's military inferiority versus the North) that absorbed $23 billion in 1990 prices for the period 1974–90. Between 1970 and 1994, South Korea increased its inventory of tanks (750 to 1,950) and tactical aircraft (200 to 520), and North Korea also increased its inventory of tanks (750 to 3,800) and tactical aircraft (580 to 850). Chung-in Moon, *Arms Control on the Korean Peninsula* (Seoul: Yonsei University Press, 1996), pp. 56–58.

17. Victor Cha, *Alignment Despite Antagonism: The United States-Korea-Japan Security Triangle* (Stanford: Stanford University Press, 1999), chap. 3–7.

18. North Korea's trade with Russia decreased from $2 billion annually in the 1980s (which was 50–60 percent of North Korea's foreign trade) to $300 million in 1991 (which was 13 percent of North Korea's trade) and averaged $90 million annually in the period 1994–98 (or 5 percent of North Korea's trade). Moscow's policy of dealing in hard currency rather than on a friendship basis caused much of the trade decrease. Political relations deteriorated with the normalization of ROK-Russia ties in 1990, and the DPRK–Russia friendship treaty was scrapped in September 1996. North Korean-Russian ties somewhat revived with a new February 2000 friendship treaty, and President Vladimir Putin visited North Korea in July 2000.

19. China was alarmed at North Korea's 1998 missile launch because this encouraged Japan and South Korea to strengthen their security and military cooperation with the United States. Further, Beijing's advocating of reforms in the DPRK was viewed with suspicion by North Korea. Kim Jong Il's view in 1998 was that China's social and economic reforms were a "dangerous policy" that undermined socialism in the PRC, which thereby deprived the DPRK of its socialist ally (China). *DPRK Report* no. 14, September–October 1998, Center for Nonproliferation Studies, Monterey.

20. Bermudez, *History of Ballistic Missile Development in the DPRK*. Another source notes that Kim Jong Il (who was appointed heir designate to Kim Il Sung in 1974) ordered the creation of a strategic rocket force in the 1970s. Such rockets were to be used both for deterrence and to launch reconnaissance satellites, because "the movement of American forces and their allies needs close watching in an accurate way and on a real-time basis." This source adds that by 2001, North Korea had several satellites in store. It next planned to launch a geostationary communications satellite and establish a satellite telecommunications network covering its mountainous regions. It eventually sought to enter the satellite launch business and earn foreign currency. This source further notes that Egyptian Scuds were transferred to North Korea as early as 1976. Kim Myong Chol, "Kim Jong Il's Military Strategy for Reunification," *Comparative Strategy* 20, no. 4 (2001): 320, 329.

21. Pyongyang would probably use rocket artillery, aircraft, and cruise missiles for chemical and biological weapons delivery on nearby targets, and ballistic missiles to deliver chemical weapons to distant targets. North Korea would also prefer to use ballistic missiles to deliver nuclear warheads, but until a compact missile-capable warhead was available, it would rely on aircraft to carry its nuclear weapons. Joseph Bermudez, "The Democratic People's Republic of Korea and Unconventional Weapons," in Peter Lavoy, Scott Sagan, and James Wirtz, eds., *Planning the Unthinkable: How New Powers Will Use Nuclear, Biological, and Chemical Weapons* (Ithaca: Cornell University Press, 2000), pp. 182–201.

22. Reflecting this view, a September 9, 1998, article in the party newspaper, *Rodong Shinmun,* argued: "It is a foolish daydream to try to revive the economy by introducing foreign capital, not relying on one's own strength. . . . We will . . . set ourselves against all the attempts to induce us to join an 'integrated' world. We have nothing to reform and open." *DPRK Report* no. 14, September–October 1998, Center for Nonproliferation Studies.

23. Dr. William J. Perry, Special Adviser to the President and the Secretary of State, *Review of United States Policy Toward North Korea: Findings and Recommendations* (Washington, D.C.: Office of the North Korea Policy Coordinator, U.S. Department of State, October 12, 1999).

24. Leon Sigal, "Averting a Train Wreck With North Korea," *Arms Control Today* 28, no. 8 (November/December 1998): 14; *Arms Control Reporter* 1993, pp. 706.B.122, 127.

25. *Arms Control Reporter* 1996, p. 706.B.200 (6-96); "U.S.-North Korean Missile Control Talks Begin," *Arms Control Today* 26, no. 3 (April 1996): 26–27.

26. The *Washington Times* reported on June 21, 1996, that North Korea delivered Scud-C components to Egypt seven times in late March and April.

27. Reuters, October 16 and October 23, 1996, cited in *Arms Control Reporter* 1996, p. 706.B.209 (1–97). U.S. and Japanese officials detected test preparations that could have been part of an elaborate game of nerves. These may also have backed up prior threats to retaliate against the ROK after the death of North Korean special forces who had entered South Korea from a grounded DPRK submarine in September.

28. *Arms Control Reporter* 1996, p. 706.B.209 (1–97).

29. Jongchul Park, "U.S.-DPRK Missile Talks and South Korean Response," *Korea and World Affairs* 20, no. 4 (Winter 1996): 612–13.

30. "North Korea Admits Selling Missiles," *Washington Post,* June 16, 1998.

31. Leon Sigal, "Negotiating an End to North Korea's Missile-Making," *Arms Control Today* 30, no. 5 (June 2000).

32. "U.S., N. Korea, Meet on Missiles; Japan, S. Korea Press on Defenses," *Arms Control Today* 28, no. 7 (October 1998): 24.

33. The Associated Press, Edith M. Lederer, "N. Korea Defiant Over U.S. Demand," New York, October 2, 1999, in *Northeast Asia Peace and Security Network Daily Report,* October 5, 1998.

34. "U.S. Team Ends Talk in N. Korea," *Washington Post,* March 31, 1999.

35. Moreover, on July 3, 1999, the North-South Vice Ministerial talks in Beijing broke down with Pyongyang demanding that Seoul apologize for sinking North Korean vessels in a naval clash in June.

36. "North Korea Vows to Continue Missile Program," *New York Times,* July 13, 2000.

37. "Chronology of U.S.–North Korean Nuclear and Missile Diplomacy," *Arms Control Today* 30, no. 9 (November 2000).

38. Wendy Sherman, "Talking to the North Koreans," *New York Times,* March 7, 2001.

39. Michael Gordon, "How Politics Sank Accord on Missiles With North Korea," *New York Times,* March 6, 2001.

40. "North Korea Sends Missile Parts, Technology to Iran," *Washington Times,* April 18, 2001.

41. Selig S. Harrison, "The Missiles of North Korea: How Real a Threat?" *World Policy Journal* 17, no. 3 (Fall 2000): 13–24; Perry, *Review of United States Policy Toward North Korea;* Leon Sigal, "Negotiating an End to North Korea's Missile-Making."

42. For a discussion of reciprocal responses to U.S. behavior by North Korea in the period 1991–94, see Leon Sigal, *Disarming Strangers: Nuclear Diplomacy with North Korea* (Princeton: Princeton University Press, 1998), Appendix I, pp. 257–60. In subsequent years, Pyongyang apologized for its submarine intrusion into South Korean waters in December 1996. In December 1997 and March 1998, it participated in four-party talks (with China, the U.S., and South Korea) to formalize the end of the Korean War. In exchange, Washington's food aid program to North Korea increased from $50 million in 1997 to $75 million in 1998. David Wright, *Will North Korea Negotiate Away Its Missiles?* Union of Concerned Scientists, April 1998.

43. Jongchul Park, "U.S.-DPRK Missile Talks and South Korean Response," *Korea and World Affairs* 20, no. 4 (Winter 1996): 615–17.

44. James Clay Moltz and Alexandre Mansourov, eds., *The North Korean Nuclear Program: Security, Strategy, and New Perspectives from Russia* (New York: Routledge, 2000), pp. 236–44; Samuel Kim, ed., *The North Korean System in the Post-Cold War Era* (New York: Palgrave, 2001).

45. Bermudez, "The Democratic People's Republic of Korea and Unconventional Weapons," in Lavoy, Sagan, and Wirtz, eds., *Planning the Unthinkable*, p. 201.

46. Scott Snyder, *Negotiating on the Edge: North Korean Negotiating Behavior* (Washington, D.C.: United States Institute of Peace, 1999), pp. 74–75.

47. Aaron Karp, "Lessons of Iranian Missile Programs for U.S. Nonproliferation Policy," *Nonproliferation Review* 5, no. 3 (Spring/Summer 1998): 17–26; Duncan Lennox, "Iran's Missiles on Parade," *Jane's Defence Weekly,* December 9, 1998, p. 23.

48. Center for Nonproliferation Studies, *Chronology of North Korea's Missile Trade and Developments: 1980–1989.*

49. On December 7, 1986, the Iranian parliament restructured North Korea's $170 million oil debt, allowing it to be repaid in five years beginning retroactively from January 1985. Iran would deduct 70 percent of the cost of North Korean merchandise purchased from the debt. IRNA (Tehran), December 7, 1986, *FBIS-NES,* December 10, 1986, p. 15. See also Kenneth Timmerman, *Mednews,* January 26, 1993, pp. 3–4. This report cites an Iranian member of parliament stating that North Korea had demanded a cash payment of $2.4 to $2.7 million apiece for the Scud-B missiles.

50. Tehran Domestic Service, April 14, 1988, in *FBIS-NES,* April 15, 1988, p. 49, cited in Center for Nonproliferation Studies, *Chronology of North . . . -1980–1989.*

51. *Iran Times,* October 12, 1989; Kenneth Timmerman, *Mednews,* December 21, 1992, p. 5, cited in Center for Nonproliferation Studies, *Chronology of North . . . -1980–1989.*

52. Anthony Cordesman and Ahmed Hashim, *Iran: Dilemmas of Dual Containment* (Boulder: Westview, 1997), p. 285.

53. *Christian Science Monitor,* December 27, 1993, p. 4; *Ha'aretz,* January 4, 1994, p. 1; in Center for Nonproliferation Studies, *Chronology of North Korea's Missile Trade and Developments: 1992–1993, 1994–1995.*

54. Anthony Cordesman, *Iran's Military Forces in Transition* (Westport, Conn.: Praeger, 1999), p. 309.

55. *The Iran Brief* no. 56, March 8, 1999. Kenneth Timmerman, "Missile Threat from Iran," *Readers Digest,* January 1998.

56. "Iran May Soon Gain Missile Capability," *Washington Post,* July 24, 1998, p. A28; "Iranian Missile Test Missed Target," CNN, July 23, 1998.

57. Bill Gertz, "Iran Missile Test Fails After Takeoff," *Washington Times,* September 22, 2000.

58. "Iran to Test Motor for New Space Rocket," *The Iranian,* February 8, 1999.

59. Fred Wehling, "Russian Nuclear and Missile Exports to Iran," *Nonproliferation Review* 6, no. 2 (Winter 1999): 134–44.

60. "Russia, China Aid Iran's Missile Program," *Washington Times,* September 10, 1997, p. 1. See also Aaron Karp, "Lessons of Iranian Missile Programs for U.S. Nonproliferation Policy," *Nonproliferation Review* 5, no. 3 (Spring/Summer 1998): 22.

61. Cordesman, *Iran's Military Forces in Transition,* p. 75.

62. Shahram Chubin, *Iran's National Security Policy: Capabilities, Intentions and Impact* (Washington, D.C.: Carnegie Endowment for International Peace, 1994), pp. 3–4.

63. "Iran to Test Motor for New Space Rocket," *The Iranian,* February 8, 1999.

64. "Tehran: No Confrontation with US, Israel," *The Iranian,* February 15, 1999.

65. Gregory Giles, "The Islamic Republic of Iran and Nuclear, Biological, and Chemical Weapons," in Lavoy, Sagan, and Wirtz, eds., *Planning the Unthinkable,* pp. 79–103.

66. The International Institute of Strategic Studies estimated Iran's defense spending to be down from $10 billion (1988) to $3.2 billion (1990), $5.8 billion (1991), $2 billion (1992), $4.9 billion (1993), $2.3 billion (1994), and $2.5 billion (1995). These compare with Kuwait's expenditures of $15 billion (for the years 1990–92) dropping to $3.6 billion (1993), and Saudi Arabia's annual average of close to $20 billion.

67. On the 1991 Scud-C order, see Chubin, *Iran's National Security Policy,* p. 48. On the 1994 Iran–North Korea talks, see Paula DeSutter, *Denial and Jeopardy: Deterring Iranian Use of NBC Weapons* (Washington, D.C.: National Defense University, 1997), pp. 22–23.

68. Michael Eisenstadt, "Living With a Nuclear Iran," *Survival* 41, no. 3 (Autumn 1999): 130.

69. Eric Arnett, "Norms and Nuclear Proliferation: Sweden's Lessons for Assessing Iran," *Nonproliferation Review* 5, no. 2 (Winter 1998): 39.

70. Rodney W. Jones and Mark G. McDonough, *Tracking Nuclear Proliferation: A Guide in Maps and Charts, 1998* (Washington, D.C.: Carnegie Endowment for International Peace, 1998).

71. Juan Romero, "Charting Reactions to the Islamic Bomb," *Jane's Intelligence Review,* March 1999, p. 34.

72. Kenneth Katzman, *U.S.-Iranian Relations: An Analytic Compendium of U.S. Policies, Laws and Regulations* (Washington, D.C.: The Atlantic Council of the United States, December 1999).

73. Eisenstadt, "Living with a Nuclear Iran," p. 130.

74. Raymond Tanter, *Rogue Regimes: Terrorism and Proliferation* (New York: St. Martin's Press, 1998), pp. 67, 279.

75. Gary Sick, "Rethinking Dual Containment," *Survival* 40, no. 1 (Spring 1998): 22–23.

76. Zbigniew Brzezinski, Brent Scowcroft, and Richard Murphy, "Differentiated Containment," *Foreign Affairs* 76, no. 3 (May/June 1997): 20–30; Jahangir Amuzegar, "Adjusting to Sanctions," ibid., pp. 31–41; Robin Wright and Shaul Bakhash, "The U.S.

and Iran: An Offer They Can't Refuse?" *Foreign Policy,* no. 108 (Fall 1997): 124–37; Fawaz Gerges, "Washington's Misguided Iran Policy," *Survival* 38, no. 4 (Winter 1996–97): 5–15.

77. Making a similar argument, Britain's foreign minister Robin Cook called for prudence in the West's rapprochement with Iran. He noted that "despite the more moderate noises from Tehran, these first signs of glasnost need to be treated with care. There is more than one center of power in Iran. We cannot afford to let our guard down until Khatami's words are matched by the acts of the Iranian authorities as a whole. This means a total end to Iranian use of assassination as a political weapon and clandestine support for terrorist organizations. It means Iran's giving up its ambitions to develop weapons of mass destruction outside international controls." Robin Cook, "The Good Fight After the Cold War," *Washington Post,* March 29, 1998, p. C07.

78. Geoffrey Kemp, "Iran: Can the United States Do a Deal?" *Washington Quarterly* 24, no. 1 (Winter 2001): 109.

79. "Iran Jubilant as U.S. Waives Sanctions on Foreign Firms," *New York Times,* May 20, 1998.

80. Shireen T. Hunter, "Is Iranian Perestroika Possible Without Fundamental Change?" *Washington Quarterly* 21, no. 4 (Autumn 1998): 23–41.

81. In the absence of American sanctions, it will become clearer that the Iranian government's economic policy, rather than external sanctions, is the cause of Iran's economic problems, and this would press Tehran to introduce structural reforms necessary for growth. Marvin Zonis and Salman Farmanfarmaian, "All in the Timing, Renewing U.S.-Iranian Relations," *World Policy Journal* 16, no. 4 (Winter 1999/2000): 47.

82. Suzanne Maloney, Brookings Institution, author correspondence, January 1999.

83. Eric Arnett, "Iran's Missile Ambitions Scaled Down, says SIPRI," *Jane's Defence Weekly,* April 16, 1997, p. 16.

8. TOWARD A TREATY REGIME

1. *Proliferation Primer,* January 1998, pp. 34-35; "Swiss Blocks N. Korea, China Scud Missile Sales to Egypt," Reuters, April 7, 1998.

2. Aaron Karp, *Ballistic Missile Proliferation: The Politics and Technics* (Oxford: Oxford University Press, 1996), p. 144.

3. U.S. Central Intelligence Agency, *Unclassified Report to Congress on the Acquisition of Technology Relating to Weapons of Mass Destruction and Advanced Conventional Munitions, 1 January Through 30 June 2000* (Washington, D.C.: February 2001).

4. *Executive Summary of the Report of the Commission to Assess the Ballistic Missile Threat to the United States,* July 15, 1998.

5. In 1990 dollars, U.S. GDP was $2,100 billion in 1960 and $3,250 billion in 1970; Soviet GDP was about $400 billion in 1960, $600 billion in 1970, and $800 billion in

1980; China's GDP was $90 billion in 1970, $160 billion in 1980, and $400 billion in 1990. For comparison, average GDP in the period 1990–97 (in 1990 dollars) was smaller for India ($360 billion), Iran ($105 billion), Israel ($70 billion), and North Korea ($20 billion).

6. Peter Zimmerman, "Proliferation: Bronze Medal Technology Is Enough," *Orbis* 38, no. 1 (Winter 1994): 71.

7. Janne E. Nolan, *Trappings of Power: Ballistic Missiles in the Third World* (Washington, D.C.: Brookings, 1991), p. 19.

8. W. Thomas Wander and Eric Arnett, *The Proliferation of Advanced Weaponry: Technology, Motivations and Responses* (Washington, D.C.: American Association for the Advancement of Science, 1992), p. 90.

9. Jose Monserrat Filho, "The Place of the Missile Technology Control Regime (MTCR) in International Space Law," *Space Policy* 10, no. 3 (August 1994): 227.

10. "UCR Deputies Reject U.S. Petition to Destroy Missile Plant," *FBIS-LAT*, March 11, 1993, p. 015.

11. "Government to Comply with Missile Control Pact," *FBIS-LAT*, February 16, 1994, p. 021.

12. Lee Jung-hoon, "The Missile Development Race Between South and North Korea, and the U.S. Policy of Checking," *East Asian Review* 9, no. 3 (Autumn 1997): 89.

13. Center for Nonproliferation Studies, *DPRK Report* no. 14, September–October 1998.

14. "India: Plans to 'Expedite' Missile Program Said Message to West," *FBIS-NES*, August 12, 1996, p. 48.

15. "India: Delhi Reportedly 'Self-Sufficient' in Missile Technology," *FBIS-NES*, July 17, 1996, p. 042.

16. "Experts Want India to Deploy Prithvi to Counter Ghauri," *Deccan Herald*, April 23, 1998. At a panel discussion following Pakistan's April 1998 Ghauri missile test, the director of India's Institute for Defense and Strategic Analysis suggested that in the short term India should deploy its Prithvi missile as a deterrence against Pakistan, but in the long term should not rule out missile disarmament through regimes such as a global INF.

17. "Boom for Boom," *India Today,* April 26, 1999.

18. "Spokesman: Prithvi Test Set Off Missile Race," *FBIS-NES*, June 23, 1994, p. 056, citing *The News*, June 5, 1994.

19. "U.S. Sanctions Over Missile Sale Draw Reaction," *FBIS-NES*, August 31, 1993, p. 053.

20. "Editorial Criticizes U.S. Sanctions on Missile Issue," *FBIS-NES*, September 14, 1993, p. 043, citing "The Latest Steps Against Pakistan and China," *Jang* (Lahore).

21. "Not Quite Understandable," *Dawn,* November 23, 2000.

22. "Saudi's Visit to Arms Site in Pakistan Worries U.S." *New York Times,* July 10, 1999.

23. United Nations General Assembly Resolution 54/54 F.

24. "Promotion of Nuclear-Weapon-Free Status of Southern Hemisphere Called for in Draft Resolution Approved by First Committee," UN Press Release GA/DIS/3192, October 31, 2000.

25. "USA Fields Scuds to Test Theater Missile Defense," *Jane's Defence Weekly,* May 7, 1997, p. 3.

26. Speech by Muammar Qadaffi, April 18, 1990, in *FBIS-NES-90-078,* April 23, 1990, p. 8, cited in *Report of the Commission to Assess the Ballistic Missile Threat to the United States* (Washington, D.C.: GPO, July 15, 1998), Appendix III, p. 370.

27. "Government Expert Panel on Missiles," http://www.reachingcriticalwill.org/missiles/missilesindex.html.

28. These groups held meetings in Canada in March 2000 and February 2001; the International Network of Engineers and Scientists Against Proliferation (INESAP) held a workshop in March 2001; and analysts stressed the role of "Citizens, Scientists and the Public" in informing policy making on the issue. Jürgen Scheffran, "Moving Beyond Missile Defence: The Search for Alternatives to the Missile Race," *Disarmament Diplomacy* no. 55 (March 2001).

29. "Draft International Code of Conduct Against Ballistic Missile Proliferation," Document MTCR/HEL/PL/oo/CHAIR/01, Helsinki, October 10–13, 2000.

30. Alexander Pikayev, "The Global Control System," in *Missile Proliferation and Defences: Problems and Prospects,* Center for Nonproliferation Studies Occasional Paper 7, May 2001.

31. Bill Gertz, "Iran Sold Scud Missiles to Congolese," *Washington Times,* November 22, 1999.

32. Before the advent of communication satellites, television broadcast receptions (which are useful educational tools) were limited to areas within 100 km of a ground transmitter. Communication satellites enabled television programs to be received in remote areas without the need for a television station or nearby ground links. In addition, satellite-based weather forecasting is directly linked to national prosperity for countries with a large dependence on agriculture—and developing countries typically have large agricultural sectors. N. Jasentuliyana and Ralph Chipman, *International Space Programmes and Policies: Proceedings of the Second United Nations Conference on the Exploration and Peaceful Uses of Outer Space (UNISPACE), Vienna, August 1982* (Amsterdam: Elsevier Science Publishers, 1984), pp. 60, 87.

The largest benefits of satellite remote sensing (i.e., earth observation) are in the areas of forestry and agriculture, followed by natural resource survey, land-use planning, and water-resource management. For example, the Indian Remote Sensing (IRS) images have been used for environmental monitoring, analyzing soil erosion and the impact of soil conservation measures, forestry management, determining land cover for wildlife sanctuaries, delineating groundwater potential zones, flood inundation mapping, drought monitoring, estimating crop acreage and deriving agricultural production estimates, fisheries monitoring, mining and geological applications such as surveying metal and mineral deposits, and urban planning. "Remote Sensing Tech Being Widely Used All Over India," *Deccan Herald,* October 3, 1997.

33. "Draft International Code of Conduct Against Ballistic Missile Proliferation," Document MTCR/HEL/PL/oo/CHAIR/o1, Helsinki, October 10–13, 2000.

34. "Statements at December 6, 1988, News Briefing," *Arms Control Reporter* 1989, p. 706.B.3 (3–89).

35. *Arms Control Reporter* 1991 p. 706.B.60 (6–91).

36. "White House Fact Sheet on Non-Proliferation and Export Control Policy, September 27, 1993," *Arms Control Today* 23, no. 9 (November 1993): 27.

37. Analysts estimated that for the period 1999–2008, a total of forty to fifty remote sensing satellites valued at $3.5 billion, and 300 military satellites valued at $35 billion, would be launched. See "Satcom Market Buffeted by Economic Uncertainties," *Aviation Week and Space Technology,* January 11, 1999, pp. 143–44. *Forecast International* estimated that 860 launch vehicles worth $50 billion would be produced in the ten-year period 1997–2006, and that 1,500 launchers would be built over twenty years (through 2016) valued at $87 billion. Forecast International, *The World Market for Expendable Launch Vehicles, 1997–2016,* July 1997.

38. See also Viacheslav Abrosimov, "Preventing Missile Proliferation: Incentives and Security Guarantees," *Disarmament Diplomacy* no. 57 (May 2001).

39. Earlier, in a January 1973 *Foreign Affairs* article on deterrence, Fred Ikle proposed that the superpowers eliminate destabilizing quick-strike ballistic missiles (Fred Ikle, "Can Nuclear Deterrence Last Out the Century," *Foreign Affairs* 51, no. 2 (January 1973): 267–85). See also Randall Forsberg, "Abolishing Ballistic Missiles: Pros and Cons," *International Security* 12, no. 1 (Summer 1987): 190–96.

40. Alton Frye, "Zero Ballistic Missiles," *Foreign Policy* no. 88 (Fall 1992), pp. 3–21; FAS *Public Interest Report,* May/June 1992, pp. 3–17; Alton Frye, "Banning Ballistic Missiles," *Foreign Affairs* 75, no. 6 (November/December 1996): 106; Jonathan Dean, "Step-By-Step Control Over Ballistic and Cruise Missiles," *Disarmament Diplomacy* no. 31 (October 1998). A 1993 FAS report outlined a four-stage approach involving U.S. and Russian missile reductions, a global conference on missiles, the negotiation of missile free zones, and the eventual elimination of missiles. The first two steps were partly realized by 2002. J. Jerome Holton, Lora Lumpe, and Jeremy J. Stone, "Proposal for a Zero Ballistic Missile Regime," *Science and International Security Anthology 1993* (Washington D.C.: American Association for the Advancement of Science, 1993), pp. 379–96.

41. *Arms Control Reporter* 1993, p. 706.B.158 (1-94); Jing-dong Yuan, *The MTCR and Missile Proliferation: Moving Toward the Next Phase* (Ottawa: Government of Canada, Department of Foreign Affairs and International Trade, May 2000).

42. Kenneth Adelman, "How to Limit Everybody's Missiles," *New York Times,* April 7, 1991, p. 19; Ken Adelman, "Going Ballistic . . . Globally," *Washington Times,* June 3, 1992, p. G1.

43. *Arms Control Reporter* 1994, pp. 603.B.225 (7-94), 706.B.170 (11–94).

44. William Durch, *Constructing Regional Security: The Role of Arms Transfers, Arms Control, and Reassurance* (New York: Palgrave, 2000), p. 226.

45. "Battling to Stop Dangerous Weapons," *Bangkok Post,* March 11, 2001.

46. Israel argued that the Code of Conduct's transparency clause, "far from encouraging restraint, will instead encourage an arms race." "Israel Hopes to Help Draft New Missile Rules," *Ha'aretz,* May 9, 2001.

47. See *Missile News,* August 1997. Bulgaria eventually agreed to scrap its ss-23, Scud, and Frog missiles in 2002, five years after its strong opposition to eliminating missiles.

48. The flight-test ban was explored in the late 1950s during international disarmament negotiations; Britain and France favored the issue, and after initial hesitation, Washington partly favored such a ban if it prevented the development of a Soviet ICBM counterforce capability. "Letter from James Killian to Dr. George Kistiakowsky, Chairman, President's Science Advisory Committee, December 11, 1959," and "Negotiations with the Soviets Relating to Testing and Control of Ballistic Missiles, Dr. Rathjens, December 21, 1959," in National Security Archives, *Nuclear Non-Proliferation, 1945–1990* (Washington, D.C.: George Washington University, 1995), slides 605, 610, 613.

49. Aaron Karp, *Ballistic Missile Proliferation: The Politics and Technics* (Oxford: Oxford University Press, 1996), pp. 139–41.

50. Test bans are useful because some problems associated with predicting ballistic trajectory bias, MIRV maneuvering, and warhead reentry can be resolved only through tests. Even if components are tested outside of flight tests, there are numerous instances when the components worked well by themselves and yet when tested together revealed incompatibilities. Lora Lumpe, "A Flight Test Ban as a Tool for Curbing Ballistic Missile Proliferation," in Peter Hayes, *Space Power Interests* (Boulder: Westview, 1996), pp. 146–82.

51. Andrew Aldrin, "Technology Control Regimes and the Globalization of Space Industry," *Space Policy* 14 (1998): 121.

52. Barry M. Blechman, ed., *Technology and the Limitation of International Conflict* (Washington, D.C.: Foreign Policy Institute, 1989); R. Kokoski and S. Koulik, eds., *Verification of Conventional Arms Control in Europe: Technological Constraints and Opportunities* (Boulder: Westview, 1990).

53. Jeffrey Richelson, *America's Secret Eyes in Space: The U.S. Keyhole Spy Satellite Program* (New York: Harper and Row, 1990), pp. 240–41.

54. In general, mobility reduces a missile's vulnerability and enhances deterrence stability, but also makes verification harder since missiles can be more easily moved. Albert Gore, "Verification of Arms Control Limits on Mobile Missiles," in Michael Krepon and Mary Umberger, eds., *Verification and Compliance: A Problem Solving Approach* (Cambridge, Mass.: Ballinger, 1988), pp. 3–16.

55. Ivan Oelrich, "Production Monitoring for Arms Control," in Krepon and Umberger, eds., *Verification and Compliance,* pp. 109–23.

56. Peter Zimmerman, "Verification of Ballistic Missile Activities: Problems and Possible Solutions," in Hayes, *Space Power Interests,* p. 215.

57. Lora Lumpe, "A Flight Test Ban as a Tool for Curbing Ballistic Missile Proliferation," in Hayes, *Space Power Interests,* pp. 146–82.

58. Rose Gottemoeler, "Verifying Controls on Cruise Missiles," in Krepon and Umberger, eds., *Verification and Compliance,* pp. 18–44.

59. Eric Arnett, "Technology and Military Doctrine: Criteria for Evaluation," in W. Thomas Wander, Eric Arnett and Paul Bracken, eds., *The Diffusion of Advanced Weaponry: Technologies, Regional Implications, and Responses* (Washington, D.C.: American Association for the Advancement of Science, 1994), p. 30.

9. CONCLUSIONS

1. Daniel Drezner argues that incentives are feasible when transaction costs are reduced, such as between democratic dyads or within international regimes. Yet even then they are not worthwhile if the sender anticipates frequent conflicts with the receiver; and even in cases of harmonious relationships, sanctions may be more cost-effective than incentives. Daniel Drezner, "The Trouble with Carrots: Transaction Costs, Conflict Expectations, and Economic Inducements," *Security Studies* 9, no. 1–2 (Autumn/Winter 1999). See also William J. Long, *Economic Incentives and Bilateral Cooperation* (Ann Arbor: University of Michigan Press, 1996). This work identifies trade and technology incentives to further bilateral cooperation. On other issues, environmentalists have long debated whether somewhat rigid technological solutions or flexible economic incentives such as taxes and transferable allowances better secure cooperation, and have generally favored the latter.

2. The qualitative evaluations of Table 9.1 can be replaced with quantitative indicators (high=1; mid=0.5; mid-low=0.33; low=0) to compute a quantitative success score of 0.44 in 1997 and 0.32 in 2002, but the small number of cases makes any percentage indicator scientifically imprecise. For column b, the impact of the MTCR is considered as roughly inversely proportional to a target's technological capability. Technologically advanced target states are less affected by MTCR embargoes, which thus only marginally constrain (say by one-third, or 0.33) such a state's missile program. MTCR embargoes would more substantially impact technologically midlevel states (by 50 percent or 0.5), and more greatly curb technologically weak states (by two-thirds or 0.67). These scores are further

adjusted to incorporate political factors such as U.S. pressure (for Brazil and Egypt) or international sanctions (Iraq).

3. Gary Hufbauer, Jeffrey Schott, and Kimberly Ann Elliott, *Economic Sanctions Reconsidered: History and Current Policy* (Washington, D.C.: Institute for International Economics, 1990).

4. See, for example, *Journal of International Affairs* 54, no. 2 (Spring 2001), special issue on "Rogue States: Isolation vs. Engagement in the 21st Century."

5. Stephen Krasner, *Structural Conflict: The Third World Against Global Liberalism* (Berkeley: University of California Press, 1985), p. 264.

6. The 1959 Antarctic treaty was negotiated among a small group of twelve states. By 1990, the treaty included twenty-eight states and twelve additional nonvoting members. Other treaties on Antarctica dealt with issues when they became relevant. The 1964 Convention on Fauna and Flora Conservation addressed scientific research and wildlife preservation, while the 1972 Convention for Conservation of Antarctic Seals and the 1980 Convention on Marine Living Resources addressed economic questions such as catch limits.

7. The seeking of an expanded scope and domain for the regime resulted in a ten-year negotiation. The resulting treaty was not initially signed by key states such as the U.S., U.K., and West Germany; these states joined the regime later. Another key international institution, the World Bank, included both the then pressing issue of reconstruction and the less urgent but still important issue of development when it was formed; it was therefore relevant and critical when new issues (related to development) emerged on the agenda.

APPENDIX

1. See Steve Fetter, "Ballistic Missiles and Weapons of Mass Destruction: What Is the Threat? What Should Be Done?" *International Security* 16, no. 1 (Summer 1991): 22–23; John Harvey, "Regional Ballistic Missiles and Advanced Strike Aircraft: Comparing Military Effectiveness," *International Security* 17, no. 2 (Fall 1992): 41–75; Stanford University, Center for International Security and Arms Control, *Assessing Ballistic Missile Proliferation and Its Control* (November 1991).

INDEX

Printed in the United States
200317BV00006B/37-108/A

9 780295 985077